The 20% Solution

The 20% Solution

Using Rapid Redesign™ to Create
Tomorrow's Organizations Today

John J. Cotter

JOHN WILEY & SONS, INC.
New York • Chichester • Brisbane • Toronto • Singapore

ISBN 0-471-13278-0

Printed in the United States of America
10   9   8   7   6   5   4   3   2   1

About the Author

John J. Cotter was born and raised in the Republic of Ireland. He has studied Experimental Physics at University College, Dublin, and Organization Design at UCLA. He has extensive operating management experience, including such positions as executive vice president and general manager, Microwave Components Division, Sterling Electronics Corporation, Houston, Texas; vice president operations, E & M Laboratories, Westlake Village, California; product design manager, Huggins Laboratories, Sunnyvale, California; and research physicist at Mullard Central Research Laboratories, Sussex, England.

Cotter was a founding member of The Center for Quality of Working Life at UCLA's Institute of Industrial Relations, the first university-based research center of its kind in North America. There he advised representatives from industry, labor, and government at the highest levels, in the United States and abroad, about the design of high-performance, team-based organizations. He left UCLA in 1978 to start his own consulting company, John J. Cotter and Associates Inc., based in Studio City, California. Since then, Cotter has taught organization design in the Executive Management Program at the Claremont Graduate School. He has also lectured and consulted all over the world.

A leading international authority on designing high-performance organizations, Cotter has published many articles on the subject in prestigious journals and collections, and produces a widely read bimonthly newsletter called *The Work Design Network News*. He is frequently quoted in *The Wall Street Journal*, *Industry Week*, *The Futurist*, and other newspapers and magazines, and has appeared in radio and television programs in the United States, Canada, Europe, and Australia.

Cotter's advisory and training activities have benefited such business giants as Alcoa, British Telecom, Colgate-Palmolive, Esso Europe, Ford, Nabisco, National Semiconductor, Nippon Steel,

Polaroid, Santa Fe Railway, Shell Canada, Sony, Texaco, United Airlines, Weyerhaeuser, and Whirlpool. He has spoken at hundreds of conferences, and has been a featured speaker at many university and business-sponsored courses and seminars. Cotter can be reached by phone at 818/762-7569 or by e-mail at JJCOTTER@aol.com.

This book is dedicated to my wife, Barbara, whose love, intelligence, and positive spirit sustains and supports me in everything I do, and to our wonderful children, Jonathan and Alysia, who continually enrich my life and inspire me in countless ways.

Contents

Chapter 3   Setting the Stage for a Rapid Redesign   51

Chapter 6   Rapid Redesign: Mapping and Analyzing   115
Social Processes

Chapter 9 Redistributing Responsibilities in the Redesigned Organization 185

Chapter 10 Managing Organizations in an Age of Paradox 207

Acknowledgments

The American author E. L. Doctorow once said that writing a book is like driving a car at night in a fog. You can only see as far as the headlights, but that's far enough to get you there. I am indebted to a great many people who helped me make it through the mist.

- ❏ Mike Snell, my agent and collaborator, encouraged, challenged, and advised me, and helped shape my ideas by reworking and rewording many of my initial thoughts.
- ❏ John Geirland, my friend and colleague, wrote the introductory vignettes at the beginning of each chapter and was an unfailing source of creative and constructive suggestions throughout the writing.
- ❏ Jim Childs, my publisher, encouraged and championed my aspirations to be an author and generously gave of his time to help me focus and clarify my thinking.
- ❏ Janice Borzendowski, my production editor at John Wiley, was extremely helpful and made many valuable suggestions.
- ❏ Carolyn Plumley, my multiskilled assistant, shortened many of my sentences, and cheerfully prepared numerous drafts of the manuscript.

I am also indebted to a great many colleagues and clients who shared their thoughts and theories with me over the years, and who provided many of the ideas and examples described in this book, especially Dick Ault, Joyce Avedisian, Ron Axtell, Jeannette Bajalia, Chuck Berezin, Eli Bernicker, Carl Bramlette, Mike Brousseau, Barry Brown, Rick Brydges, Tom Chase, Tom Christensen, Nancy Cobb, Margaret Code, Barry Coffey, Bob Coleman, Steve Davidson, Lou Davis, Bill Duffy, Jan Elsea, Joel Fadem, Bob Ferlauto, Kim Fisher, Al Fitz, Bill Flatt, George Gates, David Glines, Terry Golbeck, Walt Golembeski, Harvey Greenburg, Felix Guillen, Kathy Gurley, Paul Gustavson, Don Hardeman, Norm Halpern,

Rick Hendricks, Hermann Jakob, Marty Jaecksch, Gwynne Jennings, Bruce Keith, Pam King, Jan Klein, Harvey Kolodny, Fred Krause, Pete Konschuh, Chris Ladas, Dutch Landen, Gail Wells Landen, Ed Lawler, Corky Lazar, Mike Leonard, Alex Lowy, Bill Lytle, Barry Macy, Barry Maley, Richard McDermott, John McGarrell, Craig McGee, Ken Meen, Jim Meier, Brian Mickley, Ted Mitchell, Bernard Mohr, John Nielsen, Denis O'Brien, George Ortiz, Bill Pasmore, Gary Peters, George Pfeil, Abe Raab, Jim Rae, Joyce Ranney, Lee Sanborn, Dick Schneider, Tom Shalin, Darwin Slindee, Paul Staley, Vito Stellato, Chris Strobel, Jim Taylor, Chuck Thompson, Steve Tighe, Judy Vernon, John Walkush, Larry Walrod, David Willett, Buzz Wilms, Stu Winby, Bob Wroblewski, and Fred Zambroski. Some of the above offered valuable comments that helped me shape the final manuscript. However, the responsibility for errors, omissions, and faulty interpretations of their input is mine alone.

Finally, I want to thank the thousands of managers who participated in my public training programs and in the Claremont Executive Management Program who gave me invaluable feedback on my ideas during the past 20 years.

Introduction

The other day, a colleague asked me an interesting question: "John, can you summarize, in one sentence, everything you've learned during the past 20-odd years from your teaching and consulting practice?" One sentence!

Since my practice has covered a lot of territory—management development and training, organizational restructuring and redesign—my friend's question startled me at first, but then I realized I knew the answer: "Figure out the 20% of what you do that will contribute the most to your success in the future, then concentrate your time and energy working on that 20%."

I went on to explain. I've spent tens of thousands of hours studying what makes organizations tick and helping people make them more productive. As a result, I've spent a lot of my time thinking about the future. The answer to my friend's tough question sprang to mind because I'm convinced that, in the future:

- **Uncertainty will be the only certainty:** The future will become increasingly difficult to predict. As technology and globalization drive the world of business to operate on a larger scale in real time, uncertainty will rule. As a result, only the most adaptable and flexible organizations will survive and prosper.

- **"Getting it right" will be wrong:** Survival in an uncertain, dynamic world will depend on continuously changing the way organizations are structured. What's right today will be wrong tomorrow. There's no permanently right way to be organized anymore, no final endpoint to structure on which an organization can rest on its laurels. Future winners in business will recognize, adapt to, and sometimes take the lead by continuously inventing change.

- **Change will continue to change:** Incremental change, by itself, will no longer guarantee an organization's success. The new world economy will require creative change efforts that transform as well as adjust. To win the race to the future, an organization will have to create stimulating new opportunities rather than simply fix its present problems.

❑ **Winners will create their own futures:** Any organization that doesn't consciously and continuously create its own future will inherit a world shaped by others and find itself falling farther and farther behind the leaders as a result.

❑ **Managing successfully will require a big-picture perspective:** The biggest payoff in the future will come from avoiding problems rather than concocting spectacular solutions to problems. Disconnected improvement efforts are likely to make things worse rather than better. In a fast-moving world, an organization must simplify complexity by understanding how problems and opportunities relate to each other from a big-picture perspective.

❑ **Success will come from new ways of organizing work:** Winners in the future will structure work quite differently from how they do today, moving from complex structures assembled from many simple building blocks, to simple structures formed with much more complex components.

❑ **Only 20% of the factors shaping the future will really matter:** In a world that's changing at lightning speed, successful companies strive to change at the same rate by staying fast, focused, and flexible. The smart ones don't attempt to stay on top of every little detail or respond promptly to every fluctuation in the marketplace. Instead, they try to spot what's really important and focus their time and energy on those factors. By constantly examining and assigning priorities to developments in their environment, they concentrate on the most significant factors affecting each area of their business. Weighing how these factors will influence their future, they continuously redesign their organizations to eliminate weakness and exploit opportunities.

That's why I answered my friend's question the way I did. I could have said it even more simply: "Don't sweat the small stuff." Simple, yes, but not so easy to do. Most of the "stuff" any organization does is truly small stuff, but few organizations know how to distinguish between what's big and what's small, what's important and what's not.

"Great answer, John," my friend said after I'd explained my thinking. "I like that: The 20% Solution." "It's just another example of Pareto's Law," I explained. Vilfredo Pareto was a French-born economist who observed 100 years ago that 20% of the factors in most situations account for 80% of what happens (that is, 20% of a company's customers generate 80% of its profits). He called it Pareto's Law, and it applies perfectly to a world driven by accelerating change, where the ability to act quickly by screening out distractions and recognizing real opportunities can make all the difference between success and failure. The future will arrive as surely as a high tide. Those organizations that heed Pareto's Law will ride the crest of the wave; those that break it will be pummeled by the surf.

What will high-riding organizations look like in the future? How will they differ from today's organizations? For a partial answer to those questions, I can cite three companies that have already adopted and applied The 20% Solution: Skaltek, Semco, and W.L. Gore & Associates.

- ◻ Skaltek, a 100-person Swedish company founded in 1974, designs machines to wrap cables onto spools. It maintains no traditional business functions and operates with no departmental structure. When an order arrives, people interested in working on that order form a project team. When the team completes the order, its members disband and move on to a new project. The company spurns hierarchy, formal titles, and conventional managerial jobs. Twelve people are selected each year to evaluate individual performance and decide on salary increases for all employees. With the company's computer system, everyone in the firm can readily access information about orders, profits, cash on hand, wages, and anything else to do with the company's performance. Skaltek only does what it does best: designing overall systems and subsystems, and servicing its customers. It produces no parts, but acts as an integrator, fitting together supplies it purchases from others. Customers deal directly with employees at all levels. Assembled machines even carry a picture of the people who assembled them and a phone number to call in case something goes wrong.

- ❑ Ricardo Semler, the majority owner of Semco S/A, a marine and food services equipment manufacturer that is one of the most successful companies in Brazil, explains the secret of his company's success. "Our first principle is that information is the ultimate source of virtually all power. For this reason, we try to make all of it available to everyone. The second principle is that responsibility for any task belongs to the person who claims it. And the third is that profit sharing for employees and success-oriented compensation for suppliers will spread responsibility across the Semco map." With income and security at risk, and with information readily available, people try to stay aware of everyone else's performance. Participation gives people control over their work, profit sharing gives them a reason to do it better, and information tells them what's working and what isn't. Semco functions as a three-level organization, with factory floor flextime, open stockrooms, self-set salaries, and six-month budgeting. Six "counselors" provide overall leadership and take turns every six months as acting CEO. Weekly divisional meetings and biweekly interdivisional meetings are open to everyone, and those who attend make decisions vital to the business. Over half the products Semco once made in-house it now subcontracts to employee-owned satellite companies.

- ❑ W. L. Gore & Associates, famous for its waterproof Gore-tex fabric, operates 35 plants and employs almost 6,000 "associates" worldwide. The company rang up revenues of a billion dollars in 1993. Four core values guide everyone in making crucial decisions at Gore: maintain fairness, honor your commitments, give everyone freedom to grow, and check for agreement before making "waterline decisions" that could sink the ship. No Gore plant employs more than 200 people. No one holds a fancy title, except as required for incorporation purposes. No one gets hired unless an associate agrees to sponsor and find work for that person. There's no permanent organization per se. Instead, project specialists form teams and get work done by recruiting other associates. Each team member possesses multiple skills and commits to performing whatever tasks need to be done. Team leaders evolve from within each team and win their positions by consensus.

All three companies, operating in countries as diverse as Sweden, Brazil, and America, applied The 20% Solution and structured themselves accordingly. They refused to let themselves get distracted from what's important, concentrating instead on developing world-class capability in selected areas of their business (the 20%) to guarantee their prosperity. As a result, each has abandoned a great many traditional business practices, moving instead to minimal hierarchies, ad hoc structures, a reliance on self-control, and the discipline of the community marketplace in jobs and responsibilities to achieve high-quality, on-time, profitable performance. They totally transformed, rather than tinkered with, how people relate to each other and how work gets done. Not only have they succeeded because of these differences, they've proven they can do it year in and year out. Gore has operated this way since 1957, Skaltek since 1974, and Semco since 1982. There's nothing new under the sun; you just need to know where to look.

In the pages ahead, I'll present many more examples of successful innovation. A word of caution, however. Rather than viewing the organizations I'll describe as a parade of strange and unusual exceptions, consider them instead as precursors of the future. Their creative arrangements, or others like them, will, I believe, dominate the world economy by the end of this century.

Many popular business books have described key elements of today's rapidly changing economy, championing new work practices to deal with these elements and advising their readers to imitate the examples they present. They say, in effect, "If these ideas worked well for Motorola, or G.E., or Xerox, they'll work for you too." While such advice may satisfy academics and business theoreticians, it doesn't work for practicing managers because it doesn't show them how to redesign their own organizations to meet the unique challenges they face. As a result, those looking for practical solutions end up with a heightened awareness of the need for and the benefits of change, but they get few cold, hard facts about how to take action. Beyond chronicling what others have done, I'll describe specific ways organizations can distinguish between what's important and what's not, so they can prosper and grow in the fast, dynamic, and complicated economy of the twenty-first century.

The 10 chapters that follow chart a map any organization can follow on its journey to the future. That map, true to The 20% Solution, doesn't describe every nook and cranny in the landscape, every possible twist and turn in the road, or every side street or blind alley. Rather, it shows the main arteries to the future, the 20% of the trip that will provide the greatest competitive edge.

- ❑ Chapter 1 discusses how the future will differ from the present and describes how an organization can gain significant competitive advantage by understanding these differences.

- ❑ Chapter 2 examines the new perspectives and mindsets that are needed before embarking on a journey of discovery and change.

- ❑ Chapter 3 describes a process of Rapid Redesign suitable for a world that's constantly changing and shows how to plan the trip to the future, from identifying the start of the journey to harnessing change mechanisms that will generate widespread input and ownership.

- ❑ Creating an organization for tomorrow is a lot like putting together a giant jigsaw puzzle; it helps to have an idea of what it should look like when it's assembled. Chapter 4 explains how to create such a vision, built around clarity of purpose and an integrated set of strategies that target future aspirations.

- ❑ Chapters 5 and 6 show how to evaluate an organization's current work systems and structures in a comprehensive way, identifying and prioritizing key strengths, weaknesses, and missing elements in the context of tomorrow's business opportunities.

- ❑ Chapter 7 describes how to invent different paths to the future, developing options for redesigning an organization around the three key areas of structure, support, and staffing.

- ❑ Chapter 8 shows how to successfully implement organizational change in a way that builds in mechanisms for continuous reflection and renewal.

- Chapter 9 looks at what it will take to manage new, more dynamic organizations.
- Chapter 10 examines new developments influencing how work will be organized in the future that have just begun appearing on the horizon.

Concentrating on the essential 20% and shunning the distracting 80% can ignite remarkable success for people as individuals and for the companies that employ them. I hope to demonstrate to all those whose lives and livelihoods depend on organizations that:

- Change can be their ally as well as their enemy.
- They can create the future from a wealth of attractive alternatives.
- They already know much of what they need to know to get started.
- They can reap huge benefits if they act quickly.

I wrote this book not just for the executives and managers responsible for steering their corporations into the future, but also for the employees, workers, associates, and union representatives without whose informed efforts these companies can't succeed. I hope this book helps all of them create an enabling vision of a new and better world. This vision will encourage them to find the energy and patience needed to complete the journey successfully.

Bon voyage.

New Ways of Thinking about Tomorrow

"We're surrounded by sharks."

Ofir Kedar pulls a well-worn Mont Blanc fountain pen from his shirt pocket, uncaps it, and begins to draw on the paper tablecloth, sketching a more or less rectangular box populated with little stick people. His lunch companion stares at the drawing.

"This is my company, MITI. We're on this raft in a big ocean." Ofir traces squiggly lines that represent little waves and whitecaps, a vast sea encompassing the rectangular box and its passengers. Then he adds little replicas of Jaws all around the raft.

"These are sharks. They're swimming around the raft, waiting for us to sink. Some of them are bumping against the raft to try to turn us over, and one or two sharks are even trying to jump onboard. They all want to eat us alive."

"Who are the sharks?" Ofir's lunch companion asks. The two men are dining at a popular outdoor restaurant in Santa Monica, California. Ofir Kedar is an energetic, Israeli-born entrepreneur in his later 30s. A former helicopter pilot in the Israeli air force, Ofir emigrated to the United States with his wife six years ago, working as a contract programmer for MITI. In a short period of time, he became the owner and CEO of the Long Beach–based high-tech firm, which develops and markets database tools for Fortune 1000 companies.

"The sharks are our competitors, other tool companies and database vendors. These sharks, they're always moving. You never know where they'll pop up, and new ones are being born all the time. At the same time, my crew is expanding." Ofir crowds the raft with more stick figures.

Less than three years ago, he tells his companion, MITI had 15 employees crammed into tight quarters in a small office building. Since then, MITI has quadrupled in size to 60 people, has relocated to new quarters in a larger building, and operates sales offices in Ohio and Germany. Since MITI's highly portable database tools can serve a variety of different database platforms, it has attracted customers easily. Many industry experts consider SQR, the company's main product, the best database report-writer on the market. MITI has also won a reputation for excellent customer service. (A corporate customer once became enamored by the classical music she heard while on hold with the MITI technical support line. The tech support person went out of his way to track down the composer and the recording, which the customer subsequently used at her wedding.) MITI is now a multimillion-dollar company on an upward spiral. So why does Ofir worry about sharks?

The waiter brings out lunch, glancing curiously at the doodles on the tablecloth. He serves the men their lunch, which is, appropriately, broiled tuna.

"Oh sure, we're successful today," Ofir says, cutting the tuna with his knife, then pausing to look at his companion. "But we're in an industry where what you're good at today may be obsolete in three months. And three years from now? Nobody knows what will happen. The sharks may have wings by then. Or maybe the sharks will be our friends and we'll have to worry about the dolphins."

The Future Surrounds Us

Like MITI, companies all over the world have entered an era in which new realities such as globalization and digital technology are forcing them to change in ways that would have seemed impossible 10 years ago:

- The cloth for a jacket gets woven in Korea, finished in Taiwan, cut and sewn in India, delivered to Milan for a "Made in Italy" label, and sold at Filene's in Boston, which is owned by a Canadian.
- Between 1988 and 1993, Converse, the U.S. shoe company, shifted its shoe production from Korea, to Taiwan, to China, to Thailand, to Indonesia, and finally to India in search of lower manufacturing costs.

- Almost half the parts used in products assembled in the United States originate in other countries. On the other side of the coin, South Carolina has attracted so many German plants in one area that locals nicknamed the road leading to Spartanburg the Autobahn. South Carolina has drawn the Germans because they spend 35% less on wages and costs there than they would in Germany. BMW's Spartanburg plant will eventually produce 100,000 cars a year with 2,000 people versus 150,000 with 6,000 people back home in Regensburg.

- Tupperware obtains 44% of its sales from Europe, 25% from Asia, and only 19% from United States companies such as Coca-Cola, IBM, and Dow Chemical get more than half their sales from abroad—increasingly from the third world. Intel and Motorola have made Malaysia a global base for manufacturing and design.

- Eighty-two percent of the world's people live in new and expanding markets outside the traditional markets of North America, Europe, Japan, and Australia.

- National boundaries no longer provide protection against foreign competition. Fred Gratzon's Telegroup Inc. in Fairfield, Iowa, can save Japanese callers as much as 50% on overseas telephone calls by routing them through the United States. Telegroup buys discounted long-distance time from Sprint, MCI, and others. Customers abroad, who register their phone numbers with the company's New York computer, can place an international call by dialing New York, then hanging up after one ring. The computer calls them back with a U.S. dial tone, then patches them through as if they were calling from Manhattan. This has helped Telegroup customer Toshiaki Ichida, president of ALMA Japan Co., a small Tokyo trading house, cut his monthly telephone bill in half.

- Twenty years ago, there were 50,000 computers in the whole world. Today, according to an NTIA report, 50,000 computers are sold every 10 hours.

- Greeting cards that play "Happy Birthday" when they're opened have more computer processing power than existed in the whole world before 1950. Sega, the game maker, will soon begin selling its Saturn system, which runs on a high-performance processor that's more powerful than the original 1976 Cray supercomputer.

Living with Continuous Change

As a result of developments such as these, most companies today find themselves caught in a time of wrenching transition. Almost 200 of the 500 largest companies in America have disappeared in the past 15 years. Big, lethargic corporations like IBM are growing smaller. Smaller, nimble organizations like Compaq are emerging as the industrial giants of the future. Markets are fragmenting, product life cycles are shrinking, and consumers are demanding products that fit their needs as if tailor-made for them alone. All these factors combine to sound a death knell for the age of mass consumerism. Nowadays, the world changes so quickly, it's become increasingly difficult to keep up with new developments, much less figure out what they mean.

In the past, companies could specialize quite successfully as regional players, dominating their business in one geographical region and thus controlling change in their business environment by effectively eliminating viable competition. As access to technology has changed their special talents into commodity capabilities, these local companies have lost control of their marketplace. Competition has increased, capabilities have proliferated, and price barriers have fallen. Specialized regional players are now forced to compete in an expanded business arena to compensate for their loss of local market share. Here they find they're no longer admired or in control, and are often culturally insensitive to local norms and customs. They also find that new customers are reluctant to be told what to do; they may in fact know more than their vendors and are only subcontracting out of convenience, not because of a lack of knowledge or expertise. These customers know what they want done, and they know how they want it done, as well as by when and for how much. As competition has increased, the ability to change and stay on the cutting edge is now a key competitive capability.

Today, change flashes across the landscape like lightning. Simple, single-focus fix-it schemes no longer work, and isolated, unintegrated, one-time improvement efforts fail miserably. Organizations require periodic revolution, not just constant evolution. But power in most large organizations remains in the hands of "caretakers," who inherited their businesses rather than invented them. Since they're not accustomed to rethinking or transforming their organizations, these managers continue to rely on incremental change, striving vainly to predict rather than to invent the future. Success in the future will come to those with the ability to cast aside old assumptions and reinvent themselves in surprising new ways.

Management and unions in the steel and auto industries didn't agree to major work-rule changes until hundreds of thousands of jobs had been lost and both industries almost failed before the onslaught of foreign competition. Overwhelmed by the ongoing pressure of day-to-day business, they failed to make time to explore alternative design choices and concentrated instead on trying to make their current choices work more efficiently. Some people find it difficult to recognize that they actually have other choices; after all, everyone in their industry is organized to do business in the same way. Others don't know how to create new choices, and still others can't find the time; their world seems too complicated and fast moving as it is. Hypnotized by the present, focused on day-to-day brush fires, and preoccupied with short-term goals, they act as if the lightning will strike everyone except themselves.

Acknowledging the lightning and moving swiftly to adapt to the new economic landscape can create a tremendous competitive advantage for any organization, but this advantage can only be gained by taking a time-out to study options for creating a better tomorrow. As organizations worry about their business today, they can't afford to forget they'll be spending most of their time in the future from now on.

Recognizing That Today's Organizations Are History

Before starting to explore choices for the future, it pays to take a fresh look at how most organizations are currently structured. No matter how familiar they may seem, organizations aren't natural entities. They haven't been around forever. Someone created each one, inventing it at a particular point in time as a collection of tasks, processes, and relationships designed to achieve a particular goal. In that sense, every organization can be considered a social invention, whose design reflects the values, beliefs, and knowledge prevalent at the time it came into being.

For every organization that's operated for any length of time, much has changed since its inception. Change affects a relatively new organization like Microsoft as much as it does an older firm like General Motors. To thrive in the future, both organizations must constantly reinvent themselves or risk losing ground to competitors. According to Robert Lutz, the president of Chrysler, "Being large doesn't mean being safe. The large won't eat the small. The new industrial law is [that] the swift will eat the slow." Good things no longer come to those who wait, no matter how big they are.

Large, long-established organizations seldom handle change adroitly because they're unable to act in a fully coordinated way. Few have successfully integrated their business strategies, policies, practices, and structures systemwide. Instead, they've evolved haphazardly, as department after department grew and developed independently of one another, copying from the past by extending or elaborating on what already existed. Although companies may have smart products, intelligent marketing plans, and marvelous manufacturing capabilities, they often fail to tie them together as a set of total business strategies that all of the organization's key players accept and support. Such organizations operate as a collection of separate departments, each striving to do the best it can within the overall structure of the enterprise, each one assuming that if it does the best job possible, then the organization's overall performance will automatically soar. That assumption usually proves false when the contributions of key departments and functions don't fit snugly together or work at cross purposes to each other. If sales sells more product than manufacturing can produce, a company will end up losing customers rather than growing its business. Haphazard organizational design invariably leads to haphazard performance.

Many organizations today remain mired in the past, able to achieve the illusion of success by ignoring much of what's happening in the world around them. But the accelerating rate of change has begun shattering that illusion for most. They're slowly coming to realize just how much "the future ain't what it used to be," and they need to adopt fundamentally new ways of organizing and working to avoid being sixties industries in a nineties economy.

Organizing for Competitive Advantage in the Future

When Corning switched production at its Blacksburg, Virginia, plant from glass to auto-pollution control parts, the company employed The 20% Solution to design a flatter management structure. Instead of the four or five layers at Corning's other factories, Blacksburg engaged just seven managers to oversee 170 employees. Work at the plant was organized around five key jobs that all hourly employees were required to learn, and these employees performed many of the jobs previously done by supervisors, from scheduling vacations and overtime to handling production bottlenecks and tracking quality. Just one layer separated these workers from Robert Hoover, the plant manager. As a result, Hoover noted, "There's a lot less formality and you can make changes on the shop floor very quickly." The leaner structure also enhanced performance because it made all employees more visible, reducing the likelihood that layers of bureaucracy could hide or protect poor performers.

Like Robert Hoover at Corning, today's managers must redefine work as radically as their predecessors did in the 1700s at the onset of the first industrial revolution, or they simply won't keep up with their more venturesome competitors. New definitions of work must recognize that in a dynamic world, the ideal work unit now consists of ever-changing teams of people who come together to deal with a particular problem or opportunity, then dissolve, only to re-form again and again into new configurations as new challenges arise. Innovation and learning have replaced obedience and conformity as the key skills needed for success. Human intelligence has become the key economic resource for any enterprise. Some formerly fundamental truths of the workplace, namely the security of the large corporation and the lifetime employment it traditionally promised, have been smashed beyond repair. High-wage, low-skill jobs have evaporated. Now higher wages require higher skills combined with the ability and willingness to continue learning.

New organizations based on these realities have already appeared. The most effective ones feature flat *pancake* structures with *empowered* employees working together in *business units*, closely linked to the customers they serve. Flexible, agile work practices in these business units help them to develop long-term competitive capabilities. Sustaining success often means forming alliances with other organizations, even to the extent of collaborating with competitors.

Creating Pancake Organizations

From the end of World War II until the early 1980s, the trend in structuring organizations ran toward multiple layers of management and staff specialists. Some organizations ended up with as many as 32 levels. That trend has now begun to reverse itself, with many organizations attempting to condense these levels, frequently aiming to reduce short-term operating costs.

- ❏ When Marshall Cogan was CEO of New York–based Knoll International Holdings Inc., he boasted about running a $2 billion organization with fewer than 10 managers, quite a feat for a company with almost 20,000 employees, 70 manufacturing facilities, and 1,000 sales outlets worldwide. In practice, Cogan decentralized the company and gave six senior executives the authority to operate separate businesses ranging from auto parts to office furnishings. These executives controlled production, marketing, hiring, firing, and the tactical market positioning of their companies. Cogan reserved for himself and a few headquarters colleagues decisions on strategy, new product introductions, and advertising, matters that involved the company as a whole.

- ❏ At General Electric in the early 1980s, 12 layers stood between the lowest-level employee and the CEO. In 1994, only five remained.

- ❏ SCI, the world's largest electronics subcontractor and a major supplier of subsystems to Apple and IBM, maintains a mere 130 managers for 7,000 employees. As a result, the firm has lower costs and greater flexibility than its customers or competitors.

- ❏ GM Europe, which includes Opel, Saab, and Vauxhall, employs over 100,000 people who speak 18 different languages; yet the entire European operation is run from a central office in Zurich staffed by just 200 people.

- ❏ Nucor, the fourth largest American steel company, ranked as the most profitable in the industry in 1993 with sales of $2.3 billion. The company has only three levels between the president and the thousands of employees who make the steel. Twenty-three people work at corporate headquarters in a Charlotte, North Carolina, office park.

- $7 billion Burlington Industries maintains a mere 77 corporate employees.
- Giant $32 billion ASEA Brown Bovari, with 5,000 profit centers and over 200,000 employees worldwide, carries a scant 150-person corporate staff.

Pancake designs illustrate The 20% Solution because they replace old top-heavy pyramid structures with leaner, flatter alternatives. These are usually centered around processes, such as fulfilling an order, instead of around functions, such as marketing or manufacturing. This focus on organizing around horizontal business processes moves the organization's attention away from its internal operations and redirects it toward meeting the customers' needs instead.

Harnessing the Power of Horizontal Business Teams

In the race for world leadership, America's auto companies continue to evolve new production methods of *agile manufacturing*, emphasizing ultra-flexible production facilities and constantly shifting alliances among suppliers, subcontractors, and partners. Suppliers increasingly become involved at the very earliest stages of product development, helping to plan and design new components. Chrysler, for example, instead of surveying consumers about seating preferences for firmness, width, and color, gives that responsibility to supplier Johnson Controls. Eventually, Chrysler may actually manufacture very little, and concentrate instead on managing the integration of the whole vehicle. Along these same lines, Toyota and Nissan used a *systems engineering* approach to produce their Lexus and Infiniti cars. They harnessed sales, maintenance, engineering, and marketing specialists together, working on the total design right from the start with an emphasis on predictive problem-solving to eliminate production and service difficulties before the hardware was actually produced. Using this systems approach, they designed each car as a single integrated unit rather than as a collection of separate components.

CEO Alex Trotman has also been pushing Ford to improve the way it develops new products. With 16 new car and truck models scheduled for introduction between 1993 and 1997, Trotman wants to cut the time it takes to get a new model into production to less than 24 months (compared to the 42 months it took Ford to develop the Taurus in 1986). He also wants a 50% improvement in efficiency. Rather than handing off the design from function to function, Ford has awarded all its new model development work to a series of 700-person multifunctional product development teams. Each team consists of as many as 25 subteams, made up of specialists from different disciplines such as body engineering and power train. When specialists complete their assignments on a particular product development program, they leave the team for another assignment. To facilitate the transfer of learning between programs, Ford has built a $150 million facility in Dearborn to house personnel from several of these new teams under one roof.

Fierce international competition combined with the hectic pace of technology enhancement drives home a hard lesson to many organizations: While new ideas are fine, they aren't worth much unless they're brought to market quickly. Doing so means getting away from the notion that a researcher only researches and a marketing manager only markets. Bonding together, a team of experts who represent all aspects of the product life cycle can cut time to market significantly and improve quality at the same time. Simultaneous engineering calls for all departments that participate in the product development cycle to work closely together from the beginning. This approach saves time and money by settling conflicts and problems earlier in the development process, which, in turn, reduces the need for product modification and recirculation of the design through numerous iterations.

Creating new and different organizations in the future means learning to think about the future in new ways. One such new mind-set comes from breaking the future down into three different categories: *predictable futures*, *intuitive futures*, and *uncertain futures*.

Planning for the Predictable

In the early 1980s, a strategic task force at Holiday Inn undertook an extensive review of future business prospects in the hospitality industry. As a result of its investigations, the task force identified an opportunity to introduce a new hotel concept, filling a gap between the moderate-priced and luxury-lodging market segments. While existing hotels offered travelers a limited number of suites at considerably higher prices than regular rooms, no one had yet created a national all-suites product. In late 1982, Holiday Inn created Embassy Suites, the first nationwide all-suites hotel chain, offering the business traveler "two rooms for the price of one."

To create a competitive advantage, Embassy moved quickly, pursuing a strategy of rapid expansion with the aim of opening properties at 100 prime locations across the United States within five years. This decision created significant capital barriers for competitors wishing to enter the all-suites market since duplicating Embassy's strategy would require a huge investment. Consequently, Marriott, Hilton, and the other major hotel chains initially watched from the sidelines while Embassy grew. In 1984, Embassy opened the first of its all-suites hotels in Overland Park, a suburb of Kansas City. It also acquired 23 suite-configured properties in California and Arizona from Granada Royale Hometels, a small hotel chain geared to long-term guest visits. Business travelers loved the new product and flocked to Embassy's all-suites alternative right from the start.

By 1994, Embassy Suites racked up revenues of $600 million with 107 hotels nationwide, 56 of them company owned and operated, the rest franchised. The company picked up many of its properties from distressed regional sellers who tried the suites-only format in the 1980s but wound up with high debt and low occupancy. These failures provided Embassy with rapid entry into the market without adding to the overall supply of rooms. With higher occupancy rates and lower costs than its competitors, Embassy helped treble the net income of its parent company, Promus, from $30 million to $90 million between 1991 and 1994.

Clearly, Embassy figured out how to create a successful future by staying abreast of the market and uncovering new business opportunities in its environment. In hindsight, its strategies seem smart and obvious. Comparable trends and opportunities unfold every day in every industry, and while it's mandatory to pay close attention to them, doing so won't guarantee advantage for long. Competitors can all access the same information, and once they see a competitor's success, they'll rush to copy its efforts. Again, it pays to pay attention to The 20% Solution: Keeping consistently ahead of the competition means learning to look beyond the obvious (the 80%) and building up competitive capability for the future by spotting new opportunities (the 20%). To thrive in the long term, an organization must, of course, continue to be better than its competition.

Emphasizing Competitive Capability

An organization's competitive capability comes from the collective skills, knowledge, and abilities that employees use to create its products and services, as well as from the structural arrangements that shape how and with whom they interact. Decisions about which capabilities to instill and develop determines an organization's competitive advantage. Appropriate structures unleash the correct capabilities to create unbeatable advantage in the marketplace. The more world class a firm's capabilities, and the more they're interwoven into its products and services, the harder it will be for competitors to match its offerings.

- ❑ Half of the 3M company's 60,000 products include a layer of material that permits one substance to adhere to another. This technology gives the company its most important competitive capability (that is, its 20% Solution).
- ❑ Honda has leveraged its capability in building advanced engines to expand its business from motorcycles to cars, lawn mowers, and generators.
- ❑ Canon's capability in optics, imaging, and microprocessor controls has enabled it to enter many diverse markets such as copiers, laser printers, cameras, and image scanners.

Think of an organization as a portfolio of capabilities rather than as a collection of businesses or departments. Competitive capabilities should drive an organization's business strategies, thus enabling it to develop world-class products and services (for example, Philip's compact data storage and retrieval system grew out of the company's core optical-media capabilities). Concentrating on products built around competitive capabilities creates the correct 20% focus for business units. Exploiting these capabilities often requires the integration of different streams of technology. For example, to produce a miniature radio no bigger than a business card, Casio had to harmonize know-how in miniaturization, microprocessor design, material science, and ultra-thin precision casting. This harmonization required Casio's employees to work together across existing functions and department boundaries, developing the new skills and perspectives that allowed them to seize new growth opportunities.

To know which capabilities to concentrate on, it's important to understand how the evolution of technology and markets interrelate for your business. Look for the emergence of new technologies that reshape the contours of competition, or where technical barriers to entry are disappearing. Search for areas where technologies are converging (such as the merging of local and long-distance phone companies, cable TV providers, and computer makers in the telecommunications services industry). Isolate areas where deregulation allows different industries to compete for the same market (for example, banks, brokerage houses, and insurance companies now compete with each other for the same investment dollars). An organization's competitive capabilities should:

- ❑ Provide access to a wide variety of markets.
- ❑ Generate significant benefits for customers.
- ❑ Be difficult for others to copy or imitate.

Successful organizations in the future will know how to identify, cultivate, and exploit the competitive capabilities that make growth possible. The nature of competition will continue shifting from high quality and low cost toward the creation of new products and new businesses. Mike Ovitz, the former chairman of Creative Artists Agency (CAA), the top Hollywood talent agency representing almost 1,000 writers, directors, and actors, anticipated the convergence of entertainment with telecommunications and computers, and therefore wanted CAA to become the vendor of choice for companies seeking entertainment to fill their cable systems, enliven their video games, and exploit their products' potential in other ways. To this end, CAA has begun aggressively developing world-class capabilities in investment banking, advertising, sports marketing, and the creation of multimedia hardware and software. Ovitz believes these capabilities will allow CAA to branch out from just brokering deals for its clients to creating entirely new ventures. "It's our job to stay ahead of the curve," Ovitz claimed. "In the near future, someone with a book or a movie project won't have to be content with just putting it on television or on film. We'd better be able to tell our clients where they can find broader markets for their work."

Businesses built around cutting-edge, competitive capabilities can more nimbly serve emerging markets. As these markets broaden and new ones open up, the most successful organizations will create new products, attract new customers, define new businesses, and engage new competitors. World-class organizations in the future will concentrate on, invest in, stay on top of, protect, and expand their competitive capabilities. Using The 20% Solution, they won't let anything distract them from developing these capabilities, and they won't ever give them away without getting something more valuable in return. If they don't possess world-class capability in a strategically important area, they'll acquire it by partnering or subcontracting with someone who does.

Forming Favorable Business Alliances

Developing a world-class competitive capability in-house means investing in a long-term process of continuous improvement and enhancement. Starting from scratch, it can take a decade or longer to develop really world-class capability. But this cycle can be speeded up tremendously by borrowing capability from others, even from competitors. The new economy increasingly calls for such nontraditional business arrangements as organizations find that it's impossible to take full advantage of tomorrow's opportunities on their own. Increasingly, they form alliances with others, bisecting today's vertically integrated industries and establishing networks of partners to shape and exploit new opportunities. Such business alliances, often stretching across industry lines and national boundaries, are becoming more the rule than the exception. The capability they provide for using and sharing information sustains growth. Smart organizations in the future will develop allies rather than enemies.

- ❑ Apple's alliance with Sony to manufacture Apple's very successful Powerbook line of laptop computers linked Apple's knowledge in designing easy-to-use products with Sony's expertise in miniaturization and compact manufacturing.

- ❑ Corning has participated in 19 different partnerships with other companies such as Mitsubishi (Comtech) and 3M (Raycom Systems), a strategy that has allowed it to speed up the development of new products (which contributed almost 13% of the company's earnings in 1992).

❑ MCI, the long-distance telephone company, has allied itself with an array of partners, such as Nextel, for wireless personal services, so it can offer customers one-stop shopping for all their communication needs, including financing their equipment purchases.

Developing strategic partnerships makes sense when the need arises for a highly specialized capability in a fast-moving field or when an opportunity poses significant risk. Alliances and collaborative relationships with other organizations can often build capability more rapidly and cost-effectively than any other way. Through these arrangements, organizations concentrate on learning their partner's skills and on erecting barriers that discourage competitors from entering their market. Some don't develop core products by themselves, but learn more about them than anyone else by working with many product providers simultaneously (for instance, at one time, Sun Microsystems claimed it knew more about circuit-board technology than any of the specialized circuit-board companies that supplied it with products).

An effective partnership offers benefits to both parties based on a common vision, and each partner clearly understands what it may gain or lose from the alliance. It's important that partners not only offer the best products or services available, but that their cultures are compatible as well. A joint venture involving managers from two organizations that work under different incentive schemes will quite likely suffer ill effects from opposing priorities. Differences in organizational structures, measurement systems, and decision-making processes can all cause communication gaps and operating tensions. Organizations that connect without sufficient ongoing discussion may find their interests diverging over time. Healthy relationships require constant attention to The 20% Solution, examining on an ongoing basis what really counts in the relationship. In the new collaborative economy, the web of business depends more than ever on deep personal connections to assure consensus and accurate communication.

Collaborating with Competitors

Instead of closing underused plants, laying off workers, and wiping out earnings with costly write-downs, IBM, Digital Equipment, and other big computer makers have found a better idea. They've kept their factories open by building products for other companies, sometimes for direct competitors. Contract manufacturing can make for strange bedfellows. IBM's Austin, Texas, plant, which makes most of the circuit boards used in IBM PCs and workstations, has produced notebook computers for CompuAdd Corporation, as well as circuit boards for a Taiwanese PC clonemaker. Contract arrangements can also include assistance in product design and testing. For small, inexperienced start-up companies, using an IBM or Digital factory can bypass decades of experimentation and allow them to leapfrog the learning curve.

- ❏ Apple and IBM have set up a joint venture called Kaleida to create software that combines video, sound, data, and graphics in multimedia CDs. Kaleida's object-oriented software tool, ScriptX, helps developers create multimedia programs that will run on both IBM and Apple platforms.
- ❏ General Motors, Ford, and Chrysler participate in 10 consortia to research everything from less-polluting paint to more humanlike crash dummies.
- ❏ An automotive consortium that includes auto and oil companies has tested nearly 100 blends of gasoline in cars of all vintages.

Clearly, collaboration between rivals makes sense when such partnerships can provide access to new markets and technologies, or allow the creation of products that neither partner could produce on its own. However, the partnering organizations must make sure that cooperation enhances rather than erodes their ability to compete. It's not enough any more simply to ask what business an organization is in. It's crucial to pose follow-up questions that address rethinking strategies and redeploying assets to track changes in the competitive environment. When does logic argue for relationships with competing companies? How can an organization in such an alliance retain and strengthen its own individual identity? Since the world of collaborative competition often raises difficult issues about what information to share and what to keep proprietary, negotiating skills become as important for success as technical or operating skills. While these skills are relatively easy to define, in an uncertain world, intuitive skills can be the most important of all.

Investing in Intuition

While anyone can create the future by extrapolating trends and developments in his or her business environment, inventing truly innovative futures depends more than anything else on intuition. Andrew Wyeth, the well-known American artist, says, "I'll spend weeks out doing drawings and watercolor studies I may never use. I'll throw them in a back room, never look at them again, or drop them on the floor and walk over them. I feel the communion that has seeped into the subconscious will eventually come out in the final picture." Like Wyeth, businesspeople can use their curiosity to fuel seemingly intuitive creativity.

In 1971, Leonard Riggio bought a small Manhattan bookstore. By 1994, he'd built it into the 937-store Barnes & Noble book chain, buying the B. Dalton chain in 1986, and later acquiring the Bookstop and Doubleday chains. Riggio pioneered discount pricing and kept his stores open seven days a week. Beyond studying industry trends and conducting detailed market analyses, he relied on his educated instincts to tell him what consumers really wanted.

Believing that shopping is a form of entertainment, Riggio introduced stores with a soft-colored library atmosphere, featuring striking architecture and graphics, and plenty of welcoming public space where customers could linger, feel at home, and meet other people. He put cafés in his superstores, hosted readings and book signings, anything that would entice and entertain and keep people browsing through the shelves. Riggio believes books are consumer products, and people buy them not just for their content, but for what they say about their taste, cultivation, and trendiness. He understands that it takes more than a structured, quantified analysis to invent the future. It takes what Wyeth might call "art."

Synthesizing experience into strategy means developing an intuitive feel for the future that eludes others. This creative process involves:

- Acquisition (taking things in)
- Association (putting them together)
- Expression (giving them voice)
- Evaluation (making them better), and
- Perseverance (staying the course)

Studying facts and figures helps, of course, but insight and instinct count as well. The most creative managers go beyond statistics, mulling over ideas that lead them in surprising directions no amount of research can stimulate. Relying on hearsay and gossip and many other intangible sources of information, they observe, internalize, comprehend, and synthesize. Gradually, through both objective study and subjective contemplation, they begin to assemble viable patterns.

In his book *Made in Japan*, Akio Morita, the chairman and founder of Sony, writes, "In order to make a rational decision, you must know all the facts and the environment that surrounds the facts. American managers are only rational on the basis of the facts that they have come to know. There are bound to be lots of facts and environmental factors that they don't know. Japanese managers...grasp a general idea of the whole and then use this information...in making decisions."

Successful managers know that business judgment depends on this intuitive sixth sense, which requires imagination as much as personal knowledge of the market. As John Wooden, the legendary former basketball coach of the UCLA Bruins, once said, "It's what you learn after you know it all that counts." The capacity to empathize with and gain insights from customers is one of the most important skills anyone in business can develop. William Campbell, the CEO of Philip Morris U.S.A., says, "Even today, I go out with the sales reps. There are things that you can learn at that level of contact that you just can't learn any other way. You can't read it in the computer or in the reports. You have to see beyond the data." Akio Morita of Sony, Leonard Riggio of Barnes & Noble, Bill Gates of Microsoft, and Sam Walton of Wal-Mart all brought this ability to the enterprises they founded. Creatively uncovering and anticipating their customers' problems, challenges, and dreams, they designed organizations that did more than deliver products and services but, in addition, really gave value to their customers' lives.

Anticipating Customers

Whirlpool maintains records on close to 15 million customers and more than 20 million installed appliances, some of them dating back to the 1960s. It uses specialized computers to scan volumes of records, seeking faint but significant patterns to better understand its customers' needs. Attachmate Corp., a $145 million PC communications software company, uses information collected from the 165,000 support calls it receives each year to plan enhancements for its established products and to shape entirely new ones. "The data gives us a very clear idea of what's going on in the marketplace," according to Mary Harwood, vice president in charge of customer support.

A company that limits itself to analyzing customer reports doesn't hear from those who aren't their customers because they're already someone else's customers. Simply remaining market- or customer-oriented by itself doesn't do the trick anymore. George Colony, the president of Forrester Research, says, "You have to be ahead of your customer. The customer can't know what he [or she] wants. No customer ever asked Ken Olsen of DEC for a VAX minicomputer. No customer ever asked Tom Watson of IBM for a 360 mainframe." A Detroit auto executive commented recently, "You could never produce the Mazda Miata solely from market research. It required a leap of imagination to see what the customer might want." Since consumers follow the most imaginative products and services, how a business defines itself must outpace both competitors and customers. Benchmarking other companies' progress isn't enough. Building on an intimate understanding of the marketplace, companies can lead rather than follow customers by creating products they need but haven't even imagined. As the J. Peterman Company mail order catalog says, "People want things that make their lives the way they wish they were."

When Toyota introduced Lexus, it didn't just offer higher quality than Mercedes and BMW at a 40% discount. Rather, Toyota built the car around a thorough review of the whole buying and service world experienced by prospective Lexus buyers. On the basis of that information, Toyota decided to sell Lexus cars through a unique new channel, one structured and managed to make customers feel special and valued. For Toyota, Lexus represented not just a new car but a whole new definition of the automobile business. As a result, exploding from a standing start in 1989, Lexus outsold both Mercedes and BMW in the North American marketplace in 1994.

Unconventional market-leading business definitions seldom arise from looking only at an existing business. Markets have to be redefined in terms of needs and benefits rather than in terms of products and customers. It's not enough just to evaluate products by asking "How can we make them better?" Instead, thinking needs to focus outside the box of present product concepts. Searching for new definitions of its business, Yamaha encourages Europe's most talented musicians to experiment with the latest electronic instruments at its listening post in London. To gain insights into needs and benefits, Yahama observes the most sophisticated and demanding customers it can find, interacting with them and absorbing their thinking. This allows it to develop an intimate understanding of unmet (and usually unarticulated) customer needs. Business is moving away from selling products to buying customers. The ideal relationship is to know customers well enough to buy them by delivering something they need or want. Such a partnership with customers allows an organization to provide them with benefits they can't get anywhere else. In this setting, knowledge about the customer becomes more important than knowledge about the product. In this kind of world, small companies have the edge over large companies because they can customize products more efficiently. The most successful managers in the future will make their share of mistakes, but they'll quickly learn to fine-tune their intuition.

Going for Growth

Winston Churchill once said that "Success is going from failure to failure with great enthusiasm." Successful organizations make a virtue out of making mistakes. Hewlett-Packard encourages its managers to "fail and learn faster than the competition." Sony introduced over 300 versions of the basic Walkman without extensive market research. It simply introduced a new model, watched how it sold, and then modified the design of the next model accordingly. Seiko prided itself on introducing a new watch every working day.

Who finished third in the Indianapolis 500 last year? Who was nominated for, but didn't win, the 1990 Oscar for Best Actress? Who came in second in the women's Giant Slalom at the 1994 Winter Olympics? In the evolving business world, few people will recall the also-rans and runners-up. In many industries today, from microchips to refrigerators, a few large companies dominate the world market. If one company emerges as the clear leader with 50% or more of the market, then the rest of the pack must settle for carving up the remaining pie into smaller and smaller slices. At the same time, while the top companies struggle to replace each other, they remain open to ambush by smaller, more nimble niche firms, specialists serving seemingly narrow markets that may in fact quickly and unexpectedly explode into mammoth ones. To top it all off, a sudden shift in technology may turn the whole market upside down, sending all the competitors chasing a whole new pie. Not even the most flexible and agile market leader can rest on its laurels any longer. Nonetheless, the battle for market dominance is more successful from the high ground. Whoever holds the top spot in a market can most easily win continued growth, profitability, and employment stability.

In the early 1980s, as Scott Cook watched his wife, Signe Ostby, pay their bills, he figured it was tedious work that cried out for automation. Since there wasn't a good computer program available, he decided to invent one. Cook, a former Crisco brand manager, created Quicken, an easy-to-use alternative to existing financial planning software. He hired Tom Proulx, then a student at Stanford University, to write the code, and, together, the two entrepreneurs rolled out their first release in 1984. Cook and Proulx were among the first software designers to use focus groups and other consumer marketing tools to develop their products. When Quicken came to market, it allowed users to cut the average bill-paying time of three hours in half. By 1993, Quicken outsold all other personal finance programs in the United States, and Cook and Proulx's company, Intuit, had climbed past $120 million in sales. When someone asked Cook why Intuit had done so well, he responded, "What worked for you last year can be death this year. The trick is recognizing change you don't even see."

Maintaining profitable growth consumes more effort than cutting costs. Growth requires vision about the direction of technology, changing consumer demands, the development of new markets, and the surprises competitors will create in the marketplace. To grow steadily and profitably, organizations need to analyze financial and marketing data as well as scanning the business environment for more subtle signals about emerging problems or opportunities. These changes must be interpreted wisely, to figure out how they could influence business strategies. Analytical skills are just the beginning; perceptual skills are also required to identify pertinent issues long before their existence becomes obvious to others.

In recent years, American managers have been preoccupied with reducing costs by downsizing, decluttering, and delayering rather than leveraging their resources to create new revenue. All too often, that tendency confused reengineering with revitalization. As PepsiCo CEO Wayne Calloway put it, "You can't save your way to prosperity." Cost reduction without a corresponding effort to expand market clout results in dumbsizing. Eventually, a business gets so lean and mean it becomes anemic, a condition that erodes agility and flexibility. An organization without the resources to reinvent itself eventually disappears. Remember, over 50% of the Fortune 500 membership has changed in the past 10 years.

Peter Drucker reminds us that the most important results in business are obtained by exploiting opportunities, not by solving problems. "For many years I have been asking new clients to tell me who their best performing people are. And then I ask, 'What are they assigned to?' Almost without exception, the performers are assigned to problems... Then I ask, 'Who takes care of the opportunities?' Almost invariably, the opportunities are left to fend for themselves.... All one can hope for by solving a problem is to restore normality.... Maximization of opportunities is...the entrepreneurial job. The pertinent question is not how to do things right, but to find the right things to do, and to concentrate resources and efforts on them." Just concentrating on doing things right is playing the wrong game.

Business success in the future will require an unprecedented amount of creativity and imagination. Intuition alone won't suffice. No one would feel comfortable just relying on their intuition to fly an airplane. It's no longer true (if indeed it ever was) that "a good manager can manage anything." Experience and skill are prerequisites for understanding. However, no amount of intuition or experience will prepare anyone to anticipate the truly unexpected. But that's what can make or break a company's future.

Facing Fuzzy Futures

In the new economy, the impossible becomes possible, the improbable becomes probable. Any Irish citizen can trade stocks, pay bills, and move cash to, from, and among American institutions at will. Quicken software and a subscription to Checkfree enables a Dubliner to maintain an American bank account and move money around freely, by wire or paper check, perhaps initiating an on-line transaction on a personal computer in Dublin, which is processed on a computer in New York City and passed on to an electronic clearinghouse in Zurich. Similarly, telecommunications systems will soon offer entertainment as well. A Beatles movie was recently transmitted over the Internet, and within a few years, subscribers will be able to obtain all sorts of information and entertainment by telephone.

Since telecommunications technology transcends geography and bypasses the traditional channels of distribution, and since the technology may develop in a number of unforeseeable ways, no one can predict with assurance exactly how organizations may profit from it. Will customers tap into databases with television sets hooked up to fiber-optic cables, or will they pull the data into their homes with miniature satellite dishes? Which companies will occupy the driver's seat on the information superhighway? Phone companies such as MCI and AT&T? Software firms such as Microsoft? Or entertainment conglomerates such as that which resulted from the merger between Viacom and Paramount Communications? Since certain aspects of the future will defy all the study and analyses and inspiration in the world, organizations must prepare themselves to deal with unknowable unknowns. While remaining tightly connected to the business environment, continually trying to spot trends that signal new directions, and always striving for creative insights into new opportunities, an organization must maintain the agility and flexibility that will allow it to capitalize on surprising and unanticipated developments. One aspect of the future appears to be quite certain: it will be uncertain.

Living with Ambiguity

The future has always developed from a collection of possibilities. Today, change has accelerated to such an extent that it's now really different in kind, not just in quantity. In today's turbulent world, choices and actions often lead in unpredictable directions as separate events occurring in unrelated areas conspire unexpectedly to determine destiny. A change in policy by the Japanese textile industry to reduce prices quickly swells the unemployment rolls in North Carolina as U.S. textile companies lay off employees because of reduced market share. This in turn increases the number of people applying for welfare benefits in Chicago as people move there from North Carolina in search of work. A pebble cast into the water in Tokyo can quickly produce ripples along the shores of Lake Michigan. Given such a far-reaching pattern of cause and effect, how can those at the edge of the pond prepare for the future? Even if the ripple's impact when it reaches the shore can be anticipated, given the certainty of uncertainty, any plans that look right today may turn out to be dead wrong tomorrow.

If a company made slide rules in the 1960s, it's out of business today. If it offered Beta-format VCRs in the 1980s, it's selling VHS equipment today. Whether it's General Motors or General Foods, IBM or Intel, Bob's Shoe Warehouse or Bob's Big Boy, someone, somewhere, has very likely already launched strategies aimed at putting it out of business. The globalization of markets, the spread of information technology and computer networks, and the dismantling of corporate hierarchies and bureaucracies are all happening at the same time. Not only do these events cause one another, they affect one another in dynamic ways. Turbulence in the business environment causes organizations and institutions across the world to evolve in a dramatically new and different manner. Evolving organizations, in turn, alter the environment yet again. This turbulence produces the kind of change that companies can neither control nor ignore. Successful gamesmanship in a turbulent environment requires new skills, because the game works less and less like a chess match and more and more like an interactive video game.

As the certainty of uncertainty increases, forms of adaptation developed by organizations for simpler environments no longer work. Organizations need to find new ways to deal comprehensively with unpredictability and uncertainty, since dynamic systems act as wholes in ways that aren't easily predicted based on the behavior of their parts. The traditional notion of long-range planning can be a trap, tying up resources in ways that thwart flexibility and agility, the two primary prerequisites for creating a successful future. In today's fast-moving world, prompt action always beats passive planning. As A.J. Kitt, one of America's premier downhill skiers, whose speed routinely exceeds 80 miles an hour and who wins races by hundredths of a second, observes, "You can't win without being a little out of control. The key is going right to the edge without slipping over." Traditional planning keeps companies away from the edge while swifter competitors are already plunging down the slope.

The conventional idea of calculated risk entails knowing all the alternatives and their probabilities. Under conditions of uncertainty, all the alternatives may be known but not their probabilities. In times of turbulence, even the alternatives may not be known. When this happens, going lion hunting gets better results than simply waiting for the lion to come pounding on the door. This tactic makes some managers extremely nervous; after all, who wants to go looking for trouble? Yet that's just what a smart manager does. While staying in the comfort zone may provide the illusion of security, going right to the edge and being a little out of control enables exploration of the full range of possible futures.

In uncertain times, organizations need ways to analyze their environment that go beyond the traditional methods of environment scanning and trend analysis. Those confronted with sudden discontinuities or major uncertainties often find scenario building useful. This involves blending trends and uncertainties to create a picture of a future world that's consistent with the facts and within the realms of possibility, then asking "What would we do if this actually happened?"

Asking "What Would We Do If...?"

During the early 1970s the management of Royal Dutch Shell recognized they were living in turbulent times. Though tempted to remain in the comfort zone of their old strategies, they decided to take charge of their fate by exploring different scenarios for the future that might uncover false assumptions behind the company's strategic plans. After headquarters staff in London laid out three global scenarios, one fairly surprise-free and the others incorporating less likely possibilities, Shell's managers broke these global pictures down into regional maps. They weren't looking for the right answers but, rather, they were trying to explore and understand the full scope of possibilities.

From this exercise, Shell found that most of its managers operated with a strictly limited and not fully thought out set of assumptions about the future. Exploring a broad range of hypothetical cases helped them test other possibilities, thinking through "What would we do if...?" in imaginary situations. This process continually surfaced the managers' assumptions, so they could question, test, and eventually reconcile them with the company's strategies and goals. While Shell urged its managers to aim for the surprise-free scenario when running their businesses, the company also prompted them to remain aware of other possibilities. Managers who did so were better prepared to deal with unanticipated change because they had developed more mental flexibility and agility. As Louis Pasteur once said, "Chance favors the prepared mind."

Given the pressure of day-to-day operations, Shell's managers, like most others, usually favored action over reflection, oral briefings over written reports. Formally exploring alternative futures helped them develop alternative conceptual interpretations of their world. Posing the right questions opened up complex situations for thoughtful consideration and encouraged people to grapple with difficult issues, to challenge conventional assumptions, and to rise above conceptual ruts. Arie de Geus, who championed the scenario-building initiatives at Shell, observed, "The real purpose of effective planning is not to make plans, but to change... the mental models that... decision-makers carry in their heads."

Building In Flexibility

When fighting major forest fires, the U.S. Forest Service appoints the person who knows the terrain best to be the fire chief, irrespective of that person's normal position in the organization. Centralized control won't work in an uncertain world because, under emergency conditions, a boss may well lack the time and knowledge to develop the right response quickly enough. In a business organization, when everyone agrees on common guidelines for responding to change, anyone can seize responsibility for taking action. When everyone follows the same general rules, they make consistent and similar responses. In an uncertain environment, people who work in flat, loosely coupled organizations with porous fuzzy boundaries can get more done, faster, than people hamstrung by traditional, rigid bureaucracies. Nurturing creative employees with strong diagnostic, problem-solving skills becomes significantly more important than enforcing obedience and conformity.

If it's not possible to plan with certainty, it's especially important to focus on The 20% Solution, figuring out quickly what really matters, then doing what really matters. One way to achieve this sort of rapid response is to keep extra or redundant capacity on hand to deal with new situations. Adding extra people who specialize in managing the conditions that are changing can also help, but doing so may complicate communication and coordination and increase payroll and overhead costs. These consequences can be minimized by broadening the change-management skills of current employees and by decentralizing control, authorizing those closest to the action to act as they see fit on their own initiative.

Sneaking a Peek at the Future

Canon, a highly successful global company, capitalizes on its ability to view the world from new perspectives. As a result, Canon does very little on its own. It buys most of its components from small outside companies. It adds value by integrating the benefits of those small companies into a highly efficient network. It doesn't run big factories. It employs little capital. It doesn't sell its products directly, but markets them through large, well-financed, global trading companies that, in turn, work through networks of independent dealers. Implementing The 20% Solution, Canon stays small in areas where it pays to be small; but, it's big in those areas where it pays to be big, such as R&D and marketing. Think big, act small, and grow bigger; that's one maxim of The 20% Solution. For successful companies like Canon, the future has already arrived, and it's definitely not what it used to be.

New Perspectives Shape New Futures

The opening scene of the movie *Star Trek II: The Wrath of Khan*, shows a young Vulcan officer named Savik (played by Kirstie Alley), at the helm of the starship Enterprise when a distress signal is received from a Federation ship in the neutral zone. The unfortunate vessel is disabled, space and life support systems are giving out, and the crew is desperately calling for assistance.

Savik is faced with a difficult decision: Does she speed to the rescue of the troubled spaceship, thereby violating the neutral zone and risking intergalactic war, or does she ignore the call for help and doom the helpless crew to certain death? Savik makes her decision. "Set a course for the neutral zone, warp-factor speed."

The ship crosses the neutral zone...and falls into a trap. The Enterprise is surrounded by Klingon warships, firing volleys of photon torpedoes. The Enterprise is disabled and victorious Klingons demand that it surrender and allow itself to be boarded.

At this point, the lights in the control room come on, a door opens, and in walks Admiral Kirk. We learn that the whole sequence was part of an elaborate training exercise—a simulation famous for having, as the Vulcan officer puts it, "no way to win."

"I found a way to win," Kirk says. "I was able to beat the distressed ship scenario when I was at the Academy." Kirk was, in fact, the only officer in the history of the Academy to beat the simulation.

"But the rules preclude you from finding an escape," the young Vulcan officer answers logically. "How did you do it?"

Kirk smiles. "I broke into the computer and changed the rules."

Understanding the Power of Perspective

Many organizations today are in no-win scenarios where the only chance for survival is to change the rules of the game. In the face of constant change and uncertainty, leading-edge companies such as General Electric, Canon, Corning, and ASEA Brown Boveri have adopted organizational configurations and structures few people would have imagined possible 10 years ago. These novel arrangements have demonstrated their effectiveness over time by consistently delivering world-class performance. What worked for them was specially designed to suit their needs and may not work for anyone else. Their solutions emerged from adopting new perspectives that in turn led them to prioritize the world differently. Before thinking about changing their organizations, these companies changed how they thought about organizations. New perspectives and new priorities provided new maps for their journey to the future.

Most people have a map of some kind in their mind describing how they believe their organization really works, but they're not always aware of what it is. Asking people to create a picture of their work world as it currently exists often produces interesting results. Figure 2.1 shows such a picture drawn by a middle manager from a division of General Motors some years ago. His drawing clearly illustrates the nature of the relationships he considered important and how he felt about authority, rewards, information, initiative, and status in the workplace. When people can share their drawings with others and clarify their feelings about the issues they raise, they can begin to think together about whether current design elements will work in the future. A keen awareness of how present arrangements will fit into the shape of the future should precede any thoughts about tomorrow. New perspectives can then spring from an understanding of old perspectives. New maps can then be created to identify, rank, and reorder the variables people believe will assure future success. It all comes back to The 20% Solution. Fresh perspectives on what really matters—managing change, emphasizing speed, harnessing people's potential, and structuring organizations for flexibility—set the stage for new design choices.

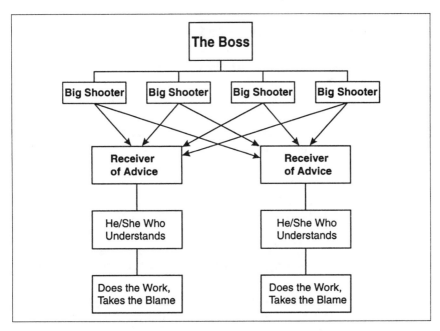

Figure 2.1 A middle manager's map of a General Motors division.

Adopting New Perspectives about Change

Life is an organic process. We're told by physiologists that 90% of the cells in our body change every year. We have a totally new liver every six months, and the cells of our stomach walls are different every five days. But most people aren't actively conscious that so much change is so close. They still view change as the exception rather than the rule and believe that constant change is a new phenomenon. Reversing these perceptions is one of the keys to survival and success in the future.

Changing the Rules of the Game

Sun Microsystems has developed a competitive advantage by changing the rules of the game in the global computer business. Sun pioneered the UNIX operating system so customers wouldn't be locked in to a particular computer vendor. The company's founders, all in their 20s, adopted the UNIX operating system because they felt the market would never accept a new workstation designed by four graduate students. That strategy allowed Sun to focus on designing the hardware and software for workstations and to limit its involvement in manufacturing, choosing instead to purchase virtually all its components off the shelf from external vendors. As a result, Sun was able to introduce complex new products rapidly and to alter its product mix continually. Sun's workstations, while vulnerable to imitation, cost significantly less to produce and thus carried lower price tags than the competition. Sun's strategy succeeded because it drew on Silicon Valley's sophisticated and diversified technical infrastructure.

Since customers preferred open systems, Sun grew rapidly, and it growth enabled it to weather the responses of larger companies when those rivals began adapting to the new rules. To pay for its large investment in R&D, Sun expanded globally by forming alliances with local companies that could add value with application software or that could provide local sales and service support. These alliances allowed Sun to grow without building its own sales and service organizations. Sun's hundreds of arrangements with original equipment manufacturers and value-added resellers to distribute its products gave it the sort of sales and service clout that once made IBM famous. Smart negotiating skills helped Sun forge relationships that spurred sales growth but kept vendors from competing with each other or with Sun's own sales force. *Vectoring*, the control of downstream sales, required extensive market segmentation knowledge and an in-depth understanding of distribution arrangements in various countries and markets.

In the new economy, prosperity comes more from creating opportunity for tomorrow than from operating efficiently today. Business school professors Gary Hamel and C.K. Prahalad call this "creating competitive space," by which they mean "a proactive attempt to harness discontinuities in technology, regulation, demographics, and lifestyles to reshape industry boundaries to the disadvantage of incumbents." Introducing a dramatic product or service innovation that redraws market and industry boundaries creates such new competitive space. Product innovation can involve adding an important new function (such as Yamaha's digital piano), developing a novel way to deliver a well-known function (such as automated teller machines), or reconfiguring functionalities to satisfy a previously unmet need through an entirely new product concept (for example, camcorders, home fax machines, all-suites hotels).

When the rules of the game shift entirely, continuous improvement and incremental change won't work. Instead, organizations need to be redesigned to match the new realities.

Either Change or Die

How long does it take to wreck a 200-year-old publishing company with sales of $650 million and a brand name recognized all around the world? One blink. Just ask the folks at *Encyclopaedia Britannica*.

In 1989, interactive computer capability in American homes seemed futuristic indeed. Now the popularity of CD-ROM players matches the 1980s boom in videocassette recorders, and the installed base of computer CD-ROM drives in U.S. homes approached 6 million by the end of 1994. Many families with CD-ROM players also own a CD encyclopedia (digital encyclopedias now outsell printed versions by more than three to one), but not the once-ubiquitous *Encyclopaedia Britannica*, which hasn't yet appeared in a complete home multimedia version. Britannica's managers saw the future of CD-ROM, but since they knew that a CD-ROM *Britannica* bearing a much lower price than the paper version would mean a lower selling commission, they chose not to risk offending the powerful Britannica sales force. As a result, CD-ROM competitors robbed *Encyclopaedia Britannica* of market share. As recently as 1990, the Britannica corporation, owned by the William Benton Foundation, a charitable trust affiliated with the University of Chicago, earned more than $40 million after taxes on the sales of $650 million. But in 1991, the business lost $12 million. For 1992, the foundation reported that the business lost money again, but it felt too embarrassed to say how much. Meanwhile, the Britannica's sales force collapsed. In 1992, it included 2,300 active sales representatives in the United States and Canada. By 1994, it had shriveled to fewer than 1,100.

It happens all the time. Western Union sent Alexander Graham Bell packing when he offered to sell the company his patents for the telephone because that technology would have jeopardized Western Union's huge investment in telegraph equipment. In the 1980s, IBM's powerful sales force blinded the company to the potential of the microprocessor because they didn't want to see their lucrative mainframe franchise business jeopardized.

Some companies, of course, don't make that mistake. Calyx and Corolla harnessed changes in technology and transportation to deliver fresh flowers at a competitive price that usually last twice as long as those available from local florists. When customers order roses or lilies or orchids from C&C's catalog, clerks log those orders into a computer. Then, the day before the order must go out, growers cut and pack the flowers, and Federal Express drivers pick them up for overnight delivery. The result? Calyx and Corolla's blossoms don't take detours. And customers get "fresher flowers, faster."

Daniel Boorstin, in his essay "The Republic of Technology," published in the January 1977 issue of *Time* magazine, wrote, "For most of human history, continuity has been the norm and change was news. Daily lives were governed by tradition. The most valued art works were the oldest. Furnishings became increasingly valuable by becoming antique. Great literature never became out of date. 'Literature,' as Ezra Pound observed, 'is news that stays news.' The new enriched the old and was enriched by the old. It was a world of the enduring and stable. Today, it's quite different. The importance of a scientific work can be measured by the number of previous publications it makes superfluous to read. We live in a world of obsolescence. Great libraries are cemeteries, not treasure houses." Applying this logic to organizations, yesterday's great companies are dinosaurs, destined for extinction unless they redesign themselves in accordance with new, future realities.

If It Ain't Broke, Break It

IBM felt relieved when 1992 went away. That year, the company recorded the biggest net loss in American corporate history and suffered a 50% plunge in its stock price. IBM's leadership position in mainframe processors and storage systems, a $50 billion worldwide business it had dominated for 25 years, lay endangered because dozens of smaller companies had succeeded in creating large-scale computers based on the low-cost microprocessor technology used in personal computers. Customers using Big Blue's mainframe processors paid approximately $100,000 for each MIPS (MIPS measures the capacity to execute 1 million instructions per second). However, Hewlett-Packard's largest minicomputers, built from the company's own microprocessors, cost about $12,000 per MIPS. According to Willem Roelandts, general manager for H-P's Computer Systems Organization, "Customers are saying 'The whole world has changed—why should I listen to just IBM?'

Companies that had Big Blue stamped on their forehead are talking to us now." James Burke, a veteran IBM board member, admits, "What I didn't understand, and what IBM didn't understand enough, was the rate of change in this industry. I don't think any of us understood the impact of that, and how much smaller, entrepreneurial companies can exploit that rapid pace of change. They move quickly, and they love to take risk."

In the 1990s, if a company doesn't drive change, breaking what isn't broken, change may drive it—all the way to the poorhouse. The most successful companies of tomorrow won't react to change, they'll act to make change happen. Success alone won't guarantee survival. As the dean of Saint Paul's, William Inge, once observed, "Nothing fails like success." Since juicy margins attract competitors, organizations must learn to make their own products obsolete before some rival does it for them. Although Intel invented the microprocessor (the silicon brain of a computer) 20 years ago, and still holds a near monopoly on the computer industry's key chip, it has continued to push its technical capability faster than its competitors, pursuing a formal philosophy of making its products obsolete before its rivals do it. Says senior vice president Paul Otellini, "Intel's history is to destroy its old products with its next products." Only innovators who keep innovating will thrive. Those who remain complacent with the status quo or who only react to change will mortgage their future to the competition. In the new economy, if at first you do succeed, you try and try again.

Adopting New Perspectives about Time

With risk, uncertainty, and complexity defining the business environment of the 1990s, nothing seems predictable anymore. Unfamiliar competitors can strike from unexpected directions at the worst possible times. From the British Empire to the Pickett Slide Rule Company, history is full of giants that failed to adapt quickly enough. As author and futurist Alvin Toffler says, "Today, it's the survival of the fastest, not the fittest."

Quick and Nimble Sets the Pace

Though most of today's technologies can operate in real time, many organizations don't. Recognizing this, Hewlett-Packard set up a Change Management Team (CMT) in 1988 to learn how its organizations should be structured to better support the company's strategy of reducing break-even time when developing and introducing new products. Stu Winby, the driving force behind the CMT since its inception, firmly believes that proprietary know-how about generating product and process improvement faster than the competition will do more than anything else to keep H-P ahead of the pack.

The CMT's initial studies revealed that traditional organizations ran into massive problems when it came to managing the business process of developing and bringing new products to market. Given the involvement of many specialized functional groups, responsibility for the overall process fell outside the ongoing central control of any clear owner. H-P's own business environment was moving so quickly, senior managers could see a need for change, but they couldn't develop appropriate responses fast enough. Worse still, they couldn't connect all the different groups required to implement change. As a result, product generation and realization times lagged behind those of competitors, with crucial decisions getting bottlenecked by organizational complexity.

To create more responsive structures, CMT members began drawing organizational boundaries around core work processes instead of functions. They explored creating multifunctional, horizontally coordinated organizations spanning the entire value chain, from identifying customer needs to incorporating feedback from customer use. They tried to create fluid, whole systems that moved power and accountability from functional organizations to product-realization business units.

Today, H-P designs organizations for speed by moving people from a functional to a process perspective, organizing work around business units focused on functionality and customer needs instead of functions and products. With this perspective, H-P's people now view business and product development teams as the core of their new organizations, striving to move customers into the design arena, then working with them to develop and test new ideas as quickly as possible. The traditional functional departments support the team's efforts to develop appropriate internal capabilities. By 1992, 55% of H-P's $20 billion annual revenue came from products that didn't exist three years before. H-P aspires "to fail and learn faster than the competition."

Used correctly, speed can reduce uncertainty by diminishing the boundary between the internal and external environments, thus bringing the customer's needs and the company's capabilities into closer, more immediate contact. The real value of competing on time comes from creating a tighter feedback loop between customers and employees. As employees learn more about the company's customers, they also learn to create additional value for them. Winby believes, "The quick and the nimble will eventually force everyone else to play this game."

Competing on speed involves more than just cycle time reduction or just-in-time inventory management. The faster a business is driven, the faster inefficiencies become apparent. Being fast also provides more degrees of freedom in selecting business strategies. UPS has traditionally won distinction as the best in the business at moving low-priority, consumer-oriented parcels where time of transit doesn't matter. But Federal Express excels at moving the most vital, high-value parcels and documents on an "absolutely, positively overnight" basis. Understanding time from the customer's perspective identifies what their time-sensitive needs are. Sometimes, overnight is overkill. Unless a drive for speed is grounded in strategy, aligned to structure, and integrated into operating practices and performance measures, it won't fulfill its competitive promise.

Rapid Response Helps Win the Race

A dozen years ago, Compaq started producing the first IBM-compatible personal computers—smaller, lighter machines engineered to accommodate IBM software and accessories, but at a lower price and with greater computing speed. Compaq prospered in the 1980s by rapidly developing and distributing new products in the personal computer industry, but it ran into trouble in the 1990s when customers began clamoring for low-cost, customized features and fact delivery. Compaq, which laid off a fifth of its employees in 1991 and 1992, has set about redesigning itself to capture the number-one position in the PC and workstation market by 1996. Its strategy depends on greatly improving its responsiveness in the marketplace, aggressively attaining higher manufacturing efficiencies, and dramatically reducing cost through economies of scale. The company knows that only the most efficient manufacturers can deliver ongoing price reductions while still achieving acceptable profitability.

Compaq uses three-person teams, or cells, to staff its assembly lines in Erskine, Scotland. One person prepares the seven or eight subassemblies that go into the computer. A second person installs the components, like the disk drive and the motherboard, into the computer's external case. A third person performs all the tests to make sure the electronics and circuits are connected properly. Each cell worker performs multiple tasks, so the work-cell approach takes up less space. Since only three people touch the parts, compared to 16 on the traditional assembly line, the process takes less time. The fewer the number of people touching the parts, the higher the quality. When an assembly line stops, work is interrupted for up to two dozen people. If there's a problem in a cell, only that cell is affected. Output per employee in a three-person cell has increased by 23% and output per square foot of factory space rose 16% compared to the company's traditional assembly-line approach. But the biggest payoff from the work-cell method is that it allows Compaq to build machines to customer order rather than to a forecast of what it thinks customers will want.

Historically, Compaq built machines according to forecast and prayed the right orders would come through. When customers requested different features, the company scrambled to rework and reconfigure existing machines. Now Compaq plans never again to build a product the customer doesn't want. In 1993, it built fewer than 5% of its computers to order, a percentage the company wants to boost to 100% by 1996. Building to order requires almost superhuman coordination among Compaq's suppliers, factories, and distribution centers around the world. When a customer's order arrives, the company must choose the factory (in Houston, Singapore, Scotland, or China) that can build the product for the lowest-cost delivery to that customer. Within hours, it must pull the right parts from suppliers to feed a round-the-clock manufacturing facility. Does that cause stress? You bet. But as Bob Stearns, Compaq's vice president of corporate development, comments, "I don't think change is stressful. I think failure is stressful."

In the business wars of the coming decade, speed of response has joined accuracy, creativity, resourcefulness, and the other traditional capabilities that lead to customer satisfaction. And in many cases, it ranks first. Research by the Boston Consulting Group shows that companies that respond to customer demands twice as fast as the industry average grow five times faster and can charge 20% higher prices.

Adopting New Perspectives about People

Somerset Maugham, the English writer, once wrote a story about a janitor at a London church. A young vicar discovered the janitor was illiterate and fired him. Jobless, the man invested his meager savings in a small tobacco shop. He prospered, bought another, expanded, and eventually owned a chain of tobacco stores worth several hundred thousand pounds. One day, the man's banker said to him, "You've done remarkably well for an illiterate. Just think of what you might have been if you had learned to read and write." The man replied "Well, I'd probably still be the janitor of St. Peter's church in Neville Square." Radical change provides radical opportunities when people are allowed to develop to their full potential.

Focusing on a Common Future

By the time many companies decide to change, it's already too late. As with fishing for trout, cast the fly where the fish will be, not where they were an hour ago. Creating the future, like fishing, takes vision. Scott McNealy, the CEO of Sun Microsystems, observes, "The bigger the organization, the more you need a vision and an architecture that allows people to make decisions that are compatible with that vision. In the future, no one will accomplish anything without a vision that extends the entire length and breadth of the corporation."

It takes a clear vision to create the future, and those who don't create one for themselves may not be around to enjoy it. A clear vision brings power, drive, and success to a company and its people as it rallies everyone in the organization and unites their efforts. Marc Porat, the CEO of General Magic, advises, "Make sure there's a vision in the company, a shared vision, that's so powerful, once a person joins the family, he or she barely has to be reminded of what to do." The vision helps people understand the company's strategies well enough to translate them into appropriate actions. That way, in the words of the poet William Carlos Williams, all employees can look to the future together and "keep the jeweled prize always at our fingertips. We will it so and so it is, past all accident."

Employee Involvement Is a Good Beginning

The Santa Fe Railway's Customer Quality and Support Center in Topeka, Kansas, combines high-performance, cross-functional work teams with some of the most advanced communication and computer systems available. The center remains in constant contact with Santa Fe customers all over the country and with trains and engine crews throughout the Santa Fe system. Employees handle about 1,500 telephone calls a day, with voice response units handling thousands more. The company has divided its customer representative teams into nine areas according to product (grain, coal, and so on). Since the information system is programmed to include customers' telephone numbers, telephone calls automatically prompt the callers' name and information about their company to appear on a customer representative's computer terminal. With a stroke on the keyboard, the representative can determine the current location of railroad cars and pull up maps of rail yards across the country. The representative can tell which rail lines a customer has used for shipping in the past and can instantly fax bills and other notices to the right parties.

Tom Shalin, the Santa Fe assistant vice president in charge of the center, says, "The current trend in customer service is to make each call a one-step, one-person stop. Customer representatives make the critical decisions that middle managers made in the past. In addition to calming an upset customer, they must pull up appropriate screens on their computers, then analyze and solve problems on the spot. The perception customers have of the company is their perception of the person who's on the telephone helping them."

Decisions about where to locate customer service operations in the future will be driven by the characteristics of the workforce, not by the technology. The ready availability of modern telecommunications services and widespread access to computers, software, and automated technologies has enabled towns as small and far-flung as Minot, North Dakota, Hattiesburg, Mississippi, and Topeka, Kansas, to compete for back-office operations. Creative people are the most important factor in getting the job done.

Employees working with automated systems must respond immediately when something goes wrong, diagnosing and correcting unexpected problems creatively and accurately. If they have to depend on others for direction to deal with events that occur with little or no warning, they won't or can't respond quickly enough. People must be free, wherever they work, to do what needs to be done without first asking permission.

Employee participation—involvement—empowerment—the idea has been renamed more times than Zsa Zsa Gabor. Call it whatever you like, it will be an essential prerequisite for quick response in the future. In addition, automated technologies demand decentralized control, and in the years ahead, the application of automation and the arrangements that support it will accelerate. Don't think of employee empowerment as a choice driven by personal values and philosophy, but as a practical requirement of operating in the future. But, although empowerment will be necessary for success, it won't be sufficient by itself. No company can achieve its business goals unless its people are committed to carry out their duties quickly and efficiently on their own initiative. Employees can be empowered by giving them access to information, authority to make decisions, and rewards that depend on the outcomes achieved. Employee commitment, however, can't be bought or forced. It results from the way people are treated and how they experience their work situation.

Driving Technology with Human Values

In 1978, Best Foods built a highly automated Skippy peanut butter plant in Little Rock, Arkansas. The task force responsible for designing and setting up the plant knew that employees would require high levels of skill and self-direction for the sophisticated technology to operate successfully. To maximize employee commitment and plant performance, Best Foods specified that jobs should be designed as much as possible to satisfy the employees' human and psychological needs. The plant design guidelines stated that work at Skippy should incorporate whole jobs, provide opportunities for advancement, allow for participation in decision-making, recognize and take advantage of individual differences, and eliminate artificial status distinctions.

When the task force reviewed plans for how the plant would receive raw materials, it discovered that design engineers planned to ship peanuts to the plant by rail in 100-pound sacks, which someone would then manually unload and store in a warehouse. This approach violated the original design guidelines because it would result in boring, monotonous, low-skill jobs quite different from those in the rest of the plant. This work wouldn't provide any opportunities for employees to learn new skills to qualify them to move to higher-level positions at a later date.

To bring this process into balance with rest of the organization, the task force directed the engineering group to rethink its material-handling plans and to devise an alternative solution that wouldn't violate the plant's design guidelines. Rising to the challenge, the engineering group developed a new system where peanuts arrived via railroad cars in bulk and could then be sucked out with vacuum technology, untouched by human hands. Receiving department employees were now required to schedule shipments and perform intricate acceptance testing of incoming raw materials, creating a much more sophisticated and fulfilling job. This system proved so much faster and cheaper than the old one, it quickly became an industry standard.

Many managers can clearly explain how technology causes a work system to produce a product or service, but they can talk only vaguely, if at all, about its impact on employees operating that work system. Technical designers frequently make unchallenged assumptions about people's tolerances, preferences, and capabilities, and then design work processes and assign tasks based on these assumptions. But organizational effectiveness depends on making more conscious and balanced choices that accommodate the demands of the organization and its technologies on the one hand, and the needs, desires, and capabilities of employees on the other.

Companies have always used technology to replace people and make work systems more predictable and dependable. People and technology are usually viewed in terms of their comparability rather than their compatibility. Machines do some things very well, especially repetitive and programmable tasks, but people also do some things very well, such as making subjective judgments and recognizing what to do in new situations Mechanical systems run best when they're least disturbed. Intellect grows most when it's challenged. Since a misfit between people and technology can throw an entire organization out of balance, it's essential to match the capabilities of both resources rather than emphasizing one at the expense of the other.

The continuing creation of new technology is a tide that can't be stopped. However, technology alone doesn't determine destiny. Eric Trist, who first championed these "SocioTechnical" ideas in a book published in 1963 titled *Organizational Choice*, once remarked, "We must use technology in ways that are consistent with the value systems we believe in." Use technology not to replace people, but to improve their effectiveness by making them faster, better informed, and more accurate.

Adopting New Perspectives about Structure

Fifteen years ago, executives could structure their companies conventionally because they operated in a relatively stable and predictable environment. Organizations typically lurched along from reorganization to reorganization, from improvement scheme to improvement scheme, alternating between periods of change and periods of recovery. Managers who saw no need to rethink or reframe their traditional beliefs merely revised rather than replaced their organizations' policies and practices. But today, local incremental improvement is seldom good enough. A fast-moving world demands more comprehensive restructuring initiatives.

Keeping an Eye on the Big Picture

A hospital consists of doctors, nurses, orderlies, dietitians, patients, and administrators. A hospital also operates kitchens, storerooms, and pharmacies, follows admitting, scheduling, and purchasing procedures, uses information systems to track medication and patient care, and works with suppliers and subcontractors who handle specialized patient testing. For a hospital to succeed, each of these components must operate efficiently, but they must also all work smoothly together. In the end, success hinges on the harmonious alignment of strategies, structures, people, and processes.

Only a comprehensive framework can address today's real-world complexity. BAE Automated Systems designed a baggage-handling system for the new International Airport in Denver, Colorado. The system was created to coax 4,000 baggage carts run by 100 computers to carry 1,400 bags a minute. When the system was first started, unexpected power surges tripped circuits and shut down its motors. BAE also discovered that a smudged bar code or a push on the wrong button could scramble the whole system, and this, in turn, could have a dramatic impact on air traffic, grounding airplanes all across the United States.

Think of an organization as a system of interdependent, connected components that must work together so that their contributions complement each other. Some of these components reside within the organization, some lie outside its walls. Identifying these components, including managers, supervisors, employees, stockholders, partners, suppliers, community groups, government agencies, and others who influence the fate of the organization, reveals the degree of connectedness that exists among all the organization's stakeholders. This picture, which looks more like an ever-expanding circle than the traditional hierarchical pyramid of boxes and lines, is more useful than the conventional organization chart for describing how all the key players in a business interact and influence each other. Studying this picture makes it clear that doing business successfully depends on the collaboration of all concerned.

The new global economy demands bridges, not walls. Individual organizations, however large, can no longer invent change successfully simply through their own efforts. Rather, each must take the purposes of a variety of other institutions into account. In an environment of persistent uncertainty, shared values help assure a coordinated response, and strategies of collaboration become as important as strategies of competition.

Breaking Down Boundaries

The long-established adversarial relationship between retailers and suppliers won't work in the new business environment that requires products to move through distribution channels faster and more efficiently than ever before. To reduce inefficiencies in the flow of supply, inventory reduction systems must maintain much closer relationships between suppliers and retailers. Essential alliances between manufacturers and retailers (such as Procter & Gamble and Wal-Mart) have sprung up in many markets because suppliers know they must develop a deeper understanding of their retailers' strategies and cost structures through direct access to their sales data. By linking their computers with those of major retail chains, top consumer product companies such as Procter & Gamble manage their inventory from the moment goods come off the manufacturing floor until the consumer takes them through the checkout line. This helps cut costs; it enables the factory to produce just what the market needs, saving inventory and warehouse space; it computes optimal truck loads and delivery schedules; and it allows the retailer to tie up less shelf space by guaranteeing a steady replenishing of stock. The *replenishment cycle*—from the time a consumer takes a product off the shelf to the time a replacement arrives from the factory—has shrunk from an average of 12 days to 5. Such speediness begins with close collaboration among partners who once eyed each other warily.

Hundreds of organizations have developed computer systems and written programs for the same types of applications, creating huge duplication of effort. Rather than tie up expensive information-system talent re-creating the wheel, smart organizations share their expertise. In just one example of this development, three Wall Street firms are building business-critical systems with the same set of computer-aided software engineering (CASE) tools. New York City–based brokerage house First Boston initially developed the tools, but to defray its development costs, it sold the technology to Bear Sterns of Atlanta and Kidder Peabody of New York City.

In its 1990 annual report, General Electric described its organizational aspirations for the future. "Our dream for the 1990s is [to be] a boundaryless company where we knock down the walls that separate us from each other on the inside and from our key constituencies on the outside." Such a company would remove barriers among traditional functions, "recognize no distinctions" between foreign and domestic operations, and "ignore or erase group labels such as 'management,' 'salaried,' or 'hourly,' which get in the way of people working together."

In the future, boundaries will continue to blur, making it harder and harder to remember where an organization begins and ends. Companies will have to think inclusively rather than exclusively, linking up with people and institutions they may have ignored in the past, but that have information that's essential for their success.

The Company with the Newest Toys Wins

In 1960, the simplest functional electronic circuit needed two transistors, five other parts, and a circuit board on which to mount them. Today, millions of functions can fit on a single silicon chip less that a quarter of an inch square. The cost per function has plummeted to a fraction of a cent, down from nearly $10 in 1960. Computer chip processing capability doubles every 18 months, while information processing costs drop by 50%. This explosive growth in capability has driven an electronic revolution, which is changing business processes more rapidly than any other development in history. With new methodologies such as reverse engineering making technical innovations increasingly easy to copy, technology has become more of a commodity than a means of sustaining competitive differentiation. Observes Tom West, Data General's senior vice president of Advanced Technology, "When you put pieces of hardware together today, the new technology life expectancy is two years at best." To retain a competitive advantage, an organization needs to constantly upgrade its technical capability, as AT&T recently discovered.

AT&T's Universal Card Services Division, based in Jacksonville, Florida, started up in 1989. Not only did Universal get off to a splendid start, meeting AT&T's profit goal of $100 million in earnings by 1992, it also won the prestigious Malcolm Baldridge National Quality Award that same year. Universal entered the market when the number of Americans carrying bank credit cards—about 41%—hadn't changed in 10 years. By 1993, in a highly competitive, low-growth environment, credit card companies were preying on each other's customers, offering low fees, no fees, or reduced interest rates to persuade them to transfer their outstanding balances. Universal's start-up strategy of providing superior customer service to differentiate it from its competitors demanded agility and flexibility. To stay out in front, Universal empowered its phone representatives to give customers credit increases and balance corrections on the spot, without first obtaining supervisory approval. To the company's chagrin, it quickly found that phone representatives lacked the tools to do the job successfully. Even though the company had been operating for fewer than five years, its start-up technology had already grown sadly out of date.

Universal's 1,900 phone representatives field over a million calls per month. At startup, they used "dumb" computer terminals that couldn't integrate information from multiple mainframes. The phone reps found themselves bouncing from screen to screen, struggling to remember different access codes for multiple mainframes while at the same time trying to keep up a cheery conversation with callers. A simple change of address required manual input to three databases. For an organization featuring customer service as its distinctive competence, dumb terminals represented a decidedly dumb technical choice.

When planning to modify the existing equipment, Universal saw that any technology that could shave a few seconds from the average three-minute phone call would translate into significant savings. So they added automatic number identification to the original customer service platform, a feature that automatically brought the customer's account information to the screen. This saved 12 seconds in keystroke time per call and greatly reduced the chance of operator-generated errors. Says chief quality officer, Rob Davis, "We have to be willing to abandon any technology, if necessary, in order to move forward." Who knows what technologies and services will be needed to captivate customers next year?

Redesigning Organizations Is a Never-Ending Story

Ford started up its world-class stamping, body, and assembly plant in Hermosillo, Mexico, in November 1986 to build the Mercury Tracer. When the company closed out Tracer production in November 1989, it hadn't planned to produce its next product, the Ford Escort, until April 1990. Normally in the auto industry, a company would lay off most employees during a model changeover. However, Hermosillo is no ordinary plant.

It began as a three-level, lean-manufacturing facility designed to support a series of high-performance work teams responsible for both car production and quality. There are no supervisors at Hermosillo, and there's only one plant-wide job classification called operating technician. These technicians can stop the assembly line if they can't complete their tasks in a way that assures world-class quality. All tasks rotate among team members, and a given technician's pay hinges on certified skills and demonstrated ability, rather than on seniority or a current work assignment. Employees participate in a continuous training program and move off the assembly line for two weeks of formal classroom training every six months.

During the six-month shut-down period in 1989–90, the technicians thoroughly examined all operating policies and practices in detail to identify strengths and weaknesses and to pinpoint needs for improvement. All 2,000 operating technicians were involved in reviewing and revitalizing the Hermosillo plant's "philosophy" (shown on page 49), which was initially developed in 1984 by the original North American launch team. By 1990, Mexican nationals had replaced all but one of the 47 foreign service managers who directed plant operation during design and startup.

Small-group discussions focused on examining current and future business requirements, clarified the philosophy statement's original intent, reviewed how living with these ideas had actually worked out in practice, and suggested modifications, additions, or deletions based on the previous three years experience. Ford's Dr. Richard Schneider, who was the organization development and training manager assigned to the original Hermosillo design team, comments, "All employees had an opportunity to challenge the original language during the revitalization process. They could have changed it, but they didn't. What started out as a Ford, Detroit philosophy, drafted in English by a group of predominantly American managers, is now a Ford, Sonora philosophy, owned by the Mexican employees. This philosophy sets forth what they aspire to. That doesn't mean everyone lives it completely every day. But everyone there knows the aspirations and is committed to trying to achieve them."

In 1990, researchers from MIT's International Motor Vehicle Program rated Ford Hermosillo as the top automobile assembly plant in the world, with better quality than the best Japanese and North American plants. Successful companies don't wait for a crisis to prompt action, but continually evaluate the appropriateness of their processes and philosophies in a conscious and comprehensive way. They know current activities simply represent "the way we do things today," and those methods will probably fall by the wayside tomorrow in favor of new and better practices. In a dynamic world, if they don't remain dynamic as well, they risk being left behind. Since the world never stops spinning, redesign efforts can never stop either. As Charles Brown, the former chairman of AT&T, once said, "You can't manage the business from memory anymore." Successful organizations in the future will view redesign as an ongoing process rather than a one-time project.

Ford Hermosillo Plant Charter
Plant Objectives

The primary objectives of the Hermosillo Stamping and Assembly Plant are to manufacture and assemble cars at a quality level of 240 UPAS concerns, at Mazda productivity levels, with organization and plant flexibility that can support market fluctuations.

In order to meet these objectives, we need all employees to take responsibility to perform their jobs with dependability and commitment. We believe that this will be achieved by managing in a way that develops and supports each individual's sense of self-worth.

Plant Philosophy

Policies and practices should reflect our belief that:

People are trustworthy.

People will behave responsibly when they have a clear understanding of what they have to do and are provided timely feedback on their performance.

People will contribute to their full potential when they have a vehicle to be heard and are not afraid to speak up.

People will grow and develop their skills and abilities when there are opportunities and incentives for doing so, and when they understand the business sufficiently to be able to actively influence what they need to learn.

People will cooperate with each other and work together effectively where there are well-defined, shared goals and where there is mutual respect and understanding of one another's responsibilities.

Key Factors in Applying This Plant Philosophy

Jobs should have broad, clearly defined responsibilities and should provide opportunities for autonomy, variety, growth, and feedback.

Informed decision-making at the first possible level should be developed and encouraged.

Rewards should recognize demonstrated knowledge, skills, initiative, quality, performance, and teamwork, and should be based on individual contributions as well as overall plant performance.

Career guidance and development opportunities should be created to encourage all employees to broaden their skills, to increase their knowledge of the business, and to develop to their fullest potential.

Working conditions in all areas of the plant should support safe, pleasant, and efficient practices.

Artificial status distinctions should be minimized.

Open, direct two-way communication should be encouraged and facilitated between all levels and all areas in the organization. Information should go first to people who need to act on it.

Every employee should understand how his or her job impacts on the total effort. Functional or departmental boundaries should not separate people who depend on one another or need to work together to produce a quality product.

The primary responsibility of supervision is to help people define and plan to achieve personal and organizational goals, to make sure they have access to the resources they need, and to interface with other groups as required.

Shaping the World with New Perspectives

How a business is designed depends on the environmental factors that shape it. Sooner or later, social, economic, and political tremors register on an organization's seismographs. Agility and flexibility should be permanently built in rather than added during a crisis. People and resources need to be constantly deployed to look for and respond to unplanned events, to learn the consequences of those responses, and to apply that learning to anticipating and shaping a brighter future. Without this learning, organizations and individuals never break bad habits and never develop new ones.

Redesign initiatives that flow from these new perspectives view customers, competitors, suppliers, and employees in a new way. New risks call for new rules. Customers now become *prosumers*, working with the organization as equal players, guiding the design of new products and services. Competitors become joint-venture partners, helping the organization achieve together what neither can do alone. Suppliers become privy to core business secrets and strategies, so intertwined with the business that their fates are interdependent with it. Employees become a high-leverage investment, an asset to develop rather than just another troublesome cost to control. New perspectives lead to rethinking business values and philosophies so that learning and leading replace controlling and copying. Creating such a future successfully requires a conscious, comprehensive, and collaborative design effort.

Setting the Stage for a Rapid Redesign

1939: Word reaches the small, tight circle of U.S. scientists that the brilliant German physicist Werner Heisenberg is heading up a nuclear research program for Hitler. A few physicists like Leo Szilard, himself a Jewish refugee who fled the Nazis, instantly grasp the implications of this news. If the Germans succeed in developing an atomic bomb, no force on earth will prevent Hitler from destroying London, Moscow, even New York and Washington. Although Szilard and a handful of American physicists recognize the danger, the U.S. government does not. Yet.

Szilard, hell-bent on remedying that situation, drives to Princeton, New Jersey, to visit Albert Einstein, carrying with him the draft of a letter for Einstein's signature that will alert President Franklin Delano Roosevelt to the threat. The two-page letter describes new strides in nuclear research and warns that new developments in nuclear fission might make possible the development of extremely powerful bombs, "capable of destroying a whole port together with some of the surrounding territory." The letter also strongly suggests that the President appoint an official in charge of marshaling the resources of the U.S. government and military to match or, better yet, surpass the German effort. Until now, a leading expert on the subject, Italian-born Enrico Fermi, has estimated that it will take perhaps 20 years to develop an atomic bomb, a time frame any U.S. project must slash considerably.

When the letter finally reaches Roosevelt, it sets off a chain reaction, resulting in the formation of the Manhattan Project, the U.S. program to develop an atomic weapon. As the war in Europe rages on, Allied concerns about the German bomb program intensify. By 1944, the United States has already invested billions of dollars in the effort, employing tens of thousands of people in vast diffusion plants in Tennessee, and hundreds of scientists in New Mexico and other sites. Philip Morrison, a Manhattan Project physicist, tunes in the BBC each morning to reassure himself that the Germans haven't yet demolished London. By mid-1945, years ahead of schedule, the Allies successfully test a nuclear device in the New Mexican desert.

After the Allies win the war in Europe, the U.S. military finally gets a good look at the German nuclear program. They discover that the Germans were still years away from testing a bomb of their own, that they had, in fact, virtually abandoned the attempt in 1942.

The moral of the story? Nothing stimulates rapid response like a crisis. Or to put it another way, a serious problem offers a wonderful opportunity to apply The 20% Solution—prioritize what needs to get done, then put all your muscle behind making it happen.

Speeding Up the Redesign Process at R.R. Donnelley

R.R. Donnelley & Sons is the world's biggest commercial printing company. In 1992, Donnelley's Hudson manufacturing division in Hudson, Massachusetts decided that rapidly changing technology and escalating customer expectations about product quality mandated significant changes in how it ran its printing plant. Though Donnelley had a long-enjoyed history of employee involvement where small representative teams of employees participated in various redesign projects, the management at Hudson wanted to get all 200 employees directly involved in the plant's redesign. Moreover, management hoped to "get something done quickly," completing the whole redesign process in fewer than 90 days, about 20% of the time that previous redesign had taken. Donnelley asked organizational consultants Dick and Emily Axelrod to help them design such a process.

Together, they designed a series of two-day conferences during which Donnelley's employees examined the emerging needs of customers and suppliers, developed a common vision about how the plant needed to evolve over the next 10 years, mapped out the strengths and weaknesses of current work processes, and listed the changes required to assure prosperity in the future. As a result, everyone ultimately agreed on a new, redesigned organization that reduced the number of departments from 20 to 4 (conversion, logistics, information, and support), and created new operating goals and philosophies. Employees assigned to the four new work units then developed plans for transitioning to the new organization, deciding how to staff, structure, and assign responsibility in their work units, and coordinating activities between them.

All 20 supervisors and managers at the Hudson plant participated in each of the redesign conferences. Hourly employees came on a voluntary basis and could choose to attend more than one conference. Each conference involved from 60 to 80 people drawn from different functions and departments, selected to bring the right mix of skills and experience to the discussions. Since the majority of the employees attended at least one conference, a good many people understood the reasons for change and eagerly offered their ideas about what to change and how.

The conferences generated a great deal of data, which was collected and synthesized into common themes by a data-assist team. This group also documented findings and conclusions and kept a record of decisions or suggestions made during the conferences. Information from each conference became available to any employee who hadn't participated in that meeting during special "walkthru" sessions involving about 20 people at a time. Issues raised during the "walkthrus" went back to the redesign conferences and were subsequently addressed in the Hudson division's monthly newsletter.

The division's director and his direct reports, together with representatives from engineering, human resources, and the data-assist team, managed the overall redesign process. Members of the group attended every conference, to provide ideas for change and to challenge the reasoning behind the recommendations being considered. As a result, they readily approved and supported all the redesign conclusions since they were already familiar with them. The whole undertaking achieved its goal of 90 days from start to finish.

Creating the Future from Strength

Employees at R.R. Donnelley realized that if they didn't respond quickly to an emerging crisis, their business could run into serious trouble in the future. Rather than fearing the crisis, they knuckled down and redesigned their operations to turn it into an opportunity for growth. In sharp contrast, management and unions in the steel and auto industries were too slow to recognize that fundamental changes in their business required entirely new ways of organizing and working in the future. As a result, those industries lost hundreds of thousands of jobs. A delayed response invariably results in stressed and preoccupied employees who spend all their energy fighting fires in order to survive and typically lack both the time and appetite for long-term planning. Any organization that waits for a crisis to force it to change runs the risk of losing its best people before it takes action. Smart organizations, like people, work on their health while they're still well. A jogging program does little good for someone who is already suffering from emphysema. In the words of the thirteenth-century English philosopher Roger Bacon, "He that will not apply new remedies must expect new evils, for time is the greatest inventor." Successful organizations make time their friend rather than their enemy, and emphasize the opportunities that the future presents rather than dwelling on the problems of the past.

Accentuating the Positive

An old saying holds that "There's nothing like the prospect of being hanged in the morning to focus the mind." In a vain attempt to enforce this dictum, many organizations try to influence employees to change by bombarding them with bad news. "Dreadful things will happen," they warn, "if you don't change so-and-so immediately." Whether these dreadful things will actually happen or not, the mere mention of them prompts many people to ignore, block out, or deflect the bad news. "Maybe it'll never happen," they reason, or "Maybe it won't be as bad as they say," or "Maybe it won't happen until after I've retired." Bad news seldom energizes people. Even if the prospect of impending calamity eventually gets their attention, it doesn't stir people to action in the same way a positive message does by detailing how to avoid the calamity and painting a picture of a more attractive future. A positive message presents time, change, and the future as a friend, not as an enemy.

Managers often feel nervous about painting and publicizing attractive pictures of the future because doing so can generate increased expectations and create additional accountability. Articulating a positive vision of the future often requires disclosing personal values and aspirations, and those who do so run the risk that others won't agree with or support their point of view. It's hard to lead a cavalry charge if you think you're going to look silly sitting on a horse. But nothing worth having comes without risk. People everywhere silently wait to follow strong leaders who boldly declare themselves and take a decisive stand, who bravely say in public what others think in private. Those who successfully lead the charge to the future invariably remain positive, clear, resolved, convincing, unequivocal, and personal in their arguments. Those who cling to negative images seldom convince people to commit to a cause. They find themselves and their organizations forced onto the shoulder of the road by competitors who are ready to change.

Assessing Readiness for Change

Some years ago, several colleagues were advising the Olivetti company about organization redesign. Working with the top management group in Italy, they led a review of the key factors influencing the company's business and found quick agreement that dramatic structural and procedural changes were needed to take full advantage of the opportunities the future offered. Delighted that the management group had reached agreement so quickly, the consultants began to talk to them about implementing these changes. However, the managers protested that they couldn't go any further until "the establishment" agreed with these findings and their implications. Puzzled, the consultants said they didn't understand who the establishment was since the officers of the company were all present at the meeting. The managers then reminded them of the company's history.

Camillio Olivetti started the company years ago. Under the leadership of his son, Adriano, the company grew and expanded rapidly after World War II, and many new managers were hired. When Adriano Olivetti died unexpectedly, these managers—the establishment—continued to run the company the way they thought he would have run it had he lived. In other words, the company was really being run by a dead man. While these middle managers didn't have the power to make much happen on their own initiative, they did have the power to effectively stop anything they didn't agree with.

The moral? Pay attention to those who must say yes to change, but don't forget those who can say no. There are more of the latter than the former, and in the long run, they have a bigger impact on introducing change successfully.

Dealing with Resistance to Change

Sixty-two percent of the presidents of large American corporations polled at the 1994 *Business Week* Presidents Forum said they were currently working to create a mind-set that would embrace change in their organizations. But, because it's always hard to take the upset out of upheaval, getting people to embrace change is tough work. Major transitions are always uncomfortable and destabilizing, whether they involve a nation, an individual, or a culture. Change transforms all kinds of relationships, as old beliefs are challenged and old jobs are destroyed while new ones are being created.

Resistance to change isn't a problem; rather, it's a symptom that some people have concerns that need closer attention. People at all levels resist change if:

They don't understand why it's necessary.

They're not really clear about what they're being asked to change to.

They don't know how to perform their new work assignments.

They're not convinced the transition is needed in the time frame specified.

They're afraid it won't be a lasting change ("It's just another program").

They feel they'll lose power and influence as a result of the change.

They don't believe they'll be rewarded for taking on new responsibilities.

They don't feel they'll be supported in their efforts to change.

Taking the mystery out of the process of changing by spelling out the steps involved as explicitly as possible make it easier to manage the issues that cause resistance. Changing is complicated because it involves not one but two processes, both taking place at the same time. One process is letting go of the past, the other is reaching out to embrace the future. Because of these dual engagements, it takes people twice as long to come to terms with what's happening. This procrastination happens at a time when people want the whole uncomfortable business of changing to be over with as quickly as possible. It's often difficult to take the time needed to alternate between mourning and stretching. People can't do both at once. But both need to occur, for each one has its own place in the process.

To provide the enabling conditions for change, it helps to create initiatives that pull the organization in the right direction, as well as to create events to push it to move faster, as illustrated in Figure 3.1. Here the organization is represented as a wavy line that seeks to move from its present condition, A, toward a more attractive future, B. The push-and-pull initiatives shown need to be coordinated in time and content so they reinforce and build on each other. If they're too radical for the organization's culture, they risk being ignored or rejected. However, failure to introduce acceptable alternatives risks losing ground to more adventurous competitors.

Pulling Organizations toward the Future

Pull initiatives are designed to move the organization in the direction of its desired future. They can take many forms and have the advantage that they can be anticipated, planned, scheduled, and coordinated in advance.

Reaching Consensus about Change

In 1990, CEO Craig Weatherup set out to transform Pepsi-Cola's business. During the next two years, he held a series of three-day meetings where every one of Pepsi's 30,000 employees could participate. Weatherup used the meetings to help people understand that the company faced a crisis, as well as to share with them his vision of a new, customer-driven organization. He also introduced tools they could use to build a better future together. Involvement in dialogs about the need for change helped Pepsi's employees understand the organization's prospects for the future. It also helped them reach a common consensus about revamping its vision, aspirations, and operating philosophy.

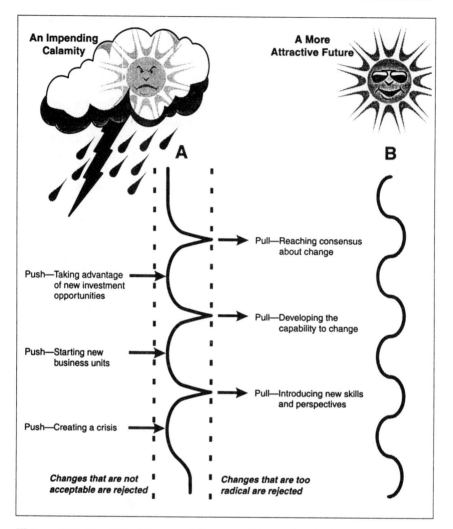

Figure 3.1 Providing the enabling conditions for change.

Developing the Capability to Change

While Weatherup was taking his redesign message to the troops, Pepsi's top 11 managers learned to use redesign methodologies such as reengineering, continuous improvement, and core business processes mapping. In most cases, this required them to become intimately familiar with a business process that needed improving. These 11 managers then used their real-world redesign experience to train the next 70 managers, who then trained the next 400, and so on throughout the organization.

Introducing New Skills and Perspectives

People are often reluctant to change because they don't know how to do what's now required of them rather than because they disagree with the content of what's being proposed. Training addresses this by giving people new skills so they can undertake new duties with capability and confidence. Visits to leading-edge companies to learn about their policies and practices also helps people develop new ways of looking at their current problems and opportunities. Following such a visit, one team of managers and hourly workers at Pepsi-Cola redesigned the way soft drinks were delivered to markets, stores, and restaurants. This saved each of its 10,000 trucks 45 minutes in delivery time each day, extra time they used to make more stops and sell more soda.

Pushing Organizations Away from the Past

Push initiatives usually arise spontaneously to take advantage of emerging opportunities. While only those organizations that have a clear vision and a well-developed sense of the future will recognize these opportunities when they arise, they can spark a number of very helpful initiatives.

Taking Advantage of New Investment Opportunities

Some initiatives come from a push for investment. In 1993, Local 763 of the International Union of Electronic Workers at General Electric's Appliance Park in Kentucky won a $70 million investment to develop a new washing machine. To engineer that coup, the union agreed to a 43-point change program that, among other things, eliminated piecework and allowed GE to broaden job definitions so workers could move more freely to different jobs in the Appliance Park complex. GE also reduced the number of supervisors and organized most of the workers into teams with a significantly greater voice in operational matters. In the past, complaints about poorly made materials from suppliers often went nowhere, but now workers could take action themselves to keep suppliers in line. "Some people have to work a little harder," said Local 761 president Norman Mitchell. "But I'd rather work a little harder and have a job."

Starting New Business Units

Push initiatives can also spawn whole new enterprises. A few years ago, Merck charged five of its employees with setting up a new U.S. marketing organization to represent anti-ulcer and high-blood pressure drugs licensed from Sweden's Astra drug company. Rejecting the traditional functional department approach to organization, the design team created 31 decentralized, cross-functional business units instead, each with its own customers and profit-and-loss responsibility. The Astra/Merck Group, with 700 employees, functions around six market-driven business processes, from drug development to product sourcing and distribution. The organization chart consists of a stack of six elongated rectangles, each representing a core business process. Along the top appear a series of functional boxes, or skill centers, that support these processes. The organization encourages all its salespeople to share with each other their information on market trends, medical research, and regulatory developments using a nationwide client-server network.

Creating a Crisis

Sometimes, push can come to shove. Ameritech, the Midwest regional Baby Bell telephone company based in Chicago, pushed itself into crisis to address the fact that as technology and competition drove down the cost of local calls, it had to find ways to reduce its costs per revenue dollar. Twenty-seven months before mandatory retirement at age 65, Ameritech's chairman, Bill Weiss, felt that although the organization's business, if left unchanged, would continue to perform well for the next three years, it would increasingly lose ground in the long term. With several seasoned executives jostling to succeed him, Weiss lacked confidence that his potential successors, all steeped in the Bell system's traditions, possessed the vision and skill required to lead the company into the telecommunications battles ahead. In February 1992, he convened a three-day meeting of Ameritech's top 30 executives at the Breakers Hotel in Palm Beach, Florida, asking each to prepare a profile of the Ameritech of the future and to share it out loud with all of the other attendees. This exercise helped identify those who felt excited by the possibilities of the future and who saw the potential of imaginatively changing the $12 billion company into something new.

At the meeting's end, Weiss thanked everyone for their contributions, then he publicly asked four relatively junior officers to meet with him in a few days to discuss how they would redesign and rebuild the organization. Within a year, Ameritech had eased most of its management committee into early retirement and, in 1993, it reorganized from five operating companies grouped by state into 11 business units grouped by customer category (residential telephone service, cellular, and small business service). "We had to create a crisis," said Richard Brown, one of the four junior officers tapped at the Breakers meeting.

The Chinese have two words for crisis; one means danger, the other, opportunity. Ameritech couldn't get properly motivated thinking competition was four years away. They had to think it was tomorrow. Organizations tend to avoid change until something catastrophic forces them to alter old habits. It's far better, of course, to choose change rather than have it chosen for you.

Choosing a Change Strategy

When Jan Carlzon took over as president of Scandinavian Airlines (SAS) in 1981, he found the company in serious trouble, demoralized, and losing money. To remedy that situation, Carlzon distributed a little red book to all 20,000 employees entitled "Let's Get in There and Fight," outlining his overall vision and strategies for reviving the organization. During his first year as president, he spent half his working hours out in the field, meeting with hundreds of small groups of employees in an effort to learn how they assessed the organization's problems and opportunities. With every group, he shared his dreams for SAS, while never failing to listen to theirs. During that time, employees joked, "Wherever three or more people are gathered together, Jan Carlzon will be there to talk with them." Carlzon worked hard to develop a fresh, realistic, shared awareness of SAS's prospects, emphasizing positive possibilities for unparalleled success in the future by applying his version of The 20% Solution, focusing on a few high-leverage issues such as customer satisfaction. This approach produced such spectacular results that in 1984, SAS snared *Air Transport World*'s Airline of the Year award.

Leading from the Top

As the SAS saga demonstrates, organizational change is most effective when it starts with clear purpose and strategies in the mind of the CEO, which are then cascaded down, level by level, through the rest of the organization. Of course, such an approach can work only when the other senior managers also believe in the need for change and commit themselves to investing the time, money, and energy it will take to explore and adopt better ways of working. Their visible conviction, commitment, and action persuades others of the need for and the benefits of changing. Nonetheless, senior management should visibly foster dialog at each level rather than dictating purpose and philosophy to subordinates. The top-down redesign process needs at least one highly visible sponsor, someone in the organization powerful enough to get people's attention, whose words and deeds signal to everyone that redesign represents the highest priority. Those involved in generating redesign recommendations can turn to this sponsor for help if, for example, someone with vital information refuses to share it.

In any top-down change scenario, the senior leadership group bears responsibility for providing a clear redesign charter for the rest of the organization, clarifying the goals, boundaries, authority, and accountability surrounding all redesign activities. They provide information about the time, cost, and scope of the redesign initiative and set limits on which issues people can and can't address. The charter determines, for instance, whether those involved in developing redesign proposals will simply recommend certain changes or whether they'll be authorized to make binding, final decisions. Either way, it's crucial for everyone to keep well informed, monitoring progress, providing input, reviewing findings, evaluating emerging proposals, and making sure that the redesign train remains on track. The sponsor oversees it all, removing roadblocks and providing additional resources when necessary.

Encouraging Widespread Participation

Someone once told me a story about an organization, let's call it Alpha Systems, that had low productivity and poor employee morale. Alpha hired a big-name consulting firm to study these problems at a cost of $250,000. The consulting firm recommended that Alpha enlarge the car park, add a second hot-food line in the cafeteria, and paint the plant's walls in pastel colors. The organization spent another $250,000 doing all this, but saw no noticeable change in performance as a result. Alpha charged a newly hired manager to find out why. On her first day on the job, she stopped a worker at random and asked him what Alpha could do to improve performance. He said that, in his humble opinion, the organization should enlarge the car park, add a second hot-food line in the cafeteria, and paint the plant in pastel colors. The new manager responded that Alpha had just spent half a million dollars doing just that, and yet, nothing had changed, to which the employee replied, "Well, they never asked me." People support what they help to create. Even when those at the top see the need for change, they don't always know exactly what to change or how to change it. This kind of expertise resides in the people lower down in the organization who do the actual day-to-day work, so making any change successfully is dependent on their participation, energy, and goodwill. That's why, in most cases, widespread participation at all levels propels change efforts more successfully than "do it or die" mandates from above.

A participative approach also collects ideas and proposals for change from customers and suppliers, who can usually provide useful insights into how an organization might redesign itself to better serve their needs. Attending training programs, courses, and seminars on organizational change and transformation, visiting other companies to study how they've improved their flexibility and creativeness, and reading books, articles, and case studies on successful work innovation helps employees learn about design choices that can satisfy their own personal needs, the company's goals, and the customer's desires. Learning from success is invariably more invigorating than fantasizing about failure.

Including as many people as possible in redesign activities helps build ownership for the change effort, providing some connection with, input into, information about, and ownership of the final redesign recommendations. In addition to reaching out to all employees, remember to use The 20% Solution. Every organization has a relatively small number of informal opinion leaders, people others go to in order to find out what's really happening. Find key roles for them in the redesign process so they'll spread the official message of change to everyone else rather than spreading rumors by guessing about what they think is going on. Try to involve every employee directly in a least one stage of the redesign journey. Bringing in new members at each stage encourages new ideas and renews enthusiasm. But enthusiasm by itself won't be enough if corporate policies continue to send the wrong messages.

Preparing the Organization for Change

In 1986, Polaroid began a work redesign program in its R2 instant film packaging plant in Waltham, Massachusetts, by asking employees to consider what they would do differently if they could relocate operations and set them up afresh someplace else (the redesign initiative subsequently became known as WINK, the initials standing for Work IN Kansas). As suggestions and ideas for change began to take shape, it was clear that new ways of working couldn't be implemented unless current policies were changed. Polaroid set up a series of corporate-level task forces to look at new options for dealing with policies about job classifications, bidding on and moving to new work assignments, and providing pay and incentives to support the team-based organizations being proposed by the WINK redesign team. Polaroid's management realized there wasn't much point in encouraging people to work together cooperatively if official company policies encouraged competitive behavior instead.

It's often necessary for the leadership group to change corporate policies in anticipation of new behaviors called for in the redesign. Employees at all levels in the organization are unlikely the change their work practices if official policies encourage or reward behaviors that are contrary to the new order.

Choices in Pacing the Redesign Process

The pace of the redesign process can be too fast or too slow. If it's too slow, it's difficult to generate and sustain any significant excitement and energy for change. People are easily distracted, and the pressures of the present drive out serious reflection about the future. The longer the redesign process takes, the more it's likely to suffer from "creeping elegance," by generating incremental but often low-yield improvements.

If the redesign process goes too fast, people don't have time to fully understand the issues being raised and can't express difficulties or questions they have about them. Unless people can clarify and express their concerns and see how these will be addressed, they won't be free to act without fear. Without opportunities to explore and understand what the future will mean for them personally, they won't know how to make it work. Troublesome issues will have to be faced sooner or later if recommendations for change are to be implemented successfully. Getting people involved from the beginning ensures that the right concerns are being addressed and develops ownership for the outcomes. It's better to use people's energy in a positive way, to avoid unwanted consequences before they happen, rather than engaging people's energy in negative ways, compensating for unanticipated events after they've occurred.

Problems with Traditional Approaches to Redesign

Over the years, many organizations have successfully redesigned themselves by actively involving a select group of employees from different functions and levels in the recommendation process. Most began by appointing a Steering Committee, made up of senior executives, to charter and guide the redesign effort. Then they assembled a cross-functional, multilevel redesign team, made up of employees representing important stakeholder groups from the rest of the organization. The senior executives defined the performance standards required for the organization to be successful in the future, while the redesign team worked out the details of how to meet these standards by examining the organization's business conditions, analyzing its core business processes, evaluating how effectively different departments and functions worked together, and assessing working conditions to see if they encouraged employee motivation and commitment. They then made recommendations about new ways to organize work based on these findings, retaining strengths, eliminating weaknesses, and creating the additional elements needed for the organization thrive in the future.

Using this approach, redesign proposals often took from 9 to 18 months to develop, especially if those involved didn't invoke The 20% Solution. Failure to identify and concentrate attention on the small number of issues with the biggest leverage for the future often resulted in an overload of data, with "paralysis by analysis" leading to frustration and burnout for the redesign team members. As a consequence, when redesign recommendations were finally approved, people involved in the redesign process had little energy left for planning how to implement them. In addition, members of the redesign team often became so engrossed in their tasks that they became isolated from the rest of the organization. Consequently, the majority of employees had a limited understanding of how the redesign recommendations were arrived at, and quickly lost sight of why change was needed in the first place. Such confusion invariably resulted in resistance to change.

Some organizations tried to avoid these problems and speed up the process by setting up multiple redesign teams that operated concurrently, each one concentrating on a different aspect of the redesign process (for example, one team analyzing the environment, another team analyzing core business processes, and yet another analyzing the organization's social systems). While this resulted in speedier analyses, it overloaded those employees not directly engaged in redesign activities by providing them with too much data in too short a time, leading once again to a lack of understanding and support for the final redesign recommendations.

In a fast-moving world, recommendations that aren't developed quickly risk becoming obsolete by the time they're approved and implemented. One way to avoid this dilemma and to circumvent the problems just mentioned is to use a Rapid Redesign process that involves many employees over a short time in a series of high-intensity activities. A redesign approach that takes only 20% of the time it traditionally took while involving almost everyone in the organization avoids a good deal of problems.

Rapid Redesign

The accelerated redesign approach used by R.R. Donnelley & Sons described at the beginning of this chapter works well in small organizations with a limited number of employees where the flow of work is easy to visualize. However, in bigger organizations, combining large group employee meetings with a dedicated redesign team is often more effective, and an additional step to examine complex social relationships and interactions is also advisable. By incorporating these additions, the Rapid Redesign process outlined here can deal with the added complexities of larger organizations while at the same time speeding up the redesign and implementation process by building broad ownership for change.

Starting up a Rapid Redesign process usually means going slowly in the beginning in order to build the organization's capability to change faster and faster later on. Sustained success in any redesign process hinges on prior agreement by the organization's leaders about the need for change, and their alignment around a common vision of a preferred future. No redesign process will work well in a politically charged environment where strong turf battles rage among leaders of different functions. In that context, individuals will be afraid to champion positions that are at odds with people at higher levels in the organization. For their own survival, employees will usually line up behind their leaders whether they agree with them or not, leading to a polarization of views that can derail the redesign effort.

Once there is a shared agreement about the future, an organization can involve large groups of employees in a series of two- to four-day meetings, invoking The 20% Solution to develop specific redesign recommendations. Because of the special facilities needed to house the large numbers of people involved, these meetings are usually held at off-site locations. To avoid shutting down the organization's regular business, meetings also often take place during weekends. The location of the meetings, their timing and continuity, and the sense of community they generate helps ignite the sort of excitement and sense of progress that builds energy and enthusiasm for change.

Keeping Everyone Informed and Involved

A small group of knowledgeable, well-respected employees should be appointed to work as a full-time redesign team, identifying key processes and interactions, collecting preliminary data about their current strengths and weaknesses, coordinating and managing the large group meetings, directing the flow of information to and from the rest of the organization, and maintaining a sense of focus and connectedness throughout the Rapid Redesign process. This role provides a wonderful opportunity for personal development as members of the redesign team quickly come to understand what very few people know—namely, how the organization works as a whole.

Individual members of the redesign team should be committed to the organization's success and should combine functional expertise with employee credibility. They need credibility because the information and recommendations they communicate will most likely challenge the status quo and, as a result, will probably generate a certain amount of resistance. Proponents of change who remain in constant communication with the rest of the organization and command everyone's respect can help to resolve most issues causing resistance if they remember that communication is a two-way street. They don't just provide others with information, they listen to and incorporate their feedback, criticism, and concerns as well.

The Rapid Redesign journey must leave enough time between meetings for the redesign team to contact and communicate with the rest of the organization. New ideas spread more slowly among individuals who hold different beliefs, values, education, or social status. Going slowly in the beginning and resolving issues as they arise results in faster progress in the long run.

All instances of progress go through stages of rejection before they're eventually accepted. Common opinion holds that anything that sounds too good to be true, or that differs from what's currently accepted, must be false. Experts, in particular, have a hard time believing anything that differs from their present view of the world. They defend the status quo and use their expertise to ridicule new ideas they're uncomfortable with. The experts said that the world was flat, that the earth was the center of the universe. Experts are often the biggest stumbling blocks for progress; don't wait for them to give the green light for change. Use their conservatism instead to guard against going head over heels into something foolish. Concentrate on and encourage the pioneers who dare to draw their own conclusions after thorough investigation.

Employing a Five-Stage Rapid Redesign Process

The Rapid Redesign process examines how an organization does business from start to finish, from product conception to customer consumption. This examination includes outsiders who have a stake in the organization's performance, such as customers and suppliers, as well as those employees who operate and support the business internally. The advantage of this kind of comprehensive approach is that it challenges existing work unit boundaries, which often results in identifying tasks and departments that shouldn't exist in the first place.

The sequence of the five-stage Rapid Redesign journey typically proceeds as follows:

Stage 1

In the first stage of the Rapid Redesign process, the organizations's leaders analyze and agree on the implications of current business trends and projected future developments. They subsequently host a large group meeting where customers and other key stakeholders explain their future plans and needs to a representative cross section of employees. This helps the employees understand the organization's purpose, aspirations, strategies, and competitive capabilities. The employee group then isolates the key behaviors and capabilities the organization must develop to realize its goals, and identifies the values and guiding principles that will encourage and support their development. These guiding principles are used to create a vision of what the organization should look like and how it should operate in the future. Building a common vision helps employees understand the need for change, the gaps between current work practices and those required for success, the time frames involved in closing those gaps, and their roles and responsibilities during subsequent stages of the redesign process.

Stage 2

During the second stage, the organization's core business processes are defined and control parameters critical to the delivery of successful products and services in the future are identified. In a large meeting, a representative group of employees focuses on eliminating process variation and improving operational control, preserving and refining efficient work practices, developing new technical skills and capabilities, and eliminating tasks that don't add value for customers. The group develops proposals for reconfiguring or replacing jobs, information systems, and work unit boundaries to structure the organization for future success.

Stage 3

The third stage evaluates the current organization to see how it helps or hinders people from working together effectively. A representative cross section of employees participates in a large group meeting to review survey data describing the organization's social processes—how goals are aligned, how people learn about and adapt to change, how the efforts of different individuals and work units are integrated together, and how employees develop long-term competitive capabilities. Recommendations to improve coordination, communication, and collaboration are developed to help people achieve better results in the future. In addition, new ways to create a healthier, safer, and more satisfying work environment are investigated.

Stage 4

In the fourth stage, recommendations are put forward to bring the present and the future into closer alignment by integrating the ideas for change developed in the previous three stages. A large group of employees selected from those who participated in the previous three meetings come together and make recommendations about where to place organizational boundaries, how to create productive and satisfying jobs, how to improve the flow of information, what to reward, and how to select and develop people. Their recommendations are reviewed with all interested parties before they're finally adopted.

Stage 5

The fifth stage formulates a general plan to introduce and implement all the recommendations developed during the Rapid Redesign process. Detailed implementation planning is carried out by local work units. In addition, plans and processes for continuous organization renewal are defined and put in place.

The Fat Lady Doesn't Sing Anymore

Larry Bossidy, the CEO of Allied Signal, says, "Yogi Berra was wrong. It ain't over when it's over, because, today, it's never over." In today's world, people will only be successful if they change their understanding of change, moving their perspective from "change is my enemy" to "change is my friend." Learning to be proactive about change will be an integral part of maintaining competitive advantage in the future. But, before it can be proactive, an organization must be clear about what it wants to be when it grows up. It must be clear and in agreement about its purpose, strategies, mission, and guiding principles.

Rapid Redesign: Clarifying Purpose, Philosophy, and Mission

When a visitor to Nick Williamson's home casually mentions that he's going to Ireland on vacation next week, Nick purses his lips. "I work seven days a week. My work is stimulating. So what if I don't take many days off. What would I do? Go fishing? I hate fishing."

By anyone's measure, Nick Williamson has built a successful career. He owns a small but prosperous architectural firm in Boston, and his growing reputation as a brilliant architect has drawn a continuing flow of business to his firm, where the staff works nearly as hard as Nick himself to keep up with it all.

"You want another mineral water?" Nick asks his visitor.

"No thanks." Nick's guest surveys the results of Nick's hard work in the den of his large, splendidly furnished 1930s-style home, resplendent with art deco furniture, lush hardwood floors, thick and snugly throw rugs, and expensive artwork.

"So when do you make time to think about the future, about what you want to do with your business in the next five years?" the visitor asks.

Nick, a handsome man with steely blue eyes, laughs heartily. Slouching there on the couch, cradling a bottle of Perrier, he looks more like a merry elf than a captain of industry. "You mean," he begins, "do I know

71

what I want to do when I grow up?" But Nick's mirth vanishes as quickly as it appears; he straightens up and leans forward, pointing with the empty bottle. "Do you really think the average guy out there, Joe Six-Pack, who goes to work and comes home and eats his dinner at the same time every day, do you think he knows what he's going to be doing five years from now? Does anybody? I don't have time to think about the future... I'm fighting fires at the office all day, every day. We go from one crisis to another. It's the nature of our work. All it takes is one major mistake, one botched job, and we're out of business."

Nick's visitor sadly shakes his head. "That may be true," he observes, "but does every day really have to be a surprise party?"

Taking the Surprise Out of the Future

Nick Williamson may well be making a fortune working the way he does, but he could accomplish much more, both in terms of personal fulfillment and business accomplishment, if he paused to consider his future more thoughtfully and set about taking the surprise out of it. Any business journey to a better future begins with that first step, a detailed and determined contemplation of all the internal and external features that will fashion the final destination. The Rapid Redesign process organizes the journey to the future into five logical stages, the first of which determines the right direction, clearly visioning what the organization should look like in the future.

Creating a Clear Vision of the Future

A research study at Stanford University's Graduate School of Business asked 170 senior managers to identify the 20 most visionary companies in America. If a dollar had been invested in each of these firms in the mid-1920s (or held with interest until the company came into being later on), by 1993, the visionary firms would, on average, have outperformed Wall Street by a factor of 50 to 1. Vision works. It worked for the 20 companies in the Stanford study, and it'll work for you.

A meaningful vision springs from a careful analysis of present and prospective business conditions. Accurately assessing current business trajectories (customers' needs, competitors' strategies, regulatory restrictions, and so on) and carefully calibrating internal capabilities (employees' skills and abilities, the appropriateness of existing functions, structures, and technologies) determines where gaps exist between today's and tomorrow's organization. The Rapid Redesign process seeks to close these gaps. Since most organizations today will find quite large gaps between where they currently reside and where they need to go, effective redesign usually calls for quick, not leisurely, change.

Many corporate leaders look enviously at the likes of Japan's Toyota, Switzerland's Swatch, and America's Wal-Mart as companies that have achieved spectacular worldwide growth and success. Their clear vision, strong sense of purpose, articulate operating philosophy, and committed employees provide models for all global, decentralized companies struggling to motivate large, scattered workforces. However, inventing a clear vision of a future involves more than imitating someone else. It requires deep self-knowledge.

Asking the Right Questions

The 20% Solution suggests that a clear and empowering vision centers around three essential components: the organization's long-term purpose, its operating philosophy, and its mission and short-term goals. To clarify these vision components, anyone setting out on a journey to the future should ask and answer the following nine critical questions.

Long-Term Purpose

What business should the organization be in?

What is the purpose of the business?

What strategies will help the organization fulfill its purpose?

Guiding Philosophy

What key employee characteristics are needed for success?

What operating philosophy will support these characteristics?

What guidelines should govern how the organization is structured?

Mission

How good does the organization aspire to be?

What performance goals should it pursue?

How will the organization operate differently in the future?

Answering these nine questions about purpose, guiding philosophy, and mission encourages the fresh perception needed to set about inventing a common vision of the future in a conscious, comprehensive, collaborative, and forward-looking way. Let's examine the components of a clear vision and the nine critical questions that lead to it more closely.

Defining Long-Term Purpose

Disney aims "to make people happy." To fulfill its purpose, Disney added adult feature films (Touchstone) to its lineup of family movies, and expanded its theme parks to Japan and Europe. AT&T, intent on providing "anytime, anywhere communications," acquired NCR and invested in a dozen high-technology startups to give it the hardware and software it needs to blaze a trail into the new era of interactive communications. Both companies asked and answered the three questions necessary to clarify their purpose, namely "What business should the organization be in? What is the purpose of the business? What strategies will help the organization fulfill its purpose?"

What Business Should the Organization Be In?

Given the accelerating rate of change today, an organization can no longer rest on its laurels, smugly assuming that the essentials of its business will remain the same over time. As a case in point, look at what happened to American semiconductor chip manufacturers in the 1980s.

Through the late 1970s, American companies dominated the manufacture of semiconductor chips. Eighty-five percent of all the machines in the world used to produce these chips came from America, and even in Japan, 80% bore American nameplates. But by 1982, Japanese semiconductor companies were making more dynamic random access memory chips (DRAMs) than American firms. As Japanese companies increased their output of chips, they turned more and more to Japanese suppliers for chip-making equipment. By 1985, Japan's total production of semiconductor products exceeded that of the United States, and American equipment makers retained barely 25% of the Japanese market, by then the world's largest and fastest-growing market. Clinging to an old definition of their business, the American manufacturers failed to envision a different future. Once they did, it took them until 1992 to reestablish market dominance.

Smart companies don't fear change in the marketplace, they seek to understand it instead because a proper understanding of change can lead to a vision of opportunity. Effectiveness in today's turbulent world entails constantly scanning the organization's environment, talking with key customers and suppliers, striving to comprehend all the implications of current trends and developments, identifying potential threats and looking for new opportunities. All this effort should result in an ever clearer definition of the organization's business. "You don't need a crystal ball to predict the future, you need a wide-angled lens."

Focusing a wide-angled lens on the business environment helps to separate areas of projected stability from those most likely to change. For example, in the early 1980s, the management of Anheuser-Busch reviewed the business environment and concluded that it wasn't working closely enough with its wholesale partners and customers. In short, it wasn't sufficiently responsive to the marketplace. This understanding prompted an examination of company-owned distributorships in an effort to grasp more fully the distributors' problems and to understand what it took for them to turn a profit. Anheuser-Busch created a joint wholesaler advisory panel to improve relationships between the company and its wholesalers. This panel tracked emerging market developments, looking for ways to respond to business trends more quickly than competitors. With everyone now sharing vital information (such as weekly sales and inventory reports), Anheuser-Busch quickly became more adept at projecting future manufacturing requirements.

In its review, Anheuser-Busch also identified proposed state and national legislation that would influence its interests in the future. It saw clearly that changes in labeling and packaging requirements, stronger penalties for driving under the influence, and increased attention to alcohol abuse were turning into major social and legislative issues. This awareness propelled Anheuser-Busch to hire lobbyists to provide information to lawmakers and others involved in discussions and decisions about these issues. Anheuser-Busch undertook this initiative with the express aim of improving the stability of its environment by preventing undesired changes from taking place in the future. In the same vein, it also developed an in-house capability to produce 30% of its own beer cans, thus increasing its pricing leverage on external suppliers.

In today's world, it pays to continuously review the organization's environment because emerging changes require fast and frequent adjustment. The review should include input from all the important stakeholders inside and outside the organization who can influence its future, and it should be global in scope, because in today's world, local responses can evoke potentially far-reaching effects. The review process helps to identify different parts of the organization that need to coordinate their responses.

To understand the organization's current and future business, analyze business developments in areas such as:

- ❑ The national business climate.
- ❑ Requirements of business sponsors and partners.
- ❑ Availability and application of new technologies.
- ❑ New product developments.
- ❑ Competitors' strategies to preempt or counter new products.
- ❑ Restrictions and demands of regulatory agencies.
- ❑ Workforce availability and current demographics.
- ❑ Consumer demands and preferences.

A thorough understanding of the business environment should provide answers to five basic questions:

- ❑ What global market developments will affect the organization's business in the future?
- ❑ What have competitors done in the past three years that has influenced these developments?
- ❑ What has the organization done in the past three years to control or counter these developments?
- ❑ What are competitors likely to do in the future?
- ❑ What can the organization do to give it a competitive advantage?

During this review, concentrate on identifying and exploring new developments unique to the organization's business (including industry trends, economic projections, availability of raw materials, distribution logistics, developments with suppliers). Hard data isn't always easy to come by, but by striving to fill in the

gaps between the known and the unknown, an overall appreciation of the business environment grows and the journey ahead
becomes clearer. Filling in the gaps also helps people determine the
real purpose of their business.

What Is the Purpose of the Business?

Many large, well-established companies have outgrown their original entrepreneurial origins and, as a result, their managers have
lost sight of their true business purpose. In mature organizations,
administrators too often seize control from the inventors, marke-
teers, engineers, or production specialists whose vision built the
business. These administrators usually define the organization's
purpose in terms of making a profit, but perceptions that "our
purpose is to make money" skirts the more fundamental factors
that drive success in the marketplace.

"We try never to forget that medicine is for the people. It is not
for the profits. The profits follow, and if we have remembered that,
they have never failed to appear. The better we have remembered
it, the larger they have been." With those words, George Merck,
son of the founder of Merck and Company, summed up a corporate
credo that exemplifies how an understanding of an organization's
true purpose can reap great rewards. Profits are like food; there's
no denying that every organization needs them to survive, but
there's more to life than eating and drinking. While a company
must remain profitable to stay in business, profit alone doesn't
drive success. Creating, selling, and delivering a product or service
that customers value does.

A comprehensive purpose statement clarifies why an organization does what it does, whom it serves, and what it provides that
others value. It delivers a timeless, broad, fundamental, and inspi-
rational message. It stretches and challenges, yet requires no ex-
planation. When stated succinctly so everyone can understand and
remember it, it helps people grasp and support the organization's
purpose.

- ❑ The McKinsey consulting group states, "The purpose of
  McKinsey and Company is to help leading corporations and
  governments be more successful." What more do the company's employees, competitors, and customers need to
  know?

- Apple, Merck, and IKEA state their own purposes equally well. Some years after Apple Computer's startup, Steve Jobs articulated Apple's purpose as "Making tools for the mind that advance humankind."

- Merck, the pharmaceutical giant, claims, "We're in the business of preserving and improving human life. All our actions can be measured by our success in achieving this."

- IKEA, the 40-year-old Swedish furniture company, has grown to more than 100 stores in 25 countries by striving "to create a better everyday life for the majority of people."

Eleanor Roosevelt once said, "The future belongs to those who believe in the beauty of their dreams." An organization's statement of purpose should capture the beauty of its dreams. However, even the most beautiful dreams will die still born without strategies to make them come true.

What Strategies Will Help the Organization Fulfill Its Purpose?

An organization's strategies should clearly define how it intends to achieve its purpose. For example, a successful product strategy offers clearly defined benefits to customers and establishes the organization in a strong competitive position in the marketplace. In this regard, McDonald's promises convenient, consistent food at a good price. The Holiday Inn chain of hotels offers convenient lodging at a moderate price. Hyatt's service strategy, on the other hand, aims to provide a luxury environment for the business traveler. Chris-Craft's recent strategy includes introducing new products to gain share in an essentially flat market. As a result of that strategy, Chris-Craft tripled its annual output of new boat designs in four years, while at the same time slashing development costs in half.

When a task force from Holiday Inn set out to create the Embassy Suites hotel chain in 1982, it based its organization design decisions on the following strategies:

- **Strategies to influence customers:** Aspiring to be "the easiest hotel in the world to do business with," Embassy created teams of multiskilled operators and rotated them through different departments so that they gained a total understanding of hotel operations. They also trained employees to develop their problem-solving and communication skills, and gave them broad authority to respond quickly to customers' needs.

❑ **Strategies to influence competitors:** Embassy planned to expand very quickly, building properties at 100 prime locations in five years in order to slow down the entry of competitors into the all-suites market. Any competitor following its lead would have to be prepared to commit hundreds of millions of dollars to enter the all-suites hotel business on a nationwide scale.

❑ **Strategies to influence stockholders:** Having obtained first-mover advantage with a product that its target market, business travelers, deemed an exceptional value, Embassy maximized room revenues by charging premium prices and promoting weekend specials, while at the same time aggressively driving down operating costs.

❑ **Strategies to influence employees:** Embassy selected employees carefully, picking only 100 employees out of 6,000 applicants, hiring those who displayed a strong commitment to providing exceptional customer service. Once hired, employees and their families spent a weekend as guests at an Embassy Suites hotel so they could understand the guests' experience firsthand. Employees received bonuses based on operating costs and guest satisfaction ratings.

❑ **Strategies to influence the community:** Embassy hired only those hotel managers who contracted to stay at their assigned property for a five-year period after startup, compared to the industry average at the time of less than 18 months. This gave the managers time to learn about the area, join local organizations, build personal relationships with members of the community, and play a visible leadership role in local activities.

Successful strategies don't come from staring at the taillights of competitors, but neither do they come from simply following the organization's own headlights. Effective strategies establish rules that guide the search for new opportunities, both inside and outside the organization. A smart organization uses these rules as road maps, not only to anticipate the obvious opportunities it should pursue, but also to invent brand-new ones. Thinking of strategies in terms of stretch rather than fit encourages creativity and discourages the temptation to scale down ambitions to fit existing resources.

Reviewing the organization's strategies involves defining how, exactly, it plans to gain competitive advantage with respect to customers, competitors, stockholders, employees, and the local community. In a dynamic organization, strategies and structure are inextricably linked and always evolving, wound together like the double strands of a DNA molecule. Structure follows strategies as product and market characteristics create operating needs, which in turn determine the logic of information flow, authority, and responsibility for work processes within the organization. In the past, structures and policies have evolved mainly in response to managements' preoccupation with internal operations. As a result, many organizations today lack sufficient external awareness and don't have the mechanisms or information systems needed to invent first-rate strategies. Internally rather than externally focused, they don't know their business environment well enough to understand how their organization should differentiate itself from others. Comprehensive strategies that take the whole playing field into account clarify the need to effect major structural and behavioral changes at every level of the organization. Implementing these strategies then becomes a people issue. However, people can't take action without the right guiding philosophy.

Building a Guiding Philosophy

Sixty-five years ago, Edgar Heermance wrote a book entitled *Codes of Ethics*, in which he espoused the belief that nothing more powerfully reinforces behavior than the written word—the organization's creed, philosophy, or code. Today, at all Ritz-Carlton hotels, each employee carries The Gold Standards, a laminated card emblazoned with the company credo and 20 basic operating principles prized by the Ritz-Carlton culture (for example "Protecting the assets of a Ritz-Carlton hotel is the responsibility of every employee"). A vibrant corporate culture needs more than sound business strategies and measures of corporate performance. It also requires rules of preferred behavior. Once an organization has defined its business, articulated its purpose, and adopted sound strategies, it can turn its attention to identifying the key characteristics that employees must possess to implement these strategies.

What Key Employee Characteristics Are Needed for Success?

When Embassy Suites opened its first all-suites hotel in Overland Park, Kansas, in 1984, its vision included becoming "the easiest hotel in the world to do business with." This implied that if a hotel guest reported a problem, any employee who learned of it would immediately take action to resolve the problem. Embassy wanted its employees to do whatever the situation called for in a timely and appropriate way, acting on their own initiative. If they couldn't personally resolve the problem, they should know whom to contact to get the situation resolved to the guest's satisfaction as soon as possible. No one at Embassy would ever say "That's not my job." The design team identified the following four employee characteristics as key elements in assuring that Embassy's hotels would be easy to do business with. All employees would behave in a way that demonstrated they were:

- Knowledgeable about overall hotel operations, not just their own department.
- Oriented toward actively serving the customer.
- Creative and innovative in responding to problem situations.
- Open to feedback, able to handle confrontation and criticism from others.

When identifying the characteristics that employees must excel at for their organization to fulfill its purpose, people who apply The 20% Solution usually conclude that, in addition to technical skills, employees must also excel in the following areas. They must:

- Be concerned about satisfying the customer at all times.
- Be able to act without fear on their own initiative.
- Accept full responsibility and accountability for their actions.
- Know how to work effectively with others.

❑ Be able to contribute to running the business to their full potential.

❑ Be willing to continue to grow and learn new skills.

Inventing the future means filling gaps between what exists today and what the organization wants to exist in the future. To close the gaps, the organization must hire people with the right talents, as well as teach the right skills to those already on board. Having identified the key employee characteristics necessary to succeed, an organization must also create policies that will support and reinforce these characteristics. Those policies should be derived from the organization's operating philosophy.

What Operating Philosophy Will Support These Characteristics?

In a well-integrated and highly effective organization, people not only understand the definitions of the business, its purpose, strategies, and key employee characteristics, they also embrace an operating philosophy that prescribes the do's and don'ts of acceptable behavior. An organization's operating philosophy revolves around its values, which are its enduring beliefs in the power of a particular way of doing business. Tom Watson, in his book *A Business and Its Beliefs*, listed IBM's three most fundamental values as respect for the individual, unparalleled customer service, and the pursuit of superiority in everything the company did. Values define how an organization works, influencing people's judgments, choices, and actions, and silently giving direction to the thousands of decisions made at every level of the organization every day. Values pump the lifeblood into the organization's culture, governing employees' actions and relationships, influencing "the way we do things around here." Unfortunately, too few organizations articulate their governing values clearly and compellingly enough.

Given the certainty of uncertainty, people need to know the boundaries of the playing field more than they need to know every single play they should or shouldn't call. If they don't comprehend the boundaries and the beliefs that circumscribe them, they can't work together to invent change. Value-driven behavior occurs as a conscious act, and for people to act consciously, they need to hear a simple, powerful message. Ed Harness, a former president of

Procter & Gamble, described the values he believed essential to that company's success as "honesty, integrity, fairness, and a respect and a concern for others." The Scandinavian Airlines System affords all employees a simple focus by emphasizing "We fly people, not airplanes." Whether they're serving meals or moving luggage, SAS employees know they must act diligently to satisfy customers. Explicit values, clearly stated, create an environment in which principle rather than procedure governs behavior, one in which employees behave properly when no one's looking over their shoulders because they know the difference between what's acceptable and what's unacceptable. A powerful operating philosophy questions answers rather than answers questions. It establishes a benchmark against which people test themselves and with which they evaluate their actions.

Mark Twain once wrote, "To be good is noble. To tell people to be good is even nobler, and much less trouble." It's not enough just to put values into words. Most people appreciate strong values, even though they may find it hard to live by those values. Significant gaps between what our appointed and elected leaders say and what they actually do evokes much cynicism in today's workplace. Effective leaders follow the maxim "Live it or lose it." They model the values, act out their convictions, and let their behavior do the talking. Like it or not, an operating philosophy serves as a company's genetic code, providing a reference that validates or invalidates leadership. People can't evaluate the relevance of leadership or question its direction unless they see the leader's beliefs in action. By the same token, before people can embrace a common philosophy, they must understand, express, and come to terms with their own individual philosophies.

Consistent with this logic, an effective operating philosophy doesn't just cascade down from the top. While the organization's leaders shoulder the responsibility for thinking through and outlining the elements of the organization's operating philosophy, they must involve all employees in shaping it. Otherwise, people won't be likely to embrace it as their own. Values work their magic only when everyone internalizes them and can invoke them instantly, in any situation. Of course, it's not easy to generate consensus when taking into account the personal beliefs held by hundreds or even thousands of individuals. People feel reluctant to reveal their deepest values and beliefs when they suspect their personal views may run counter to those of others. Taking a public position on such personal matters invites the discomfort of confrontation and conflict. Since many people fear conflict, any exploration of values should first defuse that fear.

Open-ended discussion about ideals of character and the purpose of existence will always ignite disagreement rather than consensus. The Rapid Redesign process should direct people's attention to exploring business values, which limits the discussion to beliefs about how people should behave in order to live and work together effectively. Unlike spiritual values, business values revolve around practicality. Most people can reach agreement on a set of common business beliefs by thinking together about the practicality of certain behaviors in a given situation. Few people fear exploring business values in that context, and they'll freely share their experiences, talking openly about what works and what doesn't without having to worry that their basic religious or political beliefs will be called into question. The quest for a guiding philosophy doesn't result in some universal truth, but in practical wisdom that can guide people in their daily activities. This practical wisdom provides the cornerstone of any powerful operating philosophy.

A clear and publicly expressed philosophy creates a constructive tension throughout the organization, heightening awareness of gaps between aspirations and current practice, and providing a stimulus to narrow these gaps. In that way, it helps drive a culture of continuous improvement. A strong values framework results in employees at all levels searching for solutions to problems that adhere to the philosophy, questioning and testing alternatives, and inventing change when necessary.

An operating philosophy sets communal boundaries on people's choices, decisions, and actions. It serves as the company's conscience, empowering employees to question each other's actions when they run counter to the values expressed by the philosophy. People can no longer do just as they please; instead, they must act within clearly understood parameters. St. Augustine once wrote, "I know what time is until I start asking myself what it is." Like time or truth and beauty, no one can see or touch values and beliefs. But these abstractions become a vibrant and tangible focus in an organization when its very structure gives form to those values.

What Guidelines Should Govern How the Organization Is Structured?

Nineteen ninety-four marks the hundredth anniversary of the former Investors Diversified Services, now known as American Express Financial Advisors (AEFA). Headquartered in Minneapolis, Minnesota, AEFA is the nation's largest, most successful financial planning firm, posting average earnings increases of 22% annually since American Express bought the company in 1984. Although highly profitable and still growing aggressively, President Jeff Stiefler notes, "We don't believe that our past success is any indication of future performance." In 1992, AEFA put together a cross-functional back office redesign team dedicated to serving the complete needs of financial planners in five Western states. The team posed itself an interesting question: it asked, "If we were to build a company that would put us out of business, what would it look like?"

Early in the redesign process, the team polled its members to develop guidelines about structuring the organization to maximize customer service, flexibility, teamwork, motivation, learning, and effective decision-making. Each team member was asked to cite an organization with which he or she had worked in the past where employees felt really turned on, where they worked together effectively, where they loved working for the organization, and where they felt fully informed and involved. They then explored the conditions that were present that caused this to be so. These questions prompted people to reflect on their experiences and the conditions that surrounded them—how people made decisions, how they were rewarded, how they interacted with others, and how they maintained high levels of performance. In the end, the AEFA redesign team members consolidated their thinking into the following guidelines:

- Ensure that those who are responsible for an outcome drive the decision-making related to it. The decision-making process should also include those who have relevant information to contribute, those who will be impacted by the decision, and those who must carry it out.

- Provide information first and foremost to those who need it to take action.

❑ Create reward systems that are consistent with the goals and objectives of the business. Reward and recognize people for their contributions, and for sharing skills and knowledge.

❑ Design meaningful jobs. Reduce, minimize, or eliminate tasks that don't create added value for customers.

❑ Constantly strive to break down barriers and promote teamwork across the whole organization. Develop open, timely, accurate, and easily understood communication processes.

❑ Eliminate boundaries that separate people who need to work together or learn from each other.

Following these guidelines, AEFA West created a new organization featuring a flat, multifunctional structure to execute its mission. Subsequent experience shows this has allowed employees to perform at a higher level and to learn far more effectively than in the past.

Similarly, any organization can ask the same questions that AEFA did during the first stage of the Rapid Redesign process to generate guidelines about how to structure its work effectively. Otherwise, the organization risks being unable to accomplish its mission.

Identifying a Mission

Most mission statements are much too general to inspire prompt and effective action. Vague, general statements such as "We intend to satisfy customers and earn their loyalty with top-quality products and services" sound like little more than public relations slogans. If you found one in the street, you wouldn't know where it came from. People can repeat such slogans over and over like mantras, but no matter how many times they do so, they amount to no more than a lot of "sound and fury, signifying nothing." Far from grabbing and galvanizing employees' attention, they merely create a comfort zone where people feel good but do little to fulfill the organization's vision. An effective mission statement, on the other hand, provides a beacon that steers people's efforts toward the future, allowing them to see and touch the vision in a tangible and quantifiable way by specifying the short-term goals for which they can hold themselves accountable.

A good mission statement:

❑ Walks a tightrope between what's possible and what's not.

❑ Sets attainable goals, even if they require superhuman effort.

❑ Establishes a finish line to measure progress toward objectives.

❑ Sets a time limit that lies within the reach of today's employees.

In essence, the mission statement captures the organization's aspirations and objectives.

How Good Does the Organization Aspire to Be?

When Domino's Pizza first started up, it aspired "to safely deliver a hot, quality pizza in 30 minutes or less, at a fair price and a reasonable profit." When Ford's world-class automobile assembly plant in Hermosillo, Mexico, started up in 1986, it set out "to manufacture and assemble cars at a quality level of 240 UPAS." UPAS is a universal product quality standard for the auto industry, and 240 UPAS represented Mazda's quality level in 1986. Today, Hermosillo competes effectively with Mazda, building cars at quality levels that surpass most Japanese and American car makers.

Clarity about the organization's mission is necessary if people are to rethink how work gets done, how the organization's structure unifies people's efforts around attaining these objectives, and how employees are trained and empowered so they can consistently produce perfect products and services every time. Mission objectives can be set by:

❑ Aiming at a well-defined target. In 1977, Sam Walton set what seemed an impossible target of doubling Wal-Mart's sales from $500 million to $1 billion in four years. Wal-Mart hit it. Even though the company had grown to over 1,500 stores and almost $26 billion in sales by 1990, Walton continued to set aggressive targets (such as to double the number of stores and increase dollar volume per square foot by 60% above 1990 levels by the year 2000).

❑ Focusing on a common enemy. Nike thrived for years on common enemy missions, but when it eventually beat Adidas, it lost its sense of purpose. It only regained it again when it was overtaken by Reebok.

❑ Choosing an appropriate role model. During its early days, Trammell Crow, the real estate company, set a mission "to be the IBM of the real estate industry."

In order to evaluate its success in meeting the objectives specified in its mission statement, the organization must set tangible performance goals.

What Performance Goals Should It Pursue?

Body Shop International P.L.C. has grown explosively in the last decade without mass media advertising, by mixing cosmetics and social consciousness, profits with principles. The Body Shop "sells it like it is," promoting cosmetics as tools to produce well-being, instead of as potions to fulfill fantasies of instant rejuvenation. The company delights in proving it can generate sizable profits while adhering to a central concern for the welfare of its employees, customers, and society as a whole. In the past, the Body Shop has conducted an American voter registration drive, a Take Our Daughters to Work Day, and an AIDS awareness campaign where it dispensed condoms, educational pamphlets, and advice. It has long prided itself on its environmental activism, stressing that it makes cosmetics only from natural ingredients and doesn't conduct tests on animals. The Body Shop pursues several bottom lines, actively seeking to make money in ways that also satisfy human rights and environmental goals.

"Whether we want it or not, a company by its acts transforms society," says Ariane Crozet, managing director of the Body Shop in France. "A company must recognize its responsibility toward society and play an active role within it. For the Body Shop, this definition is the foundation of our organization. In this light, we publish an environmental statement each year which underlines our progress and weaknesses at all levels and measures our objectives. One of our goals is to build waste water treatment facilities to purify more than 80% of the water coming out of our manufacturing plants. Another is to build wind farms to produce the necessary energy for our plants."

The Rapid Redesign process should take into account the interests of all the organization's stakeholders, not just its stockholders, and develop quantifiable performance goals to measure its progress in all areas where its activities affect others. Johnson & Johnson's Credo provides a good example of how an organization can set and monitor progress toward a full spectrum of performance goals.

Excerpts from Johnson & Johnson's Credo

Customers:

Our products must always be of the highest quality. We must constantly strive to reduce the cost of these products. Our orders must be promptly and accurately filled. Our dealers must make a fair profit.

Employees:

They must have a sense of security in their jobs. Wages must be fair and adequate, management just, hours reasonable, and working conditions clean and orderly. Employees must have an organized system for suggestions and complaints. Supervisors and department heads must be qualified and fair-minded. There must be opportunity for advancement for those qualified, and each person must be considered an individual standing on his [or her] own dignity and merit.

Stockholders:

Business must make a sound profit. Reserves must be created, research must be carried on, adventurous programs developed, and mistakes paid for. Adverse times must be provided for, adequate taxes paid, new machines purchased, new plants built, new products launched, and new sales plans developed. We must experiment with new ideas. When these things have been done, the stockholder should receive a fair return.

Communities in which the company operates:

We must be a good citizen—support good works and charity, and bear our fair share of taxes. We must maintain in good order the property we are privileged to use. We must participate in the promotion of civic improvement, health, education, and good government, and acquaint the community with our activities.

J&J's performance goals include four key stakeholders whose interests the company seeks to satisfy, now and in the future: customers, employees, stockholders, and local communities. Other organizations might also include business partners, or competitors with whom they've formed joint ventures. Regardless of the stakeholders, the organization should set its performance targets within the framework of how it will operate differently in the future.

How Will the Organization Operate Differently in the Future?

Once the leadership team has defined the organization's business purpose, set forth its strategies, created its guiding philosophy, and established its mission, people can then begin to paint a picture of what the organization should look like at some point in the future (typically 5 to 10 years out). This helps employees calibrate the difference between what exists today and what the organization will be like after the redesign. The bigger the difference, the earlier employees need to come to grips with the changes required. In today's dynamic environment, the smaller the difference, the more likely something has been overlooked that will blindside the organization downstream.

Following a one-week visit to a traditionally run Holiday Inn in San Antonio, Texas, the Embassy Suites design team created a series of short case studies illustrating policies and practices they didn't want the new Embassy Suites hotels to follow. They then used these cases to create a common vision of how they wanted the organization to operate in five years time, describing the structural mechanisms and cultural characteristics that would allow customers to differentiate Embassy from its competitors.

Bringing It All Together

With all the elements of the vision in place, the Rapid Redesign process can now proceed with a better sense of the future. People with vision can see the forest through the trees, and organizations with vision can see the position they eventually want to occupy in the marketplace. Before publishing a vision statement outlining the organization's purpose, philosophy, and mission, all employees should have an opportunity to debate and discuss every aspect of it. Oral and written communication from on-high won't lead to change, even at the highest level of the organization. Ownership of the vision at every level requires that all employees embrace it as if they created it themselves. Only honest and free discussion can bring out the full meaning and implications of any written documents.

An organization's vision should always be a living, breathing thing, where the wording of the various elements can be amended as greater clarity emerges from actual experience and reflection. For instance, in one organization, the aspiration to "Inspire active participation in the growth of the business to benefit everyone" has evolved over time to read "Inspire active participation in the growth of everyone to benefit the business."

All employees should participate from time to time in assessing how successfully the organization is living up to its statements of purpose, philosophy, and mission, because their ongoing feedback can help formulate future change initiatives. A formal statement outlining the company's vision represents a virtual contract that all employees have signed. Without such a contractual commitment, an organization can't expect people to explore different design options for creating a better future. It's not what the vision is that matters, but what the vision does.

If you can't imagine the future, you can't possibly create it. And if you can't create it, you probably won't be around to enjoy it. To go faster later, it's necessary to go slower in the beginning. As always, it's worth remembering Peter Drucker's advice; he says significant strategic choices "should never be made on their plausibility alone, should never be made quickly, and should never be made painlessly." That's why it's important to concentrate on The 20% Solution, getting the right people to participate in debating the right issues and asking the right questions, working together to build a common sense of the future. If people interpret results differently, get additional data; if people have different judgments, test the differences; if people guess about the future differently, agree on one scenario until additional information comes along.

All the interpretation and judgment and guesswork involved in creating a vision is more than just an intellectual exercise. People need to develop a visceral conviction about the vision if they're to sustain their efforts in pursuing it, persevering, and overcoming the inevitable hurdles that will cross their paths, and picking themselves up when they fall down. In successful organizations, there's consistency between what people believe and what they do, and there's a constant tension between vision and possibility. That's why "Visionary organizations are like great works of art. They're never finished—they're abandoned."

The next chapter shifts attention to the second stage in the Rapid Redesign process, judging the current strengths and weaknesses of core business processes, following a design map that uses The 20% Solution to isolate the success variables that really matter.

Rapid Redesign: Finding Strengths and Weaknesses in Core Business Processes

Dick O'Brien feels a headache coming on. He's been standing on his feet for six and a half hours, sweat has painted dark circles under the arms of his Brooks Brothers shirt, and his stomach churns from too many cups of bad coffee.

The war room looks like a cyclone has swept through it: a dozen equally tired and frustrated redesign team members slouch in their chairs or rest their heads on their folded arms. The long mahogany conference table is littered with manuals, printouts, Magic Markers, balled-up pages from yellow legal pads, and Styrofoam cups. Along the walls stand a dozen flip charts covered with boxes, arrows, numbers, stick figures, and almost indecipherable scrawls.

O'Brien heaves a deep sigh and sweeps out his arms. "Well, folks," he mutters, "have we finally laid it all out?"

An observer who hadn't spent the day in this room might conclude that Dick O'Brien and his weary team were planning the invasion of Normandy but, in fact, O'Brien is an internal consultant at a major West Coast bank, and his team consists of clerks, supervisors, and managers who have gathered to document the bank's Visa application process.

For a long minute no one meets his eyes. Silence reigns. Finally, a young supervisor named Angelica leans back in her chair and yawns. "Pretty much," she says.

"Pretty much?" O'Brien snorts, unable to keep the sarcasm out of his voice.

Angelica fumes. "Yeah. Well...sort of."

"Sort of?"

An audible moan comes from the back of the room as Angelica stands up and stretches.

"Sure, it applies to most of our customers," she says with a hint of belligerence.

Dick shakes his head. "Most?"

People stir uncomfortably in their chairs, faces wince, heads burrow deeper into folded arms.

"You see," Angelica says, her voice rising, "this applies to everyone... except for new customers. About a third of the way through this process, they branch off. We've got a whole different way of handling them."

Cries of agony resound through the room. Dick's eyes sweep across all the chart pages surrounding the table. Then he stares at his hands, freckled with red, green, and black Magic Marker colors.

"Let's take a ten-minute break," he says wearily.

Analyzing How Organizations Do Business

Scenes like this are not uncommon when organizations sit down and try to analyze how they really do business. Even a process as seemingly straightforward as dealing with a credit card application can quickly grow as complicated as planning a major military action. But it doesn't need to be that way, as the Ritz-Carlton Hotel found out when it tackled the simple problem of delivering guests' luggage to their rooms.

When guests at the Ritz-Carlton in San Francisco complained about the time it took for their luggage to reach their rooms after check-in, management assigned the problem to the bellhops since they were, literally, the ones left holding the bag. Working together, they mapped out what actually happened from the moment luggage came through the front door until it arrived in the guests' rooms, and they identified the factors that caused delays. Armed with this information, they developed a plan to reduce delivery time that included redesigning the luggage storage room to provide easier access to each bag, hiring a page to deliver messages (a task that took up too much of their time), and ordering new types of carts, designed to speed up luggage delivery. "Our goal is to do things right the first time," says Horst Schulze, the president of the Atlanta, Georgia-based luxury hotel chain. "The people who know where the system isn't working are on the front line. We have to give them the tools to do their job and make it easier for them to report defects."

To accomplish this goal, the Ritz-Carlton created a daily defect report that employees fill out from guest incident action forms and maintenance requests. When employees using this system documented continual problems with the toilets, the hotel convinced the manufacturer to replace them at no cost. Schulze believes that the surest quality control comes from the constantly reinforced value system of the organization. Each Ritz-Carlton employee receives 126 hours of quality improvement training and can spend up to $2,000 without a supervisor's approval to correct situations that cause guest dissatisfaction. Employees post their ideas about cutting costs or improving service on the hotel's bulletin boards, and, within a week, they file a report spelling out the potential economic impact of their suggestions. For the employees at the Ritz-Carlton, analyzing how the organization does business has become a routine daily activity, far simpler than the invasion of Normandy.

No one can eliminate a weakness without first revealing it. Yet, in most organizations, an unspoken code of silence conceals the full extent of their competitive weaknesses. To create a more competitive future, start by drawing a comprehensive picture of how the organization really operates today. People can't possibly envision what they're changing to if they can't describe what they're changing from. It all depends on adopting a process perspective.

Adopting a Process Perspective

Eurocar created redesign teams to draw a comprehensive picture of its operations several years ago. Each team audited a crucial issue, such as the company's competitive position, the current status of its most important business processes (renting automobiles and tracking information), and the consequences of different structures and operational approaches in many different countries. From the audit, a picture of a highly fragmented organization emerged in which people lacked any clear idea of what it meant to work together as a whole. By invoking The 20% Solution when analyzing its key business processes, Eurocar soon saw clearly what worked and what didn't.

Looking at an organization from a process perspective provides a much more dynamic view than a departmental or functional perspective. Think of a process as a series of steps that transform an input into an output by progressively changing its characteristics. For example, a metal fabricator transforms raw material into a product by rolling a block of metal into a thin strip, cutting the strip into parts, then shaping the parts into cooking pots. A hospital transforms sick people into healthy people by admitting them as patients, assessing their mental and physical condition, analyzing this information to diagnose their illness, prescribing medicine and treatment for that illness, and then discharging the patients when their condition improves. A process perspective focuses not on the individual tasks employees perform, but on the sequence of transformations that produce an intended output. In this context, sales isn't a process; it's a department, a function, a group of people. Order entry isn't a process, it's just one task, which, by itself, doesn't create real value for customers. Order fulfillment, on the other hand, is a process. It involves lots of steps, tasks, and activities, which, when integrated together, create value for customers.

The work of every organization consists of many different processes, but in line with The 20% Solution, only a few relate to the key business strategies that determine competitive success. In order to maximize effectiveness, an organization should concentrate on improving these vital or core business processes. They deserve the most attention and should receive the highest level of scrutiny and emphasis.

Identifying Core Business Processes

Much of the conventional cookbook advice about improving the effectiveness of core business processes reads like the recipe for rabbit stew that begins, "First catch a rabbit." Sure that makes sense, but it's easier said than done, as Dick O'Brien and his banking colleagues discovered.

The same was true for AT&T's Universal Card's Services Division in Jacksonville, Florida, when it established a redesign change council in the summer of 1993. To catch the rabbit, council members strove to answer some basic questions one might expect a Malcolm Baldridge National Quality Award winner to have already resolved—such as how many major business processes the organization had. Interviewed at the time, executives at Universal voiced the following opinions:

- Senior Human Resources vice president Pam Vosmik: "My intuitive response is to say we have thousands of processes. In my own organization there are 15 major ones. Customer service probably has five or six times that number. Marketing might have 15 to 20. I'd say there are 100 major processes in the organization as a whole."

- Executive vice president of Marketing Hans Hawrysz: "There are probably about six or seven processes."

- Quality manager Robert Hughes: "How many major processes? I look at it on a very high level. First is acquisition of accounts. Next, there's transaction processing. The third major process is customer service, responding to customer inquiries."

That's quite a range, from three to thousands, but the debate revolved around much more than figuring out how many angels can dance on the head of a pin. Just how finely should a company break down its processes, where does one start and another end, and which deserves the most attention? Those tough questions demand tough answers.

People find it difficult to examine and challenge a familiar business process because they tend to take it for granted. Since it's "the way work gets done around here," they seldom even think about it. As a result, many organizations concentrate on redesigning those business processes with the most problems, or those that are easiest to deal with (for example, work that takes place in a single department, such as testing). But doing so can lead to perfecting minor processes, even some that shouldn't exist in the first place (for instance, creating a more effective quality inspection department may be a dubious achievement since inspection, by itself, adds no value to the product), or those that the company should outsource rather than carry out internally. To identify core processes, look at how the organization does business from the customers' point of view, gauging the relative importance of processes in terms of how well they deliver value for customers, provide competitive advantage, and create a viable future. This forces an objective and fundamental appraisal: "Why do we do this work at all? What's the benefit to the customer? Why do we do it this way? Would the customer approve of the way we do it?"

AT&T's Network Services Division reviewed some 130 processes before settling on 13 core ones. It then assigned an owner and a champion to each one. While the owners focused on day-to-day business, the champions made sure that the key processes remained linked to the company's overall business strategies. When identifying core processes, it helps to think about an organization as an electric cable (see Figure 5.1). The cable's inner strand carries the current; the central strand supports and insulates the inner strand; and the outer strand guides the cable, buffering if from the environment and holding everything together. Wherever the outer strand goes, the rest of the cable follows. No one strand outranks the others in importance. All three must fit together and work harmoniously with the others. If any one frays or breaks, the cable as a whole is in jeopardy.

Applying the cable metaphor to organizations, one strand concerns itself with running the day-to-day business (the operating level), one supports these operations and keeps the business healthy over time (the coordinating level), and one charts the direction of the business and manages its connections with the external world (the strategic level).

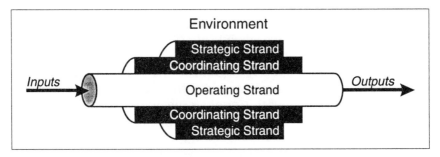

Figure 5.1 The cable structure.

Using the cable model to identify core business processes suggests that:

- People who work at the strategic level are responsible for monitoring and influencing the environment (strategy development), creating new businesses, balancing the organization's portfolio of businesses, investing and distributing resources, and developing and assigning business leaders.

- People who work at the coordinating level are responsible for identifying customers, developing competitive capability, capturing and applying learning to continuously improve the organization's performance, and creating and deploying new products and processes that will grow the business.

- People who work at the operating level assume responsibility for booking orders, managing supplies, producing and delivering the organization's products and services, and providing after-sales service to customers.

Some core processes apply to most organizations (order generation and fulfillment, for example); others only apply to specific industries (the management of relationships with regulatory agencies). Some core processes, such as new product development, cut across many different departments and involve customers and suppliers external to the organization. Hewlett-Packard, for example, found 17 shifts of responsibility some years ago when the company examined some of its product development processes. This fact, coupled with the lack of any single owner accountable for overall performance, resulted in important decisions sometimes falling through the cracks. H-P has since redesigned some of these processes to involve four transfers of ownership, with the various owners reporting to one business process manager. The company aims to eventually get this down to two. Assigning accountability for a complete business process to a single owner meant setting up reporting relationships horizontally rather than vertically. People now report to the process owner rather than to their functional department heads, a move that dramatically altered the organization's structure.

Having identified the organization's core processes, the next task is to specify how well they should perform.

Benchmarking Performance Requirements

People who say you can't teach an old dog new tricks haven't been keeping up with Union Carbide. In 1990, CEO William Joyce set out to make Carbide the low-cost producer of polyethylene and ethylene glycol (used to make polyester fibers and antifreeze), which comprised almost 30% of the company's revenues. With this goal in mind, Joyce set up teams to benchmark core processes in other successful businesses, studying their best practices and applying these lessons to Carbide's operations in distribution, inventory control, maintenance, and production.

One of Joyce's teams studied how L.L. Bean, the mail-order catalog company, ran its global customer service operation out of one center in Maine. Learning from Bean, Carbide consolidated seven regional customer service offices, which shipped orders for coatings and solvents, into one center in Houston, Texas. By making employees fully responsible for the center's operation and design, Carbide can now ship products in 24 hours with a third fewer people. Employees at the Houston center now schedule production, move tankers to the proper terminals, line up container companies to move the product, and see that letters of credit end up in the right hands. This centralization has enabled the company to improve its order accuracy while reducing finished goods inventory by 20%.

Another team studied Federal Express to learn more about global distribution. It found that Carbide's shipping costs, assumed to be less than one cent per pound of chemicals, actually ran six cents per pound because inefficient routing practices more than offset potential savings on shipping rates. When yet another team studied methods for tracking inventory at companies such as Wal-Mart, Carbide ended up making significant changes in operating practices as a result. Today, when First Brands needs ethylene glycol to make Prestone antifreeze, Carbide's computer system alerts the plant, which adjusts production to minimize inventory and routes railcars in the most efficient way to keep them fully utilized. As a result of these and other changes, between 1990 and 1994, yields on Carbide's top-grade chemicals improved by 2%, plant fixed costs dropped 18% overall, and selling and administrative expenses fell by almost 30%, for overall savings in excess of $400 million.

When Digital Equipment compared costs in its manufacturing operations with those in other companies, it discovered they ran 30% to 40% too high. Seeking out organizations that have achieved world-class status, studying their methods and practices, and examining how to apply their ideas provides a target for improvement and helps to establish minimum thresholds for performance. On the other hand, comparing performance with competitors doesn't always lead to an appropriate standard to measure success; whole industries in the United States have disappeared (microwave ovens, to name one), because companies in those industries only aspired to be as good as each other. In the long run, none was good enough to compete in a global marketplace. The most successful companies look at best practices outside their industry and calibrate where they stand against the best in the world at operating their core business processes. They then concentrate on only doing work that adds value for customers.

Mapping How Core Business Processes Really Work

An ideal business process produces what's needed, when it's needed, in the shortest time with the least work at the lowest cost. It's predictable, programmable, and operates like clockwork every time. Mapping what actually happens in each core business process calibrates how well it compares to this ideal. To understand how this kind of mapping works, imagine attaching people to a unit of work, propelling them through the process, and asking them to describe how each processing step transforms them. They could then assess which activities they encountered had the greatest influence on the process's end product or service.

Always Adding Value

U.S. bankers fret about costs. Banking today has grown so competitive that banks can't attain significant growth in earnings from their core business processes of taking in deposits and making loans. Fleet Financial Inc., a $48 billion bank with almost 6,000 employees based in Providence, Rhode Island, recently set about examining how its employees added value to their business. What they found shocked and surprised them. For example, they discovered that although each of Fleet's 800 branch offices prepared 28 monthly reports, no one read 22 of them. Four employees worked full-time collating credit card reports that they Federal Expressed daily to managers who could already access this same information on their computer terminals. Thomas Tomai, a senior vice president involved in the study, commented, "A lot of people did rinky-dink things we didn't need." Added Michael Zuchinni, Fleet's chief of retail banking, "There were very traditional ways of banking ingrained in the culture. If you looked closely, you could find ways to save millions of dollars in costs."

Surprising as it may seem, most organizations can make similar discoveries:

- When asked how they spent their time, nurses at Brigham and Women's Hospital in Boston reported that half of the handwritten doctor's orders they dealt with required them to contact the doctors later to translate illegible writing or provide missing information about times and dates.

- Ryder System, the truck leasing company, found it took almost six months to purchase a truck, as documents moved through 17 handoffs from department to department, first at the local and then at the national level.

- Blue Cross of Washington and Alaska determined that a typical health insurance claim took 10 days to complete, but required only five minutes of actual work time.

- A financial reporting team at Ameritech roamed the company asking employees, "Do you really need these financial reports?" As a result, they eliminated 6 million pages of unnecessary paperwork—a stack four times higher than Ameritech's 41-story headquarters building in Chicago.

Managers often think their operations are working efficiently only because they've never stopped to examine just what's really going on. Work processes tend to acquire extra steps as time passes, sometimes to divide up responsibility among functional specialists, other times to cope with problems that arise. In most cases, informal practices develop when employees can't accomplish their work by following the formal system (for instance, when parts don't arrive on time, people go out of their way to expedite hot items). As this sort of elaboration grows over time, more and more energy goes into making a business process work rather than on making sure the process does the work it was originally designed to do. Once people add additional steps, even if they intended to do so only temporarily, they soon find them taking on a life of their own and quickly becoming permanent. These tasks now belong to someone who jealously guards them since they help justify that person's employment.

A value-adding activity is either required by law, or it contributes to making the product or service more valuable to the customer. Non–value-adding tasks including filing, reworking, moving, copying, tracking, expediting, reviewing, approving, verifying, inspecting, processing change requests, and so on. Rapid Redesign recommendations should identify and propose dropping any activities that don't provide added value from the customer's perspective. Abandon the expendable. In organizations, as in gardening, weeding is fundamental.

Any organization can improve its business processes, and the longer it has been around, the greater the potential for improvement. When a team of people with different professional perspectives study it, they'll invariably find ways to make it work a lot better.

Controlling Variation

All 750 employees in 3M's medical and surgical products plant in Brookings, South Dakota, regularly meet face to face with their customers, the doctors, and nurses at three local area hospitals. Employees, from production-line workers to senior executives, have gone into the operating rooms to see how their surgical tapes, drapes, and prep solutions work in real-world settings. During these visits, the employees observed that customers couldn't easily open a package or close up a product for reuse. Consequently, they incorporated zip-lock type opening and closure arrangements that made their customers' jobs easier to perform. Valerie Smidt at Sioux Valley Hospital commented, "The 3M people gave us pointers on how to better utilize some items, and we in turn suggested how to make some of their products more user-friendly." According to manufacturing engineer Gary Borgstadt, "We got to feel the pulse of our customers. We saw their problems and frustrations up close." This face-to-face interaction made every employee at the Brookings plant more conscientious about getting things done right the first time, using The 20% Solution to shoot for 100% satisfaction.

Impossible, you say. Perhaps, but think for a moment what it would mean in our daily lives if things went right only 99% of the time:

- Pharmacists would process at least 200,000 wrong drug prescriptions every day.
- Nine misspelled words would appear on every magazine page.
- Unsafe drinking water would flow from the tap four days each year.
- Telephones would go dead for 15 minutes every day.

One percent defects are the enemy of perfect processes, just as variation is the enemy of quality. Long setup or change-over times, machine breakdowns, late arrival of supplies, out-of-spec materials, errors on forms—these variations introduce waste into any business process by adding time, cost, and interruptions, while at the same time reducing flexibility and responsiveness. To isolate variations, identify the key parameters that can vary in each step of the organization's core business processes, then specify the acceptable range of variation that allow those processes to operate smoothly and successfully. Next, examine how different steps in the process link together, mapping how variation in one area causes problems in others. This impact analysis identifies the control points around which the organization should structure and organize its work systems. Mapping patterns of cause and effect helps to define boundaries around interdependent process segments, and this allows the creation of work units with a high potential for self-regulation. If employees in these work units are responsible for controlling variation in critical parameters and must live with the consequences of their actions, they'll naturally strive to keep variation under control and operate the process with minimum defects.

Understanding core business processes at this level of detail makes it possible to set up work units with clearly identified inputs and outputs, and with clearly assigned responsibilities for controlling each processing step. People's roles, tasks, and relationships can then be defined in ways that produce perfect products and services every time, screening out unsuitable inputs and controlling variations in processing that can compromise top-quality output.

"We Have Met the Enemy, and They Is Us"

Some time ago, a division of Ajax Computers decided to shorten the time it took for their customers to pay them. Bringing in money from customers sooner would generate additional funds for short-term investment, producing more income for the company. A redesign team began to study the order generation and billing process, to determine how the division could speed up collections. Examining each step from the time an Ajax sales representative first contacted a customer (or a customer contacted Ajax) about a potential requirement, until Ajax received payment for the services it provided, the team eventually defined the transformation sequence as: analyzing the customer's requirements, preparing and submitting a proposal for work to be performed, entering an order, fulfilling the order following the terms of the contract, submitting an invoice, and collecting payment for products and services rendered.

The redesign team then charted the parameters that could vary in each step of the order generation and billing process (Figure 5.2). As a result, they could evaluate these parameters one by one, to see how often they varied and the consequences that arose when they did. Using The 20% Solution, they ranked the variables into a smaller subset of key parameters with the greatest impact on the timely payment of accounts. One of these (#10 on the diagonal in Figure 5.2) was "Incomplete customer reference data," which the redesign team judged to be particularly important because it happened quite often and greatly influenced subsequent processing steps. Investigating why this happened, team members found that Ajax's sales representatives, eager to book new orders at the end of each accounting period in order to qualify for performance and bonus points, collected vital information so hastily that they often ended up with incomplete or incorrect information. As a result, contracts based on this information frequently specified incorrect customer contacts or included unclear descriptions of the work to be performed. Later, invoices prepared from these contract documents went to the wrong people, or even if they went to the right people, the recipients didn't always understand what they were being billed for. This made it difficult for customers to process the invoices promptly, which delayed payment until Ajax corrected the errors or clarified the ambiguities.

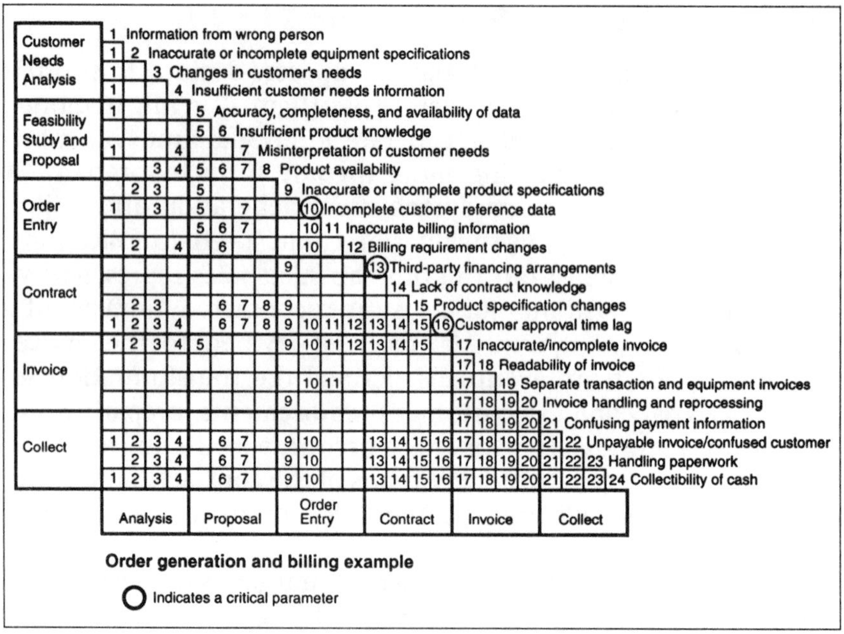
Customer Needs Analysis
Feasibility Study and Proposal
Order Entry
Contract
Invoice
Collect
1 Information from wrong person
2 Inaccurate or incomplete equipment specifications
3 Changes in customer's needs
4 Insufficient customer needs information
5 Accuracy, completeness, and availability of data
6 Insufficient product knowledge
7 Misinterpretation of customer needs
8 Product availability
9 Inaccurate or incomplete product specifications
10 Incomplete customer reference data
11 Inaccurate billing information
12 Billing requirement changes
13 Third-party financing arrangements
14 Lack of contract knowledge
15 Product specification changes
16 Customer approval time lag
17 Inaccurate/incomplete invoice
18 Readability of invoice
19 Separate transaction and equipment invoices
20 Invoice handling and reprocessing
21 Confusing payment information
22 Unpayable invoice/confused customer
23 Handling paperwork
24 Collectibility of cash
Analysis
Proposal
Order Entry
Contract
Invoice
Collect
Order generation and billing example
Indicates a critical parameter

Figure 5.2 Critical parameter matrix.

At the start of the study, redesign team members assumed they could blame customers for delayed payments and that solutions to the problem would probably involve finding ways to pressure them to pay more promptly. At the end of the study, they saw, however, that customers would happily pay for the services they received if only Ajax would stop making it difficult for them to do so. Like Pogo in the comic strip, Ajax found "We have met the enemy and they is us." It can happen to any organization, and when it does, The 20% Solution comes in especially handy.

Applying The 20% Solution

To evaluate variation according to The 20% Solution, separate the significant few from the trivial many, and identify the most critical parameters by asking "What parameter variations can cause the output to be unsatisfactory for the customer?" Then, for each transformation step, rank the importance of the parameters that can vary by asking "How do these variations affect subsequent steps in the process?" A square matrix, such as the one shown in

Figure 5.2, reveals interdependencies among different steps in the transformation process by showing connections between the major parameters, which are listed along the diagonal of the matrix. Working from top to bottom, the impact of variation in each parameter on those that follow it can be evaluated by asking "If parameter #1 varies, and if it isn't controlled within proper limits, how will it influence parameter #2, #3, #4, and so on?" Where variability in one parameter affects another, the number identifying the initiating parameter marks the point on the matrix where the two intersect. It's important to extend this analysis as far downstream as possible in order to capture the full range of consequences each variation can cause, quantifying its financial impact by asking: "How often does it happen? What problems does it cause? How much longer does the process take when this parameter isn't controlled? Must the process be repeated? How much waste does it generate? How much does all this cost?"

The matrix diagram functions as a master craftsman's blueprint, showing all aspects of the process at once. By clarifying vital relationships and linkages, it identifies the key upstream issues that drive downstream problems, thus helping to isolate the small number of critical parameters that most heavily impinge on process performance. Sometimes a variation outside of acceptable limits can cause immediate and even catastrophic consequences. A variation in "quantity of fuel," for instance, ignites more than theoretical interest among aircraft pilots. "Incomplete customer reference data," variance #10 in the Ajax case just mentioned, doesn't do a lot of short-term damage but it does create great difficulty in the long term. Regardless of the short- or long-range consequences of a given variation, identifying and correcting variations in the critical parameters will generate significant progress on the path to perfection.

The collective cost of not exercising perfect control (sometimes called the "cost of noncompliance" or the "cost of quality"), the amount of money the process owes the organization, can rob a company of its future. That's why companies such as Motorola and Xerox work hard to reduce these costs to less than 10% of revenues. Between 1992 and 1994, task forces at Tenneco whittled the cost of noncompliance down from more than 20% to less than 15%, adding $461 million to operating income in the process.

The god of efficiency lives in the details. Understanding the causes, consequences, and costs of variation simplifies the search for process perfection. Controlling critical parameters can resolve a number of structural problems, like an architect who eliminates several design flaws by moving the location of a single closet. Perfecting core business processes means answering the question "How can we entirely eliminate variation in key parameters?"

Eliminating Variation Wherever Possible

Boeing used a digital, paperless approach to help its designers create and build its new 777 airplane which involved 10,000 employees and more than 500 suppliers. Normally, the company would build mock-ups of a new plane to make sure its millions of parts would fit together properly, but in the case of the 777, Boeing chose not to assemble a trial airplane in favor of going straight to a fully functional flying machine. The mock-up existed, not on a runway, but in the form of information stored in Boeing's mainframe computers. Using the computer's three-dimensional representations of parts and components, engineers constantly checked that the whole plane would fit together as the design progressed. By doing away with paperwork, the new design system reduced the need for engineering changes and component rework by more than 50% compared to Boeing's earlier, more conventional 767 program. Previously, if two components interfered with each other, no one discovered it until the assembly phase, causing costly and extensive redesign. Now, with electronic preassembly, engineers solved many of these conflicts before manufacturing and assembling original parts. In addition, transmitting drawings directly from Boeing's computers to those of its suppliers greatly reduced misreadings and other errors normally associated with paper drawings.

Boeing worked to eliminate variation by improving its social engineering as well, combining designers, aerodynamicists, finance people, and manufacturing experts into more than 200 cross-functional teams to improve communications. Everybody learned new skills. Engineers learned to share their designs while they were in progress rather than after completion. With eight airlines participating in the design process, prospective customers also got a chance to help shape the plane they would eventually operate and maintain. British Airlines, infuriated by countless minor faults on the 747-400 series, insisted on over 100 changes during the 777's design. If Boeing hadn't invited these customers in through the front door as partners in design, it would have ended up watching them stream out the back door, taking much of Boeing's 60% market share with them.

To permanently eliminate variation, an organization must fix the process, not the problem. A rotating group of 50 hourly employees helped Oldsmobile's design engineers fix the process with which the company assembled the new $800 million Aurora. During a three-year collaboration, they made major changes in how the automaker put the Aurora together before the project ever left the engineering center, avoiding costly changes later at GM's Lake Orion, Michigan, plant. A team of doctors at Brigham and Women's Hospital in Boston, Massachusetts, led by physician Jon Teich, studied 3,000 patient charts picked at random, pinpointing 136 instances of potentially avoidable adverse events ranging from rashes, to seizures, to death. The hospital could have avoided at least 20% of these hazards through a computer-generated warning system that would have alerted a doctor to problems when he or she entered an order for treatment. Says Teich, "The best time to point out a problem with an order is at the time the doctor is giving it."

It pays to follow the advice of Mannie Jackson, one of the owners of the Harlem Globetrotters, who says, "When I do things, I always ask, 'What would it look like done right?'" If you can eliminate variation, you'll automatically see what it looks like done right. If you can't knock variation out altogether, then you can at least spot it the moment it occurs and move to control it immediately.

Controlling Variation at the Source

At Chrysler, the old way of aligning the rear wheels on some car models involved fitting the parts loosely together, forcing the wheels into alignment, and quickly tightening all the bolts to hold everything in place. Unfortunately, this crude process sometimes bent the car's undercarriage. When Chrysler's engineers began designing production lines for the company's new Neon, they prepared a $15 kit of parts to fix the rear alignment problem before it could compromise quality. Stan Larrabee, a 28-year assembly veteran, reviewed the fix with a couple of co-workers, then suggested putting those parts on during assembly. This added only $2 to the cost of the car and guaranteed that mechanics needn't take the rear suspension apart later to install the $15 kit.

If an organization doesn't grapple with variation when and where it occurs, a little pebble can cause far-reaching ripples through subsequent processing steps. In the past, clerks at McKesson Corporation, the San Francisco–based health care products company, flipped through long paper printouts with lists of orders, crossing out items as they packed them in boxes for shipment to stores. They sometimes made mistakes. McKesson calculated that while it cost $8 to perform the initial pick, correcting a bungled store order cost 10 times that much to correct bills and reship the correct products. Today, guided by hand-held computers, the clerks have improved product picking accuracy by 90%. The computers even figure out the most efficient route through the warehouse for putting together each order.

At the operating level, a company can best control variation by training people to recognize it, teaching them how to prevent or correct it, and empowering them to take action when it occurs. It makes sense to encourage and empower local problem-solving because it places the appropriate knowledge, skill, and insight in the right place at the right time, allowing the organization to deal with varying conditions without undue bureaucracy and red tape. However, empowering people to control variation doesn't mean abandoning them. A telephone repairperson may not be able to do his or her job because the garage failed to put gas in the car, or because a faulty diagnosis of the trouble sent him or her out with the wrong tools. Giving people permission to take action when they don't have what they need to do the job properly just sets them up to fail. Such false empowerment invariably degenerates into anarchy.

Using this approach to analyze work at the coordinating and strategic levels is more complicated than doing so at the operating level because strategic and coordinating work involves many more "stop and think" decisions. Here, availability and use of knowledge is the key factor determining the organization's effectiveness. Since it's difficult to detect variation in people's knowledge or information by direct observation, perfecting core work processes at these levels requires additional methods of analyses.

Dealing with Stop and Think Variation

Linear, routine operating processes like making margarine, adjudicating and paying insurance claims, or manufacturing liquid detergent lend themselves to rather simple flowcharts. They involve straightforward, sequential work with recognizable transformation stages and easily identified patterns of variation. In contrast, knowledge work involves nonroutine, hard-to-define activities that resist easy depiction. What someone chooses to do next depends on the results of previous actions. Managing problems and discontinuities involves considerable uncertainty. Sources of variation in knowledge work exist in people's heads in the form of incorrect assumptions, guesses, misinformation, misunderstandings, and trade-offs. Redesigning this sort of work means getting deliberate about deliberations.

Getting Deliberate about Deliberations

When working with free-form, nonroutine business processes, people often meet and deliberate with others who have a stake in the outcome or who may possess additional information about what needs to be done. Deliberations concentrate on turning Jell-O–like issues into concrete problems. They help people direct their actions, indicate what they should do next, and center on building commitment to support a particular point of view. Deliberations can result in actions, agreements, decisions, or new knowledge. Deliberations focus on choice points in a business process involving a judgment call when no one necessarily knows the right answer. This may require just one interaction, or involve a sequence of activities over time. Regardless, the interactions address multiple viewpoints and interests, and typically involve many people from different disciplines, functions, and departments. For example, in the product definition stage of H-P's core product generation business process, deliberations typically focus on resolving conflicts over different perceptions of the product, establishing criteria for product specifications, and allocating funds for further development.

To find problems and bottlenecks in nonroutine core business processes, decompose these processes into a series of self-contained stages with clear, measurable outputs, and list the deliberations that occur in each processing stage. Then identify the people who currently participate in each deliberation, noting the critical information they contribute to the deliberation as well the critical information they need to take away, checking to see if any information gaps exist. Identify the divergent orientations and values

that different participants bring to the deliberations (sales pro-
claims "we want it now," while engineering yells "you'll get it when
it works properly"). Pinpoint people not currently involved in the
deliberation who should participate, given their information or
expertise, or the need to have them support the outcomes later on.
In some cases, people may be involved in a deliberation for the
wrong reasons (politics or past history may dictate their participation).

It's important to ask "Who brings or takes away critical information? Who does not?" This may suggest changes in membership
or in how a deliberation happens. Examine how and where each
deliberation takes place. In a formal, scheduled meeting? In an ad
hoc, unscheduled conference? With people talking to each other
individually, in person, or on the telephone? Via electronic mail,
fax, or computer conference? Or by privately reviewing reports,
memos, or other written documents? Evaluate if the deliberation's
forum is appropriate for its purpose. Finally, estimate how well
people obtain, share, and use critical information or knowledge,
because failure in these areas causes some of the biggest problems
associated with deliberations.

Identifying Deliberation Problems

Problems associated with key deliberations include missing information or knowledge, the absence of people with necessary knowledge, unresolved conflicts over values or ideologies, lack of
agreed-upon procedures, people who are unwilling to take a clear
position, unclear responsibilities, lack of cooperation, and blocked
communication. Once the severity of deliberation problems has
been diagnosed and the major problems ranked according to The
20% Solution, their causes can then be investigated. For example,
if lack of knowledge was found to cause problems in a particular
deliberation, then the next step is to figure out what specific
knowledge was lacking and why.

Resolving these problems may involve creating new forums for
deliberations or introducing new members to existing ones to help
produce balanced trade-offs among opposing interests. Drawing
up a chart of responsibilities (see Figure 5.3) can be helpful in
diagraming current activities, as well as illustrating the preferred
contributions of the different parties in the future.

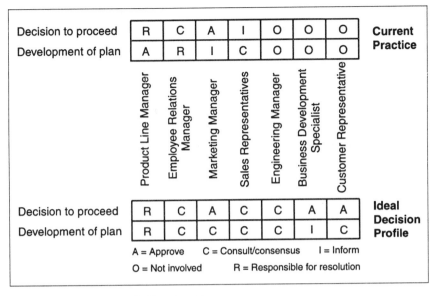

	Product Line Manager	Employee Relations Manager	Marketing Manager	Sales Representatives	Engineering Manager	Business Development Specialist	Customer Representative	
Decision to proceed	R	C	A	I	O	O	O	**Current**
Development of plan	A	R	I	C	O	O	O	**Practice**
Decision to proceed	R	C	A	C	C	A	A	**Ideal Decision**
Development of plan	R	C	C	C	C	I	C	**Profile**

A = Approve   C = Consult/consensus   I = Inform

O = Not involved   R = Responsible for resolution

Figure 5.3 Responsibility charting.

Linking These Findings to Create the Future

A problem, properly defined, is half solved. Understanding the performance requirements of the organization's core business processes and knowing how they add value for customers is the first step toward making them predictable and perfect every time. By using variation and deliberation analyses, disruptions in the process become visible, and this allows informed judgments to be made about how to structure the organization more effectively in the future. This level of understanding helps people rethink, get rid of, add to, or otherwise alter core work processes so that tasks, interactions, decision-making, and information systems function together in a parallel, integrated way rather than separately and sequentially. Core business process analysis creates a meaningful agenda for changes in technology, structure, responsibility, information, rewards, training, or people, in ways that focus all these elements on better controlling core processes. Options to consider include: reconfiguring and reordering work activities so users become doers, minimizing the number of interconnections and interfaces, coordinating and combining activities from separate functions, and relocating work to customers, vendors, and partners. As a result of these analyses, organizations can often identify quick hits or low-hanging fruit that appear easy to harvest. Be careful that these initiatives won't disrupt later stages of the redesign effort.

The Rapid Redesign process can now turn its attention to examining the social processes that link up individuals and groups inside and outside the organization, allowing them to interact and do business together. This is the subject of Chapter 6.

Rapid Redesign: Mapping and Analyzing Social Processes

"We're snowed in here." Even over the phone line, you can hear a little shiver in Lee McCormack's voice. "It's the worst storm we've had in Virginia in years."

Lee is talking about the winter of 1994. That afternoon, from points all over Fairfax County, Lee and other members of the Fairfax County Human Services redesign team left their warm homes and apartments and set forth into the storm. Struggling through snow drifts, downed power lines, and icy roads, the team members converged on the red brick building that houses the Community Services Board, where an afternoon redesign meeting was scheduled. As team members pulled off snow-dampened overcoats and wiped the frost from their faces, they faced a task that seemed as daunting and bewildering as the elements outside.

"The social processes part of this project is giving everyone a headache—me included," Lee recounts later that evening in a phone call to her home. An effusive, outgoing woman, Lee is the unit director of Outreach Detention at the Fairfax County Juvenile Court. During that terrible storm of '94, Fairfax County was in the beginning stages of an ambitious plan to redesign the whole human services system in the county. Over 20 separate agencies and a far larger number of programs would be affected.

115

"Trying to get a handle on the interactions between all the different agencies and programs is really frustrating." She adds, "There are literally hundreds of different connections and interrelationships between all these agencies and programs."

"It sounds like you're thinking about all those interrelationships from the inside looking out," her caller replies. "What if you were a customer— say, a mother with dependent children—on the outside peering into the inner workings of the county? What interrelationships would be important to you then?"

A moment of silence . . . laughter. "We haven't been thinking about it that way at all. What a great notion."

"I bet only 20% of those interrelationships would be important," her caller says.

"Maybe even fewer than that!"

Mapping Social Processes

Lee McCormack ran into the stumbling block that every redesign encounters sooner or later; organizations employ lots of people and all their activity looks like a mess of buzzing confusion without the right framework to make sense of it. As Professor Harold Hill said in *The Music Man,* "You gotta know the territory." When it comes to redesigning organizations, that means you must quickly understand just how and why people interact together.

The High-Performance Framework

The high-performance framework, described in this section, uses The 20% Solution to analyze an organization's social processes by concentrating on four basic paths through its territory, the four key factors that influence high performance. These are:

Agreeing on and aligning goals. Do people clearly understand and agree on the organization's goals? Do their individual goals and priorities support the organization's overall goals? Do all the individual goals coincide with each other? Do employees adjust their activities based on progress made toward achieving these goals?

Adapting to change. Do employees fully understand the need for change? Are they sufficiently flexible and adaptable in responding to change? Do they respond to change quickly enough? Does the organization support and reward their efforts to change?

Integrating the efforts of different stakeholders. How well do different individuals and work units communicate, coordinate, and cooperate with one another? Do people confront, explore, and resolve differences and disagreements in an open, constructive way?

Developing long-term competitive capabilities. How well is the organization developing its employees' long-term competitive capabilities? Do employees have opportunities to acquire new knowledge and skills?

Any organization's success depends on how well people perform in these four areas. Great Western Bank, Capital Asset Management, Fairfax County's Human Services Department, and Blue Cross Blue Shield of Florida used this high-performance framework to focus on the critical success factors that enhanced their performance.

Examples of the High-Performance Framework in Action

- The Audit Division of Great Western Bank underwent a change of management after 25 years under the same executive. The incoming manager brought a new direction that was a radical departure from the past. Using the high-performance framework to obtain agreement about and alignment around goals, the new manager involved all employees in developing action plans for the future, automatically creating positive momentum for change. As a result, the organization transformed itself from a 1970s-style audit shop into a leading-edge strategic performer.

- Capital Asset Management grew by an explosive 300% in a 12-month period. Given this rapid growth, the organization found it difficult to quickly assess the effectiveness of new work systems and procedures. Using the high-performance framework to clarify the picture, the organization gained more control over its business processes by consolidating employees into action planning teams, instituting better planning methods, eliminating one layer of management, and increasing its responsiveness to its customers.

❑ The Human Services organization in Fairfax County, Virginia, consisting of 20 separate agencies, redesigned itself to deliver improved, more integrated services to its customers. Using the high-performance framework, the county identified coordination and communication problems between administrative units and their service counterparts, conflicts between agencies sharing common customers, and structural disconnections that inhibited the effective delivery of human services. An understanding of these key issues enabled the organization to address them early on in the redesign process.

❑ The Private Business division of Blue Cross Blue Shield of Florida planned to evolve one of its business units into a team-based organization. By using the high-performance framework, it defined specific career paths for employees, improved supervisory and management development, and revamped technical training.

Although people's activities in these four key focus areas are determined primarily by how the organization formally structures its work, people also have a tendency to act independently and do their own thing, regardless of established processes and procedures. It's important during the third stage of the Rapid Redesign process to assesses how well these formal and informal interactions will satisfy the organization's business needs in the future.

Mapping Interaction Patterns

Thoroughly examining all possible interactions involving everyone in an organization would consume an inordinate amount of time. Invoking The 20% Solution to picture relationships between key occupational groups provides a quick way to check the most important interaction patterns. This map provides information about the frequency and type of interactions employees have with customers, suppliers, and each other, illustrating how the organization actually works rather than how it's supposed to work. Mapping who does business with whom about what (Figure 6.1) and tracking both formal and informal interaction patterns helps identify key structural and informational problems and bottlenecks.

❑ The closer groups in the map are positioned relative to each other, the more frequently they interact.

❑ Solid lines symbolize formal interactions, such as required reporting relationships; dotted lines represent informal interactions, which are often forbidden (such as contacting friends for information that's not available through formal channels).

❑ Arrows indicate direction. Some interactions are one-way, allowing for no feedback or response; others flow both ways, involving some form of back-and-forth communication between the parties. The symbols G, A, I, and L (Goals, Adaptability, Integration, and Long-term development) next to each arrow record the primary purpose of the interaction.

Scanning this picture helps to identify who participates in too many or too few relationships, as well as indicating where there's a lack of interaction about one of the four key focus issues. When used during the third stage of the Rapid Redesign process, this mapping tool can help prioritize areas of further inquiry. For example, in a health care setting, the map might look like that shown in Figure 6.1.

This picture suggests that public health nurses don't have sufficient or timely information to do their jobs properly, as indicated by their ongoing informal interactions with the records department. The chief nurse appears to have surprisingly little contact with the nursing staff, and is pictured as providing them

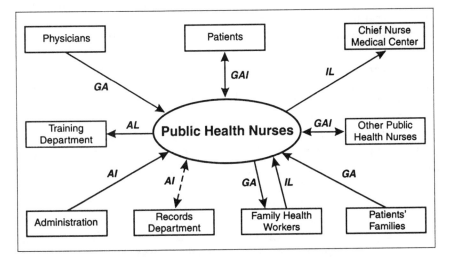

Figure 6.1 Interaction map for public health nurses.

with no direction (interaction about G is absent), while being unresponsive to their requests for training and development (interaction about L is one way) or help in resolving differences (I). The nurses don't appear to initiate any contact with the patient's families, and the picture suggests they may be unresponsive to the families' needs since the arrow linking them only goes one way.

This kind of information helps identify the strengths and weaknesses of how people associated with the organization interact together.

Learning about the Organization's Strengths and Weaknesses

Further information about the social processes depicted in the interaction map can be collected by using pencil-and-paper questionnaire surveys, by interacting with focus groups, or by conducting personal interviews.

Using Questionnaire Surveys

A questionnaire can effectively measure people's collective attitudes and opinions about a large range of issues by capturing their response to the same statements and questions. In stage 3 of the Rapid Redesign process, surveys can present questions and statements gleaned from the interaction map, asking for answers to the questions (such as "What goals do these two units share?") or assessing ratings of the accuracy of the statements ("The physical layout makes it easy for people to coordinate their work together"). Easy to administer, questionnaire surveys quickly and efficiently collect data that's easy to quantify (for example, "Seventy-six percent of those polled agreed that the organization's social goals are poorly communicated"). The data can be analyzed for specific work units, levels, or processes in the organization, and summary graphics, such as those shown in Figure 6.2, can be used to display the results of the analysis.

While generally effective, a questionnaire approach poses certain dilemmas. Answers to questions in any survey always depend on the kind of questions raised. Swiss voters once replied no when asked if they approved of smoking while praying, but the vote turned to yes when the same people were asked if they approved

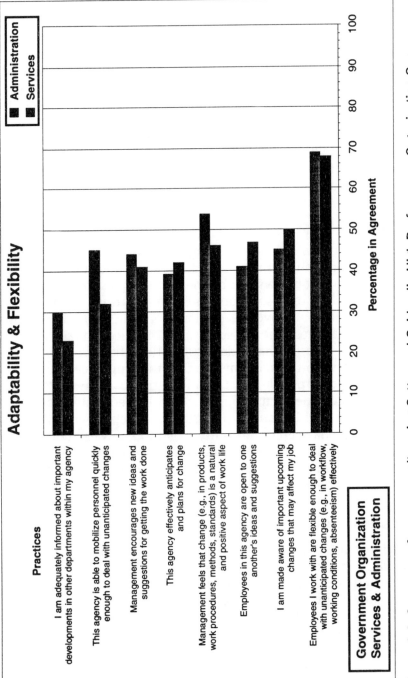

Figure 6.2 Summary of survey results using Cotter and Geirland's High Performance Organization Survey.

of praying while smoking. If respondents feel uncertain about the meaning of a question (and some percentage will feel that way about even the clearest question), their responses may mislead those averaging the results. Additionally, questionnaires afford little opportunity to build personal rapport with respondents through direct contact. People need to understand beforehand just how the results will be used. Their enthusiasm to participate will boost the thoughtfulness of their response. Key areas of interest or concern identified in the survey can then trigger a more focused approach to data gathering.

Focus Groups

This approach involves interviewing panels of from 5 to 12 people to gather more penetrating information about social processes by guiding them through a series of open-ended questions that allow for a great deal of discussion and amplification. Focus group discussions often uncover deeper issues and insights than those identified by a questionnaire survey. For instance, one such group clarified that questionnaire data suggesting that people wanted stricter supervision actually meant that the employees were concerned that some people weren't pulling their weight.

On the plus side, focus groups include the perspectives of many people at once, which can help to stimulate each other's thinking, and members have an opportunity to get to know each other and build rapport. On the minus side, some people feel reluctant to speak frankly in a group situation, which is why personal interviews may also be required.

Personal Interviews

Individual interviews not only elicit people's opinions but they also flesh out additional details surrounding important issues uncovered by questionnaires or focus groups. Interviews work best when they follow an open-ended questioning format (for instance, "Tell me, what's it like to work here?"). On the other hand, directive or loaded questions (such as "Why is this organization such an awful place to work in?") build a bias into the response.

Asking for additional comments at the end of each interview session (asking "What issues haven't we covered that are important to you?") can sometimes produce surprising results. For instance, in a U.S. government agency, these closing questions produced an unexpectedly large number of comments about racial discrimination and affirmative action. These issues hadn't surfaced in previous data since key managers viewed them as politically sensitive subjects and didn't want to publicly acknowledge them. Resolving these hidden problems became a crucial component of the final redesign recommendations.

The advantages of the interview method is that it generates highly detailed information and provides an opportunity to probe individual opinions. Prior training in interviewing skills is essential for success, particularly facilitation and active listening skills. The disadvantages of this method is that individual interviews take a lot of time, typically one to two hours to complete, and require copious note taking. Even when tape recorders are used, transcribing the tapes later can be very time-consuming.

Since each of these methods for analyzing social processes offers certain advantages and disadvantages, it's best to use a multimethod approach that incorporates the best of each.

Using a Combined Approach

The high-performance framework and the interaction diagram can be used to identify those employees who interact with each other in managing the organization's core business processes and to identify strengths and weaknesses in social interactions that will significantly impact the organization's future success. Following this, a survey can be designed and circulated that addresses these strengths and weaknesses with clear and succinct questions that have been customized to reflect the organization's language and culture. The survey results then drive discussions with focus groups and individual employees, and the outcomes can be consolidated into a *relationship grid*.

Maintaining the high-performance framework, the relationship grid, shown in Figure 6.3, maps strengths and weaknesses along four key avenues of social interaction:

❑ Relationships between people up and down the organizational hierarchy.

❑ Relationships between people in the same department.

❑ Relationships between people in different departments.

	Superior/ Subordinate Relations	Relations within Workgroups	Relations between Workgroups	Relations with Outsiders
Agreeing on and aligning goals	Supervisors convey information one-way— top down.	Results shared, but little participation in setting goals.	Supervisors are linked. Others are not.	Contact is at the top only. Customers are not included in goal setting.
Adapting to change	Notification is usually a surprise. Response depends on quality of input.	Better planning for change needed.	Information is received, but usually after the fact.	Changes in other product areas not known until problems arise.
Integrating the efforts of different stakeholders	Employees expect their supervisor to solve all their problems.	Good communications. Conflict resolution is not effective.	Frustrating. Unclear about how to resolve problems.	Little opportunity to work on external issues. Time is never available.
Developing long-term competitive capabilities	Supervisor is key to learning, but is not active in personnel development.	Informal communication only.	Little cross-training.	Little awareness of future needs and skills required.

Figure 6.3 High-performance relationship grid.

❑ Relationships between employees and important stakeholders outside the organization, such as customers, partners, and suppliers.

A completed grid describes how the organization currently operates and evaluates its status in each of 16 cells. Analyzing this picture provides information about what the organization should add, subtract, or improve in the future.

Moving from Analysis to Action

With a clear picture of the organization's social processes, recommendations can now be developed to improve how these processes function in the future. Once again, the high-performance framework (G, A, I, and L) provides a concrete way to move from analysis to action.

Agreeing On and Aligning Goals

Prior to 1990, each department in Motorola's Government Electronics Group operated in isolation from, and often at cross purposes to, one another. While the organization evaluated purchasing agents in terms of cost savings, it measured the performance of quality assurance technicians in terms of defect reduction. As a result, when defects ran high, quality assurance blamed purchasing for buying materials too cheaply, and when the purchasing department exceeded its budget, it blamed quality assurance for setting product specifications needlessly high. To mediate these disputes, the company involved no fewer than eight levels of management.

Unhappy with its results, the Electronics Group thoroughly redesigned its operations between 1990 and 1993, breaking supply management into three departments, with quality and purchasing employees assigned to all three teams. With work now divided by commodity, a single team followed a technology all the way from design to delivery, so team members had common goals and common measurements for tracking progress against those goals. This redesign encouraged people to communicate openly about how to achieve their goals rather than trying to outfox each other in a race toward different goals. Training gave team members the wide range of skills they needed to resolve problems on their own without much assistance from management, and this allowed a reduction of the management hierarchy from eight levels to four. Every employee participated in evaluating all the other members of their team, and the final evaluations determined bonus payments. Motorola found that peer evaluations resulted in fair and equitable rewards and encouraged both team cooperation and individual excellence. As a result of the redesign, total operating expenses in the supply management operation fell by 45%, while the product quality rate rose by over 100%.

Conventional organizations designed around independent departments and multiple layers of management invariably create cumbersome and unnecessary social processes where people interact at cross purposes to one another and fail to achieve meaningful breakthroughs in profitability or productivity. Purchasing buys parts cheaply but manufacturing needs them strong. Shipping moves goods in bulk but sales promised them fast. To focus people on working together to achieve common goals, some Japanese organizations encourage all their employees to concentrate on one specific annual breakthrough goal for the organization as a whole. This is called a Hoshin goal, and each individual's performance goals specifically include activities that contribute to achieving this breakthrough. The Hoshin approach drives the selection of process improvement opportunities as well. Rewards for suggestions are tied to the Hoshin goal, and the more a suggestion contributes to achieving that goal, the more it's rewarded.

Answering the following questions helps to evaluate the degree to which people are agreed on and aligned around the organization's goals:

❑ What goals and priorities do individual work units currently strive to achieve? Do they support the overall mission and strategies of the organization?

❑ Did employees help set the goals? Do they clearly understand them? Are they committed to achieving them?

❑ Do different departments and functions share the same goals and priorities? Do different work units help each other achieve their goals?

❑ Do people know how well their efforts help the organization meet its goals? Do they get accurate and timely feedback on the organization's performance? Do those who contribute the most get rewarded for their achievements?

❑ How can the organization improve its goal-setting and alignment capability?

Improvement, whether it involves adding something new, removing something old, or altering the social processes that govern the ways in which people interact, means change. And change requires adaptability.

Adapting to Change

Traditionally, zoos have organized their exhibits around taxonomic groupings (birds with birds, reptiles with reptiles). The best zoos have also tried to house and present their collections as naturally as possible, to the benefit of both the animals and their human visitors. The San Diego Zoo, however, has gone one step further by transforming itself into 10 bioclimatic zones. Using this scheme, the zoo assembles animals, birds, reptiles, and sometimes even insects in the same area with the plants, flowers, and trees found in their native habitats. So far, the zoo has created three of these zones. The first, Tiger River, representing an Asian jungle, was opened in 1987. A wooded area, Sun Bear Forest, followed in 1989, and an African rain forest exhibit, Gorilla Tropics, came along in 1991. These new exhibits not only provide a safe nurturing place for species reproduction, they also give visitors a chance to view the animals in their natural surroundings.

Part of the zoo's mission is educational, and aims to increase its visitors' awareness of the environmental concerns facing our planet. Attractive displays, located throughout the exhibits, explain interesting facts about many of the species on display, including information about endangered animals and conservation efforts. Consistent with this new bioclimatic design, visitors may or may not see certain animals during their visit because the zookeepers periodically give the animals a rest by removing them from the exhibit areas. As a result, employees spend more time interacting with visitors, elaborating on the information in the displays, and answering questions, as well as explaining the animals' absences or behaviors.

In the three redesigned organizations, each exhibit's employees are grouped in teams, and team members receive training that ensures a broad education about the exhibit's features. A groundskeeper feels comfortable explaining the habits of a Sumatran tiger, and an animal handler doesn't hesitate to pick up a gum wrapper a visitor has carelessly tossed aside. Performing a variety of jobs helps alleviate the boredom of repeatedly working at the same tasks over and over again. It also allows team members to cover for each other when someone's absent, and provides them with a greater appreciation of how the different aspects of the environment affect the animals, which in turn improves their ability to care for their charges.

Answering the following questions helps to evaluate how well people in the organization adapt to change:

- ❑ How do employees find out about important changes that affect them (including changes in product design specifications or changes in staffing)? Do people receive timely and accurate information about these changes?

❑ Who plans the organization's overall response to change? How do individual responses impact one another?

❑ When changes require a rapid shift in workload, do people respond with flexibility and agility? How do they make these internal shifts? When unexpected changes occur, do people feel excited and challenged, or angry and overwhelmed?

❑ How can the organization improve its ability to respond to change?

Whether change occurs as a planned event or strikes the organization unexpectedly, success depends on having social processes that enable the right people to interact together in the right way at the right time. Successful response depends on how well they communicate, cooperate, and coordinate their efforts.

Integrating the Efforts of Different Stakeholders

Anyone who has suffered through a mortgage application process remembers the seemingly endless approvals their application had to go through and the myriad corporate officers who, at one time or another, participated in the undertaking. Given the number of different people who took part, who do you think was responsible for seeing that the whole application process was completed properly? The answer, usually, is nobody. Each of the individual specialists involved completed his or her tasks, passed the application to someone else, and then forgot about it. Each department or function worried about its own responsibilities and nobody worried about the whole. Each department solved problems in its own best interests with little regard for the interests of the total organization. Even the bank and the escrow company worked at cross purposes to each other, with each one following its own priorities and schedules.

In many organizations, engineering and manufacturing people reside in different buildings or in separate cities, so it's difficult for them to establish the personal rapport needed to work together effectively. Budgeting practices sharpen rivalries as manufacturing engineers seldom receive funding to work on a product until after it's released, at which point funding for the design people ends. But although design expenditures may be only a small part of a product's total cost, how a product is initially designed fixes half of its total life cycle costs and determines a huge proportion of manufacturing, testing, and servicing costs. It's difficult for manufacturing engineers to influence design decisions when the organization is designed to stop them from doing so.

Most older, larger organizations have formalized their operations in such functional isolation that it short circuits conversations across preset boundaries. Separate functional departments end up with conflicting agendas because they're isolated from customers and from each other, and unaware of how they affect the business as a whole. As a result, employees have grown accustomed to the "ready, fire, aim, and blame" sequence that produces presentations followed by inquisitions. Finding constructive ways to deal with this kind of institutionalized conflict has perpetually preoccupied progressive managers. At Honda, any employee, however junior, can call for a "waigaya" session where he or she can lay his or her cards on the table and speak directly about issues that concern him or her. All issues are fair game, and none lies out of bounds. Waigaya helps to surface difficult issues so the organization can learn to confront and resolve its problems.

Traditional bureaucratic arrangements that define turf narrowly won't work in the future. Success will require a newly negotiated order that legitimizes many different interests and bridges between them to reach mutual accommodation. A multiplicity of departments creates barriers that get in the way of common objectives, timely communication, and efficient workflow. Successful organizations in the future will find ways to redesign themselves to become arenas that encourage cooperation rather than conflict. People naturally tend to vacillate between cooperating and going it alone, and many of the procedures they create to protect them from each other mask their mutual interests. This will change only if employees at all levels develop common interests to bridge their differences and understand how collaboration is necessary for common gain.

Wal-Mart is an $80 billion company that's led from the top but run cooperatively by people lower down. While five levels exist between CEO David Glass and individual store managers, every Saturday morning at Walton Hall auditorium, all those layers collapse when 300 managers come together in an open forum to discuss current issues. They applaud the week's top 25 stores and set to work fixing the bottom 25.

Answering the following questions helps to evaluate how well the organization integrates the efforts of different individuals and work units:

- ❑ How good are the relationships between key work units? To what extend do different work units agree on the work that needs to be done? How do different individuals and units coordinate their efforts? Who is responsible for seeing this coordination takes place?

- ❑ What's the relationship between managers, supervisors, and the employees who report to them? How well do they communicate with one another? What formal and informal communications channels do they use?

- ❑ To what extent do employees coordinate their work directly with one another rather than through higher levels in the organization? How does the physical layout of the work space affect communication and coordination between individuals and work units?

- ❑ How could people integrate their efforts and activities more effectively?

According to Casey Stengel, the legendary coach of the New York Yankees, "It's easy to get the players; getting 'em to play together—that's the hard part." Unless an organization knows how to foster collaborative relationships internally, it won't succeed at developing partnerships with suppliers and customers on the outside. These relationships are key in determining an organization's long-term competitive capability.

Developing Long-Term Competitive Capability

Every two years, each one of the more than 70,000 employees at Emerson Electric is asked to fill out a lengthy opinion survey, answering questions such as "If you were starting over again, would you come to work for this organization?" If more than a third of the employee responses are negative, division managers must come up with proposals to remove the defects. If the thoughts and feelings of the workers are important at Emerson, so also are those of the managers. CEO Charles (Chuck) Knight keeps passport-sized photos of the company's 650 top managers nearby, each bearing a short resume of their current and past postings with color-coded stickers to indicate their experience and potential for promotion.

Horst Schulze, the president of the Ritz-Carlton Hotel chain, personally conducts orientation sessions at all new hotels. On the first day, he delights in the wide-eyed stares he gets when he declares, "My name is Horst Schulze. I'm the president of this company, and I'm a very important person." He pauses dramatically before adding "So are you."

BMW believes the quality of its employees will distinguish it in the marketplace, so it develops them as a source of long-term competitive capability. Its personnel marketing program presents the company as an attractive place to work with all the vigor it uses to market its cars, encouraging students (and their professors) to take summer jobs even before they graduate. Since BMW is structured around a network of multifunctional committees (for investments, product development, and diversification), employees who display managerial ability must rotate to another function before they can be promoted. As part of their long-term development, managers must remain in a job at a particular level from three to five years, and can't move up in the organization unless they've also spent time working at the same level outside their department.

Answering the following questions helps to evaluate how well the organization is developing its employees to create long-term competitive advantage:

- How much emphasis does the organization place on learning and personal development? What kinds of learning opportunities are available for employees?

- What skills do employees need to make an even bigger contribution to the success of the organization than they currently make? Does the reward system (pay, advancement, recognition) encourage them to do what's right for the organization as a whole?

- What additional skills or abilities will employees need to maximize their effectiveness and efficiency in the future?

- How should the organization develop and deploy its people for success in the long term?

The analysis of the four key high-performance issues—goals, adaptability, integration, and long-term competitiveness—concentrates on people's connected, collective experience at work.

However, it's also important to evaluate how well the organization satisfies people's needs as individual human beings. People's greatest fulfillment comes from participating in meaningful, healthy, and secure work activities.

Encouraging Employee Commitment

In 1927, D.J. DePree, the founder of office-furniture maker Herman Miller, visited the home of one of the company's craftsmen who had died. When the grieving widow showed DePree her husband's handicrafts and poems, the business owner felt stunned. Recalling that experience later, DePree said, "As I walked around the block... I realized that we were all extraordinary, and this changed my whole attitude toward 'labor'.... These people were my peers." This realization, that all employees had similar needs and aspirations as he himself had, forever changed the way DePree viewed his business.

What Are "Good" Jobs?

Kevin Clark started Cross Country Healthcare in Boca Raton, Florida, in 1986. Since then, he has built his company into a $70 million business, linking nurses, therapists, and other health care workers with job opportunities all over the United States. Nurses typically take positions for 6 to 12 months, either to gain teaching-hospital experience or just to spend the winter in a warm place. After they complete their tours of duty, they move on to another assignment or go back to their old jobs. The nurses travel to develop their capabilities and satisfy their needs.

Every employee brings unique needs, capabilities, desires, and aspirations into work with him or her every day. People who feel they're productively developing and applying their capabilities and who feel the organization is committed to their welfare invariably commit themselves to helping the organization succeed. Frustrated and unfulfilled workers seldom give the company their all.

The 20% Solution suggests that people's needs and expectations at work generally center around the three Cs:

- ❑ Competence—having the skills and capability it takes to do their work well.
- ❑ Contribution—knowing how what they do adds value for the organization and its customers.

❑ Centrality—knowing that what they do is important and makes a difference.

People consistently report the following job characteristics as the top ten that generate commitment. They say that a well-designed job:

❑ Uses their skills and abilities.

❑ Provides opportunities for learning and development.

❑ Specifies a well-defined area of responsibility.

❑ Poses reasonable demands and challenges.

❑ Creates opportunities for social interactions with colleagues.

❑ Contributes to the product the organization makes or the service it provides.

❑ Incorporates some variety in their tasks.

❑ Allows them to make a worthwhile and meaningful contribution.

❑ Leads to some sort of desirable future (more pay, a promotion, and/or job security).

❑ Provides them with opportunities to participate in decisions about their work.

Different people value these characteristics differently but, taken as a whole, they describe jobs that fulfill people's needs, keep them productive, and don't stress them out.

Managing Stress

In their book *Healthy Work*, Robert Karasek and Tores Theorell conclude that stress arises as a function of what they call the "decision latitude" of the job, which includes the chance to learn and use skills, exercise initiative, and otherwise control working conditions. A demanding job doesn't cause stress as long as the worker enjoys latitude in making decisions. That's why the bossed, rather than the bosses, suffer most from job stress. When work combines heavy psychological demands with little decision latitude, the result usually proves corrosive. Workers in such high-strain jobs will most likely burn out and lose their sense of commitment to the organization. Occupational stress doesn't just harm workers; research suggests that the medical costs of dealing with stress and its symptoms in the United States run over $100 billion a year, not including the indirect costs of absenteeism and lost productivity. Even more damaging in the long term, stress inhibits learning. In an economy increasingly characterized by rapid change and new technologies, stalled learning can destroy an organization's future.

People who cope with stress in a constructive way share three general attitudes: First, they see life as a challenge; second, they're committed to what they're doing; and third, they feel they have control over their lives.

Achieving Personal Well-Being at Work

People instinctively try to impose order and structure on their world, seeking to define themselves by shaping the context in which they live and the events in which they participate. Doing so helps them discover and explore their talents, skills, and abilities. By using their skills and abilities, they develop a sense of power and competence, which in turn shapes their image of who they are and what they can expect from life. Eventually, this sequence of development determines whether or not they commit themselves to becoming contributing, responsible members of an organization or a society.

How work is organized obviously influences this cycle. Working amounts to much more than just a way for employers and employees to make money. It also provides a way for people to discover and test the limits of their abilities, and to develop a sense of their own uniqueness. The universal desire to engage in activities that facilitate self-definition and personal development drives people to get involved in some kind of structured activity even after they've won the lottery and no longer need to hold a job in order to make a living. A healthy sense of personal self-esteem depends on a feeling of competence and success. A sense of mastery and satisfaction causes people to feel powerful and influential. People without influence seldom develop a meaningful identity because they lack a positive sense of their own worth. They haven't experienced themselves as important people, able to make a difference at work and in the world. The most effective people, the healthiest people, those who know themselves and commit themselves to challenging goals, invariably strike a good balance between their work and their life.

Striking a Balance between Work and Life

Most people want time in their life for work, family, friends, and themselves. They want an interesting job, one that will provide financial security and a chance to get ahead. Sometimes, they want all these things equally, at once; more often, they want different things at different points in their lives. Regardless of their particular desires at any given point, however, what they want most of all from employers is a paradoxical blend of flexibility and security. Resolving that paradox is at the heart of organizational redesign. Highly motivated employees grow frustrated when their jobs fail to provide opportunities and rewards for taking initiative. Slow-growing companies can seldom offer these opportunities. As a consequence, an unprecedented number of people today are opening their own businesses and a high percentage of workers say they would like to quit working entirely.

At the same time, the average American works 160 more hours a year than he or she did 20 years ago, an increase driven primarily by financial concerns. Although the Bureau of Labor Statistics reported 6% of Americans held a second job in 1992, Gallup polls suggest the figure was closer to 16%. Close to half hold two jobs in order to meet regular household expenses and pay off debts. Others hold several jobs to acquire skills that will make them more marketable in case they lose their current job.

Working partners contribute greatly to younger workers' frustration. The surge of women joining the workforce during the 1970s and 1980s dramatically altered the balance of work and family life. Men today are far less likely than their fathers to have dinner waiting for them when they come home from work, and millions of women wish they could find a more satisfying solution to the work and family dilemma as new patterns of family responsibility have created frustrating conflicts.

- According to a 1990 Gallup poll, 87% of employed Americans between the ages of 30 and 49 expressed some feelings of conflict between work and family issues. This figure dropped to 63% for people 50 and older.

- On average, Americans reported they could afford 37 hours of leisure time every week, but dual-earning couples and working women reported only 27.

- In 1991, 69% of working fathers ranked work as one of the most important aspects of their lives, but according to Gallup, only 49% of working mothers did so.

- Working women don't all feel the same about work. Single women more often rate the opportunity to learn new skills and to further their career as an important element in their lives.

Any organization redesigning itself for the future must understand these trends and project their consequences on the way it organizes work, studying the demographics and lifestyle desires of all employees to assess their current aspirations and frustrations. Redesign proposals can then balance the need for business efficiency with the needs of developing strong families and vibrant communities, assuring gender equity in the workplace, and providing a good fit between work demands and personal lifestyles. Otherwise, organizations will find themselves lacking healthy, committed workers, operating in crime-ridden and drug-infested communities, and falling ever further behind more sensitive, forward-looking rivals. Complicating this picture further is the prospect that employment in the future will revolve around a whole new definition of job security.

Redefining Employment Security

On November 12, 1994, the business section of *The New York Times* reported that Continental Airlines had decided to cut over 1,600 maintenance jobs in Denver and Los Angeles, subcontracting this work to outside companies to save $30 million a year. The article went on to say that the plan was communicated to employees as part of a recorded telephone message, while top management was meeting with financial analysts on Wall Street to explain the carrier's operating strategy for 1995.

Employees at British car maker Rover, on the other hand, now receive a version of the Japanese "job for life" pledge; in return, they must remain fully flexible in what they do, how they do it, and when they do it. IBM once made the same pledge, but its definition proved outdated in a world of lightning-swift change. The number of employees at IBM dropped to 220,000 in 1994, down from over 400,000 in 1986. Like IBM, more and more organizations can no longer promise that they'll remain a secure and stable place to work.

Concentrating on Cutting Short-Term Costs

Once used almost exclusively by retailers and other firms faced with seasonal demand, *contingent* workers (that is, temporary, part-time, or on short-term contracts) are increasingly being used by companies to reduce employment costs. Many organizations that say "people are our most important asset," on the one hand, are focusing their efforts on downsizing and creating a contingent workforce to reduce the cost of employee benefits on the other. Consequently, employees live in an uncertain and turbulent world, and managers often find their compassion and humanity in conflict with the pressures of competition and ambition. A sense of fear has invaded the factory floor and the corner office, and loyalty often takes a backseat to survival and personal advancement.

However, the old-fashioned bond of loyalty between employees and the organization that employs them has grown stronger than ever at Southwest Airlines because of the way it has successfully redefined employment security.

Living and Working the Southwest Way

Southwest's CEO, Herb Kelleher, has helped make working there an attractive adventure for its employees, allowing the airline to differentiate itself through its focus on service, operations, cost control, marketing, its people, and its corporate culture. Southwest has never laid off employees and has suffered only one strike, a decade ago, when machinists went on a six-day walkout. Southwest employees, all 12,000 of them, eagerly pitch in wherever they're needed. When bottlenecks occur at the boarding gates, pilots step in to help out; ticket agents don't mind moving luggage if doing so will improve customer service.

In 1992, 1993, and 1994, Southwest won the Department of Transportation's service triple crown: most on-time flights, best baggage handling, and highest customer satisfaction. All of this is a direct result of Kelleher's efforts to identify with the people who work for him. As he said, "I feel that you have to be with your employees through all their difficulties, that you have to be interested in them personally. They may be disappointed in their country. Even their family may not be working out the way they wished it would. But I want them to know that Southwest will always be there for them." David Ridley, who joined Southwest as director of marketing and sales after previously working for two more traditionally designed Fortune 500 companies, comments, "I have come to appreciate a place where kindness and the human spirit are nurtured."

Southwest isn't alone in its concern for its employees. Other highly successful companies also work hard to hang on to their people in the bad times as well as the good.

Keeping Employees around for the Long Term

Toyota, instead of slashing employment when business gets tough, works to generate more savings through relentless frugality in design and manufacturing. Cost-cutting aims to trim excess from cars already in production—an inch of extra wire here, a plastic clip there; it all adds up. The company aims to trim costs by designing cars differently from the ground up. For example, the new Corona and Carina share windshield glass as well as front and rear door panels, and both use the same instrument panel as the Celica. As a result, Toyota saved $1.5 billion in 1994.

Sidney Harmon, a former Commerce under-secretary and chairman of Los Angeles–based Harmon Industries, believes that commitment and productivity increase when employees believe their jobs are secure. Harmon's $675 million-a-year consumer electronics company employs 1,500 production workers and features a full employment program called Olé, an acronym for Off-Line Employment. To avoid layoffs, Olé seeks to create an internal labor pool to buffer for periods of slack demand. Under this program, for example, the company uses scrap wood from speaker cabinets to make clock faces. These are sold in outlet stores staffed by Harmon employees, thereby employing production workers who would otherwise be idle during economic downturns. Production workers rotated to Olé assignments keep their seniority, health benefits, and connection with the organization. When demand picks up again, Harmon doesn't have to train a whole new batch of people.

But in a rapidly changing business environment where fluctuations in staffing levels are often inevitable, the reality is that lots of jobs aren't forever anymore.

Benefitting from Contingent Employment

Over 35 million people, almost 30% of the U.S. workforce, were contingent employees in 1994. Of these, nearly 11 million were self-employed (including doctors, lawyers, writers, and others who were contingent because they wanted to be or because their chosen profession demanded it), and this percentage has changed very little in the past 25 years. Another 22 million contingent workers were part time, and of these, 17 million were working part time because they wanted to go to school, or raise a family, or pursue another career. Another 6.5 million worked for contractors that supplied janitorial, secretarial, computer programming, engineering, or other business services. Among these, 2 million people were registered with temporary service agencies and worked for different employers for a limited period of time. Thirty-eight percent of Manpower Inc.'s temporary employee pool were offered permanent positions in 1993.

"We're in mind power, not manpower," says Edward Kopko, the chairman of Butler International in Montvale, New Jersey. Butler runs a temporary help business with 61 offices around the United States and a permanent payroll of 500 people. Instead of renting out secretaries and clerical office help for $12 an hour for a few days at a time, Butler leases out engineers, computer programmers, and managers to big companies for assignments that usually last from six to nine months. AT&T contracts with Butler for workers to install complex phone network systems; Boeing used these temps for its new 777 airliner. Butler keeps about 6,500 people working on assignment at any one time and has more than half a million resumes on file.

Contingent employment provides American business with a source of labor flexibility that makes it more efficient than many of its foreign counterparts.

Changing the Contract between Organizations and Employees

The changing nature of company-customer relationships demands a new breed of worker, one who is empathetic, flexible, informed, articulate, inventive, and able to work with little supervision. Successful companies recognize that learning, loyalty, and retaining good employees go hand in hand with winning and keeping good customers. Relying on temporary workers in the long term risks losing knowledge and experience when employees leave, as well as wasting the organization's investment in training. In addition, there's little incentive for people to go the extra mile when they're uncertain about their future. Wal-Mart knows this. Despite its discount strategy, it uses fewer part-timers and temporary workers than virtually any of its competitors because it knows that customer service as well as low prices are the key to its success.

The increased need for flexibility and the cost pressures of global competitiveness require changes in the old contract between organizations and their employees. The old employment contract traded employee loyalty for job security. The new one no longer sustains that traditional pledge. Instead, it honors the principle that employees will keep their jobs only as long as they add value and continually find new ways to add value. In return, the organization will provide interesting and important work with the freedom and resources to perform it well, honesty about their employment status and opportunities, and access to the experience and training required to stay employable—somewhere. Looking for a job, inside or outside the organization, has become a regular part of the new job. The new definition of corporate loyalty is not looking for your next job on company time.

Wrestling with the Problems of Contingent Employment

In 1943, the psychologist Abraham Maslow proposed his now-famous theory of motivation based on a five-level hierarchy of human needs. Maslow postulated that people progressed from satisfying their security needs for food and shelter at the lowest level of the hierarchy through subsequent stages of security, friendship, and status, until they sought to satisfy their need to be creative and innovative at the highest level. However, Maslow pointed out that people's needs must be satisfied at each level before they move up to the next one. Organizations that seek to impose the new contract just described will have to resolve the contradiction inherent in asking people to act on their highest-level needs to take initiative and express themselves freely on the one hand, while denying them the opportunity to satisfy their lowest-level security and survival needs on the other. Organizations involved in a redesign process must meet and wrestle with these dilemmas head on.

Conclusion

Discounting the importance of employee loyalty and commitment while operating a business is a big-ticket proposition. Someone told me recently about a forklift operator who dropped a newly manufactured appliance onto a concrete floor. After the fall, the carton containing the product looked like all the others except it was about three inches shorter. Before he lifted it into a truck, the operator smiled, pulled out his Magic Marker, and wrote "compact model" on the side of the box. Workers who feel less important than the products they make use their creativity to find ways to goof off and to get even with those in charge. Disgruntled workers in America steal $50 billion a year, and turnover costs another $11 billion annually.

Having explored the organization's future opportunities and having figured out what's causing the technical and social problems that compromise current performance, the next stage in the Rapid Redesign process develops recommendations for change that accentuate the positive and eliminate the negative. This is the subject of Chapter 7.

Rapid Redesign: Radically Redesigning the Organization

Organizational design consultant John Geirland has been chatting with his client, Joe Camara, for over an hour. Camara manages over 100 data processing professionals at Fincom, a leading financial services company in the Midwest. His team has been developing a whole new generation of computer software, but progress has stalled to the point that Camara has hired Geirland to analyze and help correct the situation.

"You've just described a classic example of what I call the Möbius effect," Geirland says, leaning back in his chair and chuckling.

Camara looks puzzled. "The what?"

"I'll show you." Geirland takes a narrow 12-inch-long strip of paper, twists it, and tapes its ends together. Marking an X on the strip with a Magic Marker, he hands it to Camara. "Put your finger on the X" he tells his client. "Then move your finger around the paper without lifting it. What happens?"

Doing as he's been told, Camara looks up at Geirland with an expression of surprise on his face. "I ended up just where I started!"

"Exactly. That's the Möbius effect. The Möbius strip is a one-sided geometrical phenomenon that endlessly loops back on itself."

"So, how does that apply to my team?"

Geirland smiles. "You just told me you don't let your programmers talk to their internal customers. Correct?"

143

"Right. We don't want our programmers to bother the operations people with a bunch of questions. Those people have work to do."

Geirland raises his hand. "Okay. But what if a programmer has a problem or a question that only an operations person can answer?"

Camara shrugs. "We've got proper channels for that. We set up a special committee to handle that sort of stuff."

"I see. How often does that committee meet?"

Camara narrows his eyes and purses his lips. "Once a week, I think."

"Okay. But you said earlier that the main problem you're facing is that the programmers on this project lack commitment. They aren't as productive as they should be, absenteeism is high, people don't want to work overtime, they lack a sense of urgency."

"That's right."

Geirland leans forward in his chair, sticking his pen behind his ear and gesturing at the Möbius strip. "Let's suppose I'm a programmer, and I have a problem that only an operations person can help me with, but I have to wait a week to bring the problem to a committee. During that delay, I'm just looping back on myself and getting nowhere with my problem."

Camara's eyes narrow. Geirland imagines how his client feels right now, probably the way anyone who's fallen asleep on the subway feels when he wakes up to discover he's back at the same station where he's boarded the train.

"I see your point. The Möbius effect, huh?" Camara says quietly. "What do I do about it?"

"You begin," Geirland says, "by redesigning the strip." He takes the Möbius strip from Camara and tears it apart.

"It's all a matter of redesign," he says. "You can't tell employees to work overtime and move forward on software development with all deliberate speed, then structure the project in a way that puts the brakes on their efforts."

"You mean, I haven't been making consistent design choices, right?"

"Right. It's time for radical change. Tear it up and start over."

Developing Radical Redesign Recommendations

Many firms suffer from the Möbius effect. They live with structures that keep people moving but returning to the same old problems, over and over again, instead of redesigning their organizations so people can move forward to accomplish greater results. Like Joe Camara, they won't or can't "tear it up and start over."

In 1880, two freight trains collided and a young man named George Westinghouse set to work to prevent such an accident from every happening again. Using the old brake design, if the compressed air system failed, the train would run out of control. By reversing his approach to the problem, Westinghouse finally came up with the following solution: heavy springs held the train's brakes on, while the compressed air pushed the brakes away from the wheels. If the air system malfunctioned, the springs clamped the brakes back against the wheels, forcing the train to come to a safe stop. By looking at the problem from a different angle, by tearing it apart and starting afresh, Westinghouse perfected the air brake, and his design soon became a standard for the entire industry. Those involved in stage 4 of the Rapid Redesign process should do just that, revisiting findings and ideas about improving the organization gathered in the previous steps and looking at them from a new angle.

Understanding the Redesign Process

The word question comes from the Latin *quaerere* (to seek), and success in developing redesign recommendations hinges on seeking answers to the kind of questions children often ask, questions of wonder ("I wonder what would happen if...") that can produce radically new ideas. For example, "I wonder what would happen if we divided the company into six smaller, stand-alone business units?" Questions such as this challenge employees to imagine a better future, not to avoid reality, but to change that reality. The organization should explore such provocative propositions, testing for blind spots and assumptions that deserve to be torn apart and reassembled differently.

Creativity and innovation are key factors in developing redesign recommendations. Creativity is the ability to look at the same information as everyone else and see something different. Innovation isn't finding the light at the end of the tunnel. It's finding a way to have no tunnel at all. Most redesigns are fundamentally about moving responsibility and information across old and obsolete boundaries. Remove artificial barriers between process customers and those who carry out the process tasks. Break up the traditional linear process flow so many things happen simultaneously. Changing your mind-set makes the impossible become possible.

Finding the Right Balance

Organization redesign is the art of accumulation and imagination. It involves understanding, shaking up, rearranging, and inventing, invoking The 20% Solution and following new ways of thinking. Beware of either-or thinking. Try instead to define and develop "and" propositions. Executive Jet created a totally new concept in executive transportation called Netjets. The idea is simple; owning an airplane is often costly and sharing one is inefficient. Netjets offers the best of both: a fractional ownership program that guarantees availability, 365 days a year. Customers pay only for their time on the airplane.

E.F Schumacher, writing in *Economics as if People Mattered* in 1973, said, "For his different purposes, man needs many different structures, both large and small ones, some exclusive and some comprehensive. Yet, people find it most difficult to keep two seemingly opposite necessities of truth in their minds at the same time. They always tend to clamor for a final solution, as if in actual life there could ever be a final solution other than death. For constructive work, the principal task is always the restoration of some kind of balance."

Redesigning the organization to introduce the right balance means using The 20% Solution to focus on six key redesign decisions.

Focusing on Six Key Redesign Decisions

Concentrating on rethinking the following six aspects of structure, support, and staffing simplifies complexity and helps to develop choices for redesign in an efficient, orderly way, without being distracted by less important issues.

The Six Key Redesign Decisions

□ Structure

1. Where will we draw organizational boundaries?
2. How will jobs be designed?

- ❑ Support

  3. How will we organize the flow of information?

  4. What rewards and benefits will employees receive?

- ❑ Staffing

  5. How will we select employees?

  6. How will we develop their capabilities?

The redesign guidelines described earlier will help shape the selection of appropriate choices in each of these six areas. In the end, a committee of people who have successfully created change in the past can review the final recommendations and critique them based on their previous experience.

Making Decisions about Structure

Finance staffs in large traditionally structured organizations average nearly 5% of total employment, and in some cases they account for more than 10% of the organization's payroll. In recent years, organizations as diverse as Johnson & Johnson and General Electric have restructured the finance function, cutting overhead by a third or more with new ways to bill customers, pay employees, and process checks. Instead of each business unit maintaining its own accounting operation, they rely instead on a centralized finance function that shares its services by using electronic data transfer and local area networks. In the process, they've increased the output of accounting clerks by mapping their core work processes the same way they did to speed up production on the shop floor. Whereas GE's Financial Services Operation once served 100 manufacturing locations with 106 people, it now processes the payroll for 40,000 employees with a scant 28 people. The finance staff are now integrally involved in setting overall business strategies instead of checking for errors in travel and expense reports. By changing their focus from processing transactions to adding value, the new breed of financial analysts spends their time developing information about company spending practices and negotiating better deals with vendors.

Decision 1: Redefining the Organization's Boundaries

The organization should consist of self-contained work units that are responsible for discrete processing segments. Boundaries should minimize the transfer of variation from one work unit to another, and shouldn't separate people who need to work together or learn from each other.

❑ Since she joined Microsoft in 1988, Patty Stonesifer has worked hard to understand and articulate customer needs by studying videotapes of typical people working and playing with computers. After studying how people used computers at home, Stonesifer, the vice president in charge of Microsoft's $200 million-plus consumer software division, restructured her staff of 500 people into work units organized around "usage occasions" or "usage opportunities," rather than around technologies such as multimedia. The new units, called Family Reference, Life Styles, Kids and Games, Personal Productivity, and Personal Transactions, center around customer needs.

❑ Cigna, the giant property and casualty insurer, has transformed its procedure for developing group policies for corporate customers, aiming to do it quicker and reduce variation with the help of artificial intelligence. Under the old method, which is still standard practice for most insurers, each proposal wandered through 10 or more departments sequentially (sales, underwriting, policy service, claims, and so on). Each department revised the proposal in light of its own responsibilities, information, nomenclature, and schedules, resulting in considerable confusion and delay.

Under the new method, teams made up of representatives from each department assemble new policies with the help of a system programmed with insurance knowledge. Flexible yet disciplined, this system calls up, correlates, and displays descriptions of all existing insurance coverage and options. The teams construct policies from alternatives the system suggests, and their proposals are then routed electronically throughout the corporation for the necessary approvals. Proposals come together faster, meet the customers' needs better, yet cost less because they reuse work the organization has already done. Perfecting the smallest frequently replicated work activities allows the organization to provide the highest possible degree of segmentation and fine-tuning for customers at the lowest cost.

Redesign options to consider when setting organizational boundaries typically include:

❑ Setting boundaries to encompass complete processing segments, so employees can clearly identify, evaluate, and control the inputs and outputs of each segment.

❑ Defining boundaries so they minimize the likelihood of passing on problems from one work unit to another.

❑ Creating multifunctional teams of employees who are responsible for producing a complete end product or a clearly defined component of the final product.

❑ Reassigning administrative or support tasks so that these multifunctional teams have quick access to all the resources they need to succeed.

When recommending changes based on these ideas, it's important that those who will be impacted by the recommendations understand the benefits of changing. Employees naturally feel comfortable doing what they're presently doing and resist the inconvenience of change. Since existing boundaries represent traditionally sanctioned fiefdoms and empires, redrawing these boundaries usually creates a sense of winners and losers. Managers' status and salaries often depend on the number of people reporting to them, so they're reluctant to give up responsibility, control, or manpower to other departments unless they appreciate how doing so will benefit them and the organization.

Developing trust and team-working skills among employees from different functions takes time and training. Some people who don't believe others can ever learn to do their jobs as well as they can need to learn how to teach others what they know. Team assignments should also take into account people's personal preferences. Some employees may not want to join a team that includes people with whom they've developed tensions or personality conflicts in the past. Further, teams should be given operating responsibility only when they've gained a full understanding of how to manage their assigned processes. In the interim, managers should give team members clear direction and feedback, gradually relinquishing control over decision-making as the team gains capability and confidence.

Decision 2: Redesigning Jobs

Jobs should combine tasks between people and machines in a way that treats their respective capabilities as compatible rather than comparable. Tasks should be combined to get work done efficiently while at the same time satisfying people's human and psychological needs. For maximum satisfaction, job content should provide variety, autonomy, personal growth, respect, mutual support, and a desirable future.

- Product quality at Frito-Lay's Lubbock, Texas plant ranks in the top six of Frito's 48 U.S. factories. Since the plant introduced work teams in 1990, the number of managers has dropped from 38 to 13, while the number of workers has increased from 175 to 220. Work teams assume responsibility for everything from potato processing to equipment maintenance. They also determine crew scheduling, interview potential employees, and receive weekly reports on their cost, quality, and service performance relative to Frito's other team plants nationwide.

- Umwelt Technik Systems in Austria, working with Borland International, has developed a robot equipped with video cameras to crawl through sewer pipes looking for damage. The robot is tethered to a long cable that supplies it with power and water (for pressure), and sends back video signals and data. This way, a human operator can sit in a nice dry van or truck, and observe the action on a TV screen.

- Advances in technology sound the death knell for many traditional jobs. At Boeing, workers formerly assembled wire bundles by painstakingly laying strands of wire across pegs on plywood boards. Today, they wear helmets that augment reality by projecting wiring schematics onto a partially reflective lens, allowing the wearers to see wiring instructions superimposed on whatever they're doing. Working with a single board, they rely on computer graphics to indicate the position of each peg and wire. Technological marvels like this don't replace people, they redefine their jobs and boost their ability to add value for customers.

Redesign options to create more effective jobs typically include:

- Assigning programmable, repetitive, or boring tasks to machines, and assigning nonprogrammable tasks that require judgment or discretion to people.

- Automating or eliminating dangerous tasks, those that pose a threat to the physical or mental well-being of employees.

- Choosing equipment that leverages rather than replaces people's abilities, allowing them to accomplish more through its use than they could achieve on their own.

Henry Ford once said, "Why is it that I always get a whole person when what I really want is a pair of hands?" When considering these ideas, it's important to find an accommodation between the demands of the organization and the technology on the one hand, and the needs and desires of employees on the other hand. Advances in technology may deal a fatal blow to many traditional jobs, but they can also give birth to a whole new world of work, one in which the activity that consumes one-third of a person's life can become much more productive and fulfilling than ever before.

Making Decisions about Support Systems

When Gene Kirila founded Pyramid Plastics in Sharpsville, Pennsylvania, in 1986, his experience quickly reinforced his belief that only well-informed employees would enable his business to grow and prosper. After asking people in each department to list five things that everyone in the company should know, Kirila and his managers then developed a quiz to test employees' knowledge. Typical questions included: "When does our fiscal year end? Why do we take inventory? What's our policy for sending replacement parts? Can you name three of our major competitors?"

Today, new employees take the quiz after their indoctrination— 40 hours of classroom and on-the-job training—and once a year after that. Kirila updates the questions periodically but never uses the scores, which average about 70%, as part of his employees' performance reviews. However, each department's aggregate results do count in the managers' performance reviews. Kirila claims the scores relate closely with efficiency. "Give me our score for a year," he says, "and I can tell you our gross profit."

Decision 3: Organizing the Flow of Information
Information should always go first to the people who need it to direct and control the organization's core business processes.

□ In 1991, every time a payroll request or an employee records update arrived at one of Sears, Roebuck & Company's 24 human resource centers, it drifted back and forth between desks and filing cabinets for days, even weeks on end. With 573 clerks, data entry operators, and supervisors spending countless hours verifying and signing off on every single piece of paperwork, employees often languished for weeks before seeing their updated records or paychecks. To remedy the problem, Sears redesigned its HR department, introducing new technology to automate the work flow, shifting tasks to other departments in the Sears organization, reducing the number of its HR centers to two and its workforce to 125 people. The move slashed almost 75% off Sears' HR costs, primarily because it enabled information to flow through the system much more efficiently.

❏ In October 1993, Black and Decker held a three-day phone-a-thon with the goal of asking 2,500 people their thoughts about its Quantum line of power tools for do-it-yourselfers. Nearly 200 employees—assembly-line workers, marketing executives, and everyone in between—flew from around the world to company headquarters in Towson, Maryland, where they set to work with an array of phone banks and computers. Munching take-out pizza, everyone associated with the Quantum products heard firsthand from their customers. Information flowed exactly where it needed to go so Quantum employees could serve those customers better.

❏ At some General Mills beverage plants, 20-person high-performance teams now get timely information about the company's marketing plans and production costs, information once reserved for managers only. These teams do everything from scheduling production to rejecting products that fall short of quality standards. Team members receive bonuses based on their plant's performance. This approach has produced such significant productivity gains that the company has begun spreading it to all plant operations.

Any business strategy depends on an effective information system for its success. Organizations have traditionally arranged themselves in functional groups and management hierarchies designed to get the appropriate information to the right managers, who could then could make decisions and issue directives. Since information once kept in ledgers and files can now flow electronically throughout the organization without human intervention, this traditional structure and hierarchy needs to be reviewed, rethought, and redesigned. Price Waterhouse maintains electronic bulletin boards that are accessible to over 18,000 employees in 22 countries on more than 1,000 different subjects. This kind of network technology flattens hierarchies, disconnecting intellectual activity from organizational level and physical location, and enables people with different skills, interests, and authority to cross barriers of geography, language, and specialization in the same way that the automobile disconnected shopping and work from residential neighborhoods. Free access of information across an organization allows people closest to the customer to think for themselves and make faster decisions.

Organizations that don't redesign their information systems at the same time they redesign their structures resemble a boxer who goes on a crash diet to make weight; they're lean and mean, but they don't have much of a punch.

Redesign options that improve information flow typically include:

□ Providing employees with wider and more immediate access to information traditionally considered proprietary to management (such as actual unit costs, projected production volumes).

□ Supplementing or translating available information so it illustrates the impact of important variables in direct business terms (for example, temperature deviations translated into dollars lost per hour).

□ Reassigning responsibility for product testing and evaluation to those who produce the product, giving them direct, real-time feedback on their performance.

When considering these ideas, it's important to appreciate and alleviate the concerns of staff specialists who may fear their jobs will eventually disappear, or activities such as testing won't be performed properly if their functions are decentralized to operating units. Managers often fear that other employees won't manage sensitive business information responsibly, but when an organization clearly ties employees' rewards to the organization's success, such fears evaporate. Competitors probably already know most relevant business information about their rivals anyway.

Decision 4: Choosing Rewards and Benefits

Rewards and benefits should encourage and support the behaviors, processes, and outcomes that the organization needs to be successful, and should include both material and psychological recognition.

❑ XEL Communications makes custom circuit boards in Aurora, Colorado. The company's success hinges on quick-as-a-flash turnaround of orders for customers such as GTE, much faster than competitors such as Northern Telecom and AT&T can manage. XEL introduced high-performance work teams in 1988, and by 1993, it had reduced the number of support and supervisory personnel by 30%, the cost of assembly was down by 25%, inventory had shrunk by 50%, while quality levels were up by 30%. The company's all-important cycle time fell from eight weeks to four days.

High-performance team-based management seldom works under a traditional compensation system that focuses only on individual performance, because workers strive to shine on their own rather than as contributing members of a team. XEL's compensation system encourages team behavior in three ways:

> It bases pay on skills, recognizing that members of successful teams need to perform a variety of tasks. Hourly wages are determined by the number of skills an employee can demonstrate.

> It provides merit increases, based on a combination of team performance and peer reviews. No one can better judge an individual's contribution than that person's teammates.

> It delivers profit sharing, paid in cash every quarter, based on the company's performance and on each worker's quarterly earnings. That way, team members succeed as individuals only if their efforts benefit the company as a whole.

❑ Aid Association for Lutherans Insurance Company has designed a pay-for-applied services system where people need to certify not only that they're technically competent in a skill, but that the skill is needed on their team. Skill blocks are based on knowledge about life insurance, disability insurance, and tasks such as claims, billing, and address changes. A base pay rate determined by aggregate skills is one element of employee compensation. A second element is individual incentive compensation, which recognizes star performers who are eligible for annual incentive bonuses based on their contribution to the success of the operation. Team or departmental performance is a third element in the form of an annual bonus based on the success of their department. Corporate gainsharing, called Success Share, is a fourth element, rewarding all employees according to the results of the entire operation.

❑ Knowledge Adventure is a $35 million, 100-person multimedia edutainment software company in La Crescenta, California. Its products, learning software that combines fun with facts and figures, could allow Knowledge Adventure to grow into a $1 billion company by the end of the century. Although his company has attracted some powerful rivals, from Microsoft to the movie studios, founder Bill Gross believes these giants can't match his small-size speed. He's spent a lot of time thinking about keeping his company entrepreneurial and avoiding the big-company lethargy that so often follows growth. As part of a reward system that encourages employees to share his concern, the company offers new recruits three salary options, ranging from all salary and little stock, to tiny salary and lots of stock. The more pay cuts people take, the more of the company they end up owning. As a result, employees own more than half the company. If it continues to act small and grow, even the lowest-paid shipping clerk could become rich when the stock eventually goes public.

Most people want to earn a high income, but employees also view employment as more than an honest day's pay for an honest day's work. Their jobs are closely interwoven with their identity, and their benefits are closely interwoven with the quality of their lives. While regular paychecks fuel daily activities, medical benefits determine whether people will remain free from the financial risks of catastrophic illness or disability, and pensions determine whether they can maintain the lifestyle shaped during their career later in life. In the past, employees joined an organization at 18 years of age and stayed aboard until they turned 65. This provided plenty of time for them and their employer to set aside money to support their retirement, a period of modest living that would last a couple of years on average. Today, people retire in their late 50s, change jobs more frequently, and need income for an active retirement that may last longer than their working career.

Given the major social and economic changes sweeping through the world—more women joining the workforce, more single parents working, dual-income families, more frequent job and career moves, longer life spans, a drive toward greater gender and racial equity in the workplace—organizations can no longer maintain a one-size-fits-all benefits package for everyone. Redesign recommendations should consider expanding their choices to include a broader array of noncash compensation options, from discounts at the company store and subsidized child and elder care, to health club memberships and free parking.

Redesign options that make rewards and benefits more relevant and effective typically include:

- Rewarding both team and individual performance.
- Linking pay levels to the number of skills an employee learns and uses. Skills can be associated with business, administrative, and interpersonal competencies, as well as with technical operations.
- Creating reward systems that recognize certified skills, the willingness to use those skills, and the results of successfully applying those skills.
- Tying pay-for-knowledge with performance planning, whereby employees regularly contract with others who depend on them, based on their joint expectations for future performance.
- Providing individual and group incentives in addition to regular pay, based on exceptional product quality, cost reductions, or other relevant performance parameters within the direct control of the employee or the employee's workgroup.
- Setting up all-salaried pay schemes to eliminate a "we-they" culture in the organization, recognizing that success depends on equality of effort and contribution by employees at all levels.

When considering these ideas, it's important to make sure that any pay-for-knowledge compensation scheme rewards only the skills people use on a regular basis to benefit the bottom line. Training without sufficient application time or proven certification procedures results in paying people for contributions they haven't actually made. If employees can earn more money without a corresponding benefit for the organization, they'll see their rewards as nothing but free money, and this will encourage exploitation rather than responsible behavior. Pay-for-knowledge, if installed as a stand-alone program without a corresponding emphasis on performance planning and time-in-grade requirements, encourages employees to spend their time in training rather than working to produce or improve the organization's product or service. Since advancement by certification challenges traditional seniority progression systems, older employees often fear that the certification process will foster special treatment for a favored few, or that younger employees will get ahead faster (and eventually earn more) than they will. Pay initiatives can cause problems if they're introduced piecemeal in a single department or work unit, as issues of inequity inevitably arise, negating the very motivation the organization seeks to inspire.

Making Decisions about Staffing

State Farm Insurance outperforms its rivals in terms of customer retention, market share, and profits, and it does so by painstakingly recruiting and training each of its 18,000 agents. Prior to 1994, applicants, preferably people who had never sold insurance before, went through 200 hours of interviewing, testing, and visiting with State Farm agents before finding out if they would be hired. Now anyone who wants to become an agent must work three years in underwriting, claims, or another department at the company's headquarters in Bloomington, Illinois, or in another State Farm office. Candidates then undergo six months of agent training. State Farm knows that no matter how brilliantly it structures itself, those structures won't work properly without the right people.

Decision 5: Selecting Employees

The first rule of staff degradation states that people who rank a seven on a scale of 1 to 10 usually hire people who rank a five or a six. Aim to break that rule, and never hire anyone you wouldn't want to work for. An organization's hiring process should be consistent with the values it aspires to live by, starting with the end in mind.

□ The core values that Hewlett-Packard has identified for high performance include: continuous process improvement, flexibility, teamwork, and continuous learning. When H-P set up a new plant in Puerto Rico, the company brought people in for interviews in groups of 20 at a time. First, they filled out applications. Next, the recruiters asked them to look carefully at the application form and to think about how it might be improved (continuous improvement). Then, they formed teams to summarize their suggestions (teamwork). Reforming into different teams (flexibility), they conferred and reported what they'd learned (continuous learning). Every applicant went through this sequence four or five times. Finally, the recruiters asked, "Do you notice something different going on here? What message do you think we're trying to get across to you?" One H-P manager noted, "They then told us about the core values; we didn't have to tell them. It's important to be explicit about what you're doing, the way you design your culture. You don't get there by default."

❑ At the Gates Rubber plant in Siloam Springs, Arkansas, all job applicants go through a five-step screening and interviewing process. First, they have a general interview with people from the personnel department. Three days later, someone else from personnel interviews them a second time, to verify information and impressions from the first meeting. The third step consists of a group interview with the plant manager and two other people from different parts of the plant who evaluate communication skills, work attitudes, and general confidence level. Since teams perform all the work in the plant, these interviews also explore the applicant's ability to respond well in a group setting.

If this panel approves the candidate, the personnel department conducts an intensive reference check. Candidates whose references check out then come back for a final meeting, which lasts a couple of hours and usually takes place on a weekend so the candidate's spouse or significant other can also attend. During this meeting, the plant manager and two other people from the plant review its policies, practices, and benefits, then show a 20-minute video on Gates Rubber's history, discussing what it means to join a high-performance work team.

Each step in the interview process strives to surface the kinds of problems that might otherwise show up only after the company has hired someone. Given the costs of quality mistakes, injuries, work slowdowns from incompetence, and overtime, Gates believes that its investment in hiring pays off. The Siloam Springs plant has an 8% annual turnover rate versus 100% in a comparable plant in town owned by another company.

Redesign options to improve employee selection typically include:

❑ Changing hiring requirements to place greater emphasis on personal values and willingness to learn, in addition to assessing current credentials and past experience.

❑ Using work simulations to assess a job applicant's attitudes and skills.

❑ Involving those who will work with new employees in their selection.

In considering these ideas, it's important to bear in mind that staffing for high-performance work teams requires hiring people who are assertive, ambitious, and have an expansive attitude toward work and life. Team members should participate in choosing the candidates because it develops team ownership for the success of new members. A formal buddy system, pairing new hires with veteran employees, also helps get people quickly up to speed on their jobs. In the long run, all the time spent screening and scrutinizing potential staff will pay off handsomely in terms of commitment, loyalty, and service to the customer.

Decision 6: Developing Employee Capabilities

Work should provide people with opportunities to learn, grow, develop, and contribute to their full potential. It should stimulate and encourage them to invent a better future for themselves and for the organization.

❑ Solectron, founded as a small assembly shop in 1977 by a group of former IBM executives, now exceeds $1 billion a year in sales. The company provides circuit boards to leading computer manufacturers like Apple Computer, Sun Microsystems, and Motorola, allowing these companies to focus their resources instead on areas such as design and marketing. Solectron's costs per employee are half those of other major circuit board manufacturers, and over the past decade, it has reduced its product defect rate to less than three parts per million. In recent years, the company has bought factories from IBM, Hewlett-Packard, and Philips, in France, Scotland, Malaysia, and the United States, and while many of these plants had been losing money before they were taken over, they now generate profits. Solectron takes pride in its nimbleness. Every day, it builds 800 different circuit boards at its Milpitas, California, factory in average lot sizes of 50 each. To help spot and correct problems quickly, it invites customers to fill out weekly report cards on the company's performance.

Since startup, Solectron's revenues have grown at an average rate of over 60% a year. Says chairman Winston Chen, "If you want to have high growth and high quality, training is a big part of the equation. Technology changes so fast, 20% of an engineer's knowledge becomes obsolete every year. Training is an obligation we owe our employees." In 1994, all 7,000 Solectron employees, including Chen himself, spent 110 hours in training sessions during regular working hours, learning everything from concurrent engineering to how to make effective presentations.

The longshoreman and philosopher Eric Hoffer once wrote that "In times of drastic change, the learners inherit the future. The learned find themselves equipped to live in a world that no longer exists." Clearly, the need for continuing education is a significant force shaping the future workplace. Yet, according to the American Society for Training and Development, a mere 15,000 employers, one-half of 1% of the total, account for 90% of the money spent on training annually in the United States. *Training* magazine estimates spending on formal staff development by U.S. companies with more than 100 employees at $50 billion in 1994, up just 11% from 1990, an increase that's less than the rate of inflation over the same period.

Corning executives, on the other hand, expect all employees to spend at least 5% of their working hours in training, which averages out to 92 hours per employee per year. Ford offers salaried employees tuition for two courses per semester in approved degree programs. When Motorola found in 1985 that 60% of its workforce struggled with seventh-grade math, it set about investing almost 4% of its payroll on training. Between 1987 and 1993, Motorola increased profits by 47% and cut costs by $3.3 billion, not by firing workers, but by training them to simplify processes and reduce waste. Motorola calculates that every dollar it spends on training delivers $30 in productivity gains within three years.

Professional basketball players work for a particular club, but their real loyalties are to themselves, their families, and their fellow players. The club owners know this but still expect all-out commitment at practice and on the court. For their part, the players know if they perform poorly, they'll be riding the bench, and their income and market value will drop. In exchange for their commitment, the players expect the club to provide training to keep them fit, coaching to improve their skills, and rewards for peak performance. This model parallels the new relationship between employees and employers.

Research by Nigel Nicholson and Michael West at Sheffield University shows that careers for many, rather than reflecting clearly defined aspirations and plans, are "myths about the past that make them feel better about the future." If employment relationships are based only on temporary contracts, then people's careers today follow very sketchy maps. True power stems from knowledge, and since knowledge quickly gets out of date, one of the secrets of career management lies in constantly extending knowledge. If security no longer comes from being employed, then it must come from being employable.

Redesign options that improve opportunities for employee development typically include:

- ❑ Cross-skilling employees so they can perform multiple tasks.
- ❑ Broadening employees' skills to allow them to contribute in areas such as administrative support, equipment maintenance, interpersonal relations, and group dynamics.
- ❑ Developing certification processes to assure that employees demonstrate expertise in their skills.
- ❑ Providing performance planning and career counseling opportunities for all employees.
- ❑ Eliminating dead-end jobs.

When considering these ideas, it's important to bear in mind that some people resist learning because they're functionally illiterate and fear they'll be detected if the organization is redesigned. Some fear they can't master new skills, regardless of the quality of the training programs provided. Functional groups often turn their backs on cross-functional skill development because they fear a reduction in overtime earnings or eventual job elimination. They also fret (sometimes justifiably) that people will end up knowing more and more about less and less. Managers, hired for their academic rather than their workplace skills, often display a different learning style (visual, verbal, and auditory) from front-line employees (tactile and kinesthetic). They mistakenly view workers as slow learners when, in fact, those workers' learning styles simply differ from their own and may accomplish more in the workplace. Redesign efforts will falter if organizations continue to rely on out-of-date programs that assume conventional training results in learning.

Benjamin Franklin once said, "Tell me, and I forget; teach me, and I may remember; involve me, and I learn." The most effective training is concise, interactive, and interspersed with group projects, role-playing, and hands-on experiences. The best teachers transmit ideas by telling war stories, personal anecdotes that relate directly to the subject at hand. When people play games that simulate the real world, they gain better insights about their decisions in a safe environment that stimulates learning. Learning shouldn't cause stress, but should please and delight people, because when learning becomes fun, growing the business becomes fun too. "Work hard, play hard" characterizes the old school of training; "learn to play, play to learn" epitomizes the new.

Bringing It All Together

As United Technologies Corporation has modernized manufacturing techniques, its Otis, Carrier, and Sikorsky units have all abandoned standard assembly-line production in favor of cross-functional teams of employees who create products together from start to finish. By giving employees more responsibility, the company has reduced mistakes and eliminated downtime. In England, Sun Life Assurance Society, a Bristol-based insurer managing $25 million in assets, redesigned once-isolated customer service representatives into teams and made them responsible for processing a customer's file from start to finish. As a result, Sun has slashed turnaround time to settle claims in half while growing new business by 45%. Infosys Technologies Ltd., a software development company in Bangladore, India, lacks any formal structure. When a job comes along, teams form, take responsibility for the work, get the job done, then disband and re-form to tackle a new job.

All around the world, proposals to redesign structure, support, and staffing are being developed each and every day as organizations continually search for more effective ways to operate. But it doesn't matter how relevant these redesign recommendations are unless they can be implemented effectively.

Rapid Redesign: Implementation and Continuous Renewal

Wednesday, January 4, 1994. Three people are sitting around a conference table with training folders open on their laps. Jeannette Bajalia, a dark-haired woman in a pinstripe suit, is the first to speak. "Steve Horowitz has always stood up under fire," she says, stabbing a finger at the folder on her lap. "But he's been jeopardizing his team's performance lately. What do you think, Midge, personal problems?"

The youngest of the group, Midge Colombo, leans forward in her chair. "Maybe," she agrees, "although it's hard to tell. His team's been under the gun for weeks, but they've managed to hide Steve's poor performance. Sooner or later, that's going to blow up and somebody's going to get nailed."

"What bothers me," interrupts Stell Bennefield, "is Steve's team has let him down. They think they're doing him a favor by picking up the slack. This situation has now created danger for everyone on the team, everyone in the organization."

Jeannette stands up. "Laying blame won't help. This is obviously a Code Red. Who should pull the trigger?"

These people aren't spies at the Central Intelligence Agency, but dedicated Blue Cross Blue Shield of Florida employees immersed in what

163

that company calls the Genesis Project. Genesis is a pilot program to explore how the organization should redesign itself to make the transition from the old way of doing business, processing medical claims and transactions, to the new way, helping people manage and care for their health.

Jeannette, Midge, and Stell have spent three days working through a series of "critical incidents," case study scenarios that reflect the sort of real-world situations work teams face when implementing redesign recommendations. The present one involves an employee whose job performance has declined, but whose teammates have chosen to cover for him rather than confront him with the problem.

Stell Bennefield stands up and stretches. "Pull the trigger?" she says. "That's pretty tough language, JB."

Jeannette laughs. "Somebody's got to do something. This situation won't improve until a teammate takes Steve aside and helps him face the fact he's letting everyone down, especially himself."

"You know what I'd do?" observes Midge. "I'd put the team through this critical incident. Seeing someone else with the problem might defuse their emotions and let them see what's wrong. You know the old saying, 'A wife never sees her husband's flaws because his face is so close on the pillow.'"

Jeannette nods her head. "That's the whole point of these simulations, isn't it? They give us a chance to navigate through problems with clear heads. Then, when real problems come up, we can go to a map that'll help us solve them without all the usual fear and denial."

"I'm with you," says Stell. "When it comes to handling change, nothing beats the old A&P formula."

The others look perplexed. "The A&P formula?" they ask, almost in unison. Stell grins. "Sure, Anticipation and Preparation."

Business is like a bicycle—it's stable only if it's moving. All the effort and energy invested in the Rapid Redesign process will be wasted if the recommendations aren't implemented effectively. Using The 20% Solution, concentrate on being consistent with the following five guidelines to assure that everyone keeps pedaling forward:

1. Make sure that employees see the redesign recommendations as their own rather than mandates that have been devised and forced on them by outsiders. A critical mass of employees must fully grasp the organization's plans prior to implementation. They must believe that implementing the

recommendations will reduce rather than increase their present burdens.

2. Concentrate in the early stages of implementation on working with people who support the recommendations, rather than on working against those who resist change. Invest sufficient resources early on to propel the organization out of its natural state of inertia. Pay particular attention to implementing recommendations that can demonstrate results right away.

3. Test proposals on a small scale first, encouraging key opinion leaders to assess, adapt, and adopt the recommendations prior to a full-scale rollout. Acknowledge and quickly resolve any problems or objections that arise. Reward and encourage employees for the effort of changing, as well as for achieving expected results.

4. Take advantage of opportunities where change is already under way. Start where new technologies are being introduced, or where new managers have come on board. Make sure these managers walk their talk and can clearly differentiate between ends and means (for example, employee participation in decision-making is a means to an end, not an end in itself).

5. Remember that successful implementation depends on three things: training, training, and training. Provide the right education at the right time so employees aren't distracted from serving customers by unfamiliar equipment, software, and work procedures.

Following these five guidelines will ensure that the bicycle remains stable and gathers momentum as it speeds toward a new and better future. The implementation journey starts by developing a widespread sense of ownership.

Developing Employee Ownership

When staging a successful Broadway play, countless auditions and rehearsals take place in the months before the curtain finally rises. The actors "prep it, then pop it." Similarly, an organization undergoing redesign must engage in many ownership-building activities long before opening night. The Chevron Chemical Company took this into account when it set about implementing a major redesign program.

Inviting Widespread Participation

In the early 1980s, the Chevron Chemical Company hired a contractor specializing in phosphate fertilizer plants to build a state-of-the-art manufacturing facility in Rock Springs, Wyoming. The plant started up in 1985 as a nonunion facility employing 200 people, and work was organized to incorporate a variety of innovative work practices culled from benchmarking high-performance organizations across the United States. Nevertheless, plant performance was disappointing during the first few years of operation, primarily because Chevron had implemented a random collection of ideas that didn't always work smoothly together. In 1987, when Bert Weller entered the scene as a new plant manager, he determined that radical redesign was required to improve the situation.

In January 1988, Weller scheduled a three-day in-house workshop for a select group of supervisors and employees to introduce the idea of participatively redesigning the plant. Participants at the workshop agreed with Weller's redesign proposal, but urged him to put others at the Rock Springs facility through the same experience before making a final decision. As a result, all employees attended a series of similar workshops during the months that followed. These highly experiential sessions allowed participants to get hands-on experience with the tools and techniques of organizational redesign, and to consider exactly what it would take to guarantee a successful outcome at the Rock Springs facility. Weller didn't make a firm decision to proceed until it was clear that most employees supported the redesign process.

In April 1988, a representative group of management and hourly employees began to redesign the Rock Springs plant by analyzing Chevron Chemical's business environment together. They outlined the plant's mission, articulated its operating philosophy, listed the organization's technical, social, and economic objectives, examined existing problems and concerns, and prepared a lengthy stakeholder analysis. During the following months, they examined the organization's technical and social processes to generate the data from which they developed redesign recommendations.

Developing Provisional Recommendations

By the fall of 1988, the redesign team had created a list of provisional recommendations for circulation and discussion throughout the plant. The recommendations proposed eliminating the boundaries between current production units and reorganizing employees into self-regulating, multiskilled teams to improve both operational control and the employees' job satisfaction. The proposals also recommended doing away with traditional supervision, expanding employee training, introducing a skill-based pay system with a group bonus arrangement, and increasing employee participation in setting goals, preparing budgets, evaluating performance, disciplining other employees, and charting career development. In the future, they proposed, employees would assume responsibility for managing the complete production process by themselves, from the receipt of raw materials all the way through production and shipping.

The redesign recommendations also proposed changing from four rotating shift-crews to five, allowing employees to spend one week out of every five in training sessions. Rather than continuing to perform maintenance and quality testing in separate departments, the new scheme included in each crew at least one person with equipment maintenance skills and one person with the laboratory skills needed for product testing. The core maintenance department remained centralized, but with 23 contract maintenance employees, down from 88. Vacancies for crew maintenance specialists were filled from the resulting pool of excess contractors. Each production team became responsible for hiring its own employees. The redesign proposals created a single boundary management team, which cut across different disciplines and hierarchal rankings, an organization support team, comprised of a cross-functional group of employees who previously reported to separate specialized departments, and a production specialist team, made up of engineers and former supervisors. Finally, a plant-wide coordinating team, with elected representatives from each of the work teams, would provide guidance and direction for production scheduling and day-to-day operational issues. With these ideas in place, the Chevron redesign team turned its attention to implementation planning.

Planning for Implementation

After employees throughout the plant had thoroughly discussed and accepted the redesign proposals, an implementation planning team developed an eight-page schedule of events designed to get the redesigned organization functioning as quickly as possible. Since the initial recommendations had been kept deliberately sketchy and outlined only the barest framework of the new work structures, the implementation planning team set about filling in the details (for example, the new pay scheme needed further work before final recommendations could go to Chevron's corporate office for negotiation and approval). The heart of the implementation planning process was the formation of 18 subsystem redesign teams. While nine of these would work on the support departments (production control, goal attainment, financial management, learning, customer support, supply, rewards, government compliance, and membership), the others would tackle the nine newly formed work teams. Team members were selected by their peers and authorized to reach consensus on how to implement the redesign recommendations.

The plant leadership team prepared a charter statement to guide the implementation process, and the 18 teams participated in week-long training sessions to get them started. During these sessions, participants revisited the plant's mission and philosophy statements with the express goal of revising them if necessary. Each team reviewed its customers' requirements and defined its relationships with other work units. The members then determined how to implement the redesign recommendations in their own work area, striving for agreement with visiting representatives from other teams about how to integrate all the implementation efforts. Recognizing the need to make redesign a habitual process, everyone sought ways to build in the notion of continuous renewal.

Building In Continuous Renewal

Thomas Jefferson once wrote, "Great initiatives cannot be built on slender majorities." Over 60% of the Rock Springs' workforce participated in one of the redesign or implementation teams, and 100% got directly involved in redesigning their own work. The new organization institutionalized continuous change by creating a way for everyone to suggest ideas for improvement in their own teams and to recommend ideas for plant-wide improvement to a coordinating team representing the whole organization. Chevron agreed that, henceforth, it would schedule a formal reexamination and renewal process at least once a year.

Three years after initiating the redesign process, Rock Springs showed a 48% improvement in productivity, a 21% decrease in operating expense, an 18% increase in production (to 115% of the original engineering design standards), and a 15% reduction in labor costs.

Working with Those Who Support Change and Improvement

To develop an effective implementation plan, start by canvassing the opinions of all those individuals and constituencies whose commitment is needed for success. Knowing how they view the change proposals helps to define their roles during the implementation process.

Developing a Commitment Plan

The most ardent foes of change are those who feel they stand to lose the most, and they usually wield enough power so that their resistance is a primary concern. To develop a plan to win their support, it's important to identify the most powerful individuals and stakeholder groups (including sales representatives, accountants, employees over 50 years old, and so on) without whose commitment the redesign recommendations will most likely fail. The current status of each stakeholder can then be assessed on the scale of commitment illustrated in Figure 8.1.

Stakeholder positions range from *oppose* the implementation to *let* the implementation happen, to *support* the implementation to will take responsibility to *lead* the implementation effort. When each stakeholder's support status is known, plans can be developed to involve them appropriately in implementing the Rapid Redesign recommendations. Since the stakeholders' commitment to support the implementation effort may vary, the organization must constantly monitor their involvement and act quickly to correct any backsliding. It often helps to involve people in test-driving new ideas on a small scale first before rolling them out company-wide.

	Oppose	Let	Help	Lead
President			O◄——X·	
Plant Manager		X————►O		
Mid-Level Managers		Don't know		
Union Officers	X————►O			

X = Where they are now
O = Where they need to be for success

Figure 8.1 Stakeholder analysis.

Using Pilot Sites to Introduce Organizational Innovations

American Express piloted and closely monitored a new incentive pay plan for a full year before rolling it out to all 10,000 employees in its consumer card and consumer lending groups in 1994. By testing the plan with 1,500 employees first, Amex learned it needed to work harder to communicate the plan's goals. It also learned to simplify the plan, and ended up basing payouts on three measures (customer satisfaction, employee productivity, and shareholder wealth-creation) instead of the six originally proposed.

When Saint Luke's Episcopal Hospital in Houston, Texas, set out to push decision-making down to the operating level, it set up a pilot project that designated the general surgery nursing department as a "super-unit," an experimental lab to test out new ideas about shared governance. The organization picked the general surgery unit because it had relatively low turnover and flexible staff that had a good working rapport with other departments. After defining expectations and educating employees, Saint Luke's set up ground rules that delineated where people could and could not make decisions. Councils of nurses were empowered to make decisions about patient care outcomes and about issues that affected the way they worked. The nurses tested and implemented many new ideas such as improving shift change procedures, adding a pharmacist to the unit, and streamlining how surgery was scheduled. Following the prototype's success, Saint Luke's designated five more super-units, each one working on a particular theme, such as nurse and physician collaboration, performing major testing in the units, and developing care partnerships between licensed and unlicensed staff members. As a result, Saint Luke's reduced operating costs while significantly improving employee attitudes and patient satisfaction. Clearly, Saint Luke's picked the right pilot sites to test out new ideas.

Picking a Pilot Site

If possible, the Rapid Redesign recommendations should be introduced on a small scale first, with the clear understanding that successful efforts will eventually cascade throughout the organization. A pilot program aims not so much to see if the redesign ideas will work, but to learn how to make these ideas work as effectively as possible. This strategy involves starting with limited implementation, which results in learning. This learning is then shared with everyone, followed by expansion of the pilot program and diffusion throughout the rest of the organization. The ideal pilot site should provide the best opportunities for learning rather than setting the greatest challenge to the concepts involved. Only a foolish test pilot would take a new aircraft on its maiden flight during the season's worst storm.

When choosing a pilot site, listen for squeaky wheels where demand seems strongest, and consider grafting new initiatives onto existing programs with a history of acceptance and success. A mainstream site that's directly related to the core mission of the organization will probably receive more attention and resources than a backwater site. A successful mainstream site will also make diffusion easier since a success there will have greater credibility in the rest of the organization. Taking local initiatives and leveraging them globally usually works better than trying to impose new ideas from headquarters on the rest of the organization. Still, no matter how well the pilot site is chosen, surprises will occur and something will inevitably go wrong.

Staying the Course When Things Go Wrong

Art Buck once said, "Though good may come of practice, this primal truth endures: The first time anything is done, it's done by amateurs." When things go wrong during implementation, the organization shouldn't allow dissatisfaction and frustration to reign unchecked. While some frustration can provide good stimulation for learning, too much can easily provoke a full-scale revolt. Emerging issues should be dealt with promptly, but never smash the piano just because the person playing it hits a few sour notes. Mistakes should be treated as learning opportunities, not as experiences to punish or ignore, and the learning loop is best closed when experiences are still fresh in people's minds. Reverting to the expert role and supplying quick solutions whenever a problem crops up undermines system-wide learning and fosters a dependent, fire-fighting approach to problem-solving. Attention should be focused instead on clarifying who is responsible for correcting the problems that invariably pop up. Those who must live with the consequences when things go wrong own the problems that caused them. The implementation process should give people the skills and authority they need to resolve the issues that cause their problems.

The organization should avoid just publicizing problems and failures. It's true that nothing succeeds like success, so it's important to provide constant feedback on what's going right, creating special events where people can celebrate and be recognized for their achievements. Public forums celebrating success give the organization's leaders an opportunity to make their own enthusiasm visible by walking their talk.

Walking the Talk

A good tennis instructor doesn't just tell a novice how to hit a backhand, he or she demonstrates the proper technique so that the student can imitate the stroke. Some astute managers at Ford kept this in mind as they developed a training strategy to implement new work practices at the company's Romeo engine plant.

Modeling New Skills

When Ford's Powertrain Division developed a new high-commitment, high-performance engine plant in Romeo, Michigan, in 1989, most of the 700 hourly employees hired had previously worked at a tractor plant the new operation replaced. Since this workforce lacked previous experience building engines or working in a high-performance organization, they needed extensive training prior to startup. In addition to providing training to develop technical and interpersonal skills, Ford's management paid considerable attention to developing employees' business skills as well, so employees could understand the reasons for, and track achievement against, the world-class goals that Romeo was designed to achieve. Romeo used many different training formats including instructor-led classroom sessions, large group off-site seminars, interactive video and self-instructional computer-based training, as well as ongoing experiential, on-the-job training.

Most important, however, Romeo's management and union leadership developed and presented a lot of the classroom training themselves. The instructors attended train-the-trainer courses before they each developed 10- to 40-hour programs in their areas of expertise, each designed to involve groups of about 30 employees at a time in simulations, discussion sessions, and team-based learning activities. The local union chairman, Pete Piccini, prepared and presented a course on the history of the United Auto Workers union. The plant manager, George Pfeil, taught Productivity 101, where he explained how to identify and remove production bottlenecks. Other managers taught employees how to carry out their work assignments consistent with the Romeo Quality Plan, how to function as members of high-performance work teams, and how to use personal computers.

Coaching for Success

By serving as instructors, the plant's leadership team demonstrated that they were competent and approachable experts in their functional areas. Over time, this allowed them to build mentoring relationships with employees, who now knew the managers personally, understood their areas of expertise, and felt increasingly comfortable asking them for help. During commissioning and startup, this approach to training allowed employees to express their concerns directly to those who knew the most about the topics involved, while keeping the managers up to date about issues developing on the shop floor. The training also demonstrated that both managers and union officials shared the same perspectives and priorities for the Romeo plant. People saw that their joint actions were consistent with the plant's operating philosophy, which stated that managers and union officials would "assure that employees would have the atmosphere, resources, and abilities to produce the highest quality production engines in the world, and to develop teams of employees who were the best engine builders in the world."

Walking the talk reaped many rewards for Ford, most notably in 1992, when the American Society for Training and Development recognized Romeo with its annual award for the best team training program in the American auto industry. Rather than trying to compress the training into a few weeks before startup, Romeo spaced it out over a one-year period, responding to the employees' learning needs rather than arranging matters for the convenience of the training department. As Dr. Lee Sanborn, the startup training and team development leader, noted, "Romeo didn't just train its people well, it trained them at the right time as well."

Delivering Timely Training

Apple Computer has transformed many of its existing training resources into ARPLE, the Apple Reference Performance Learning Experience and Presentation Library. Every one of Apple's 20,000 employees around the world can avail themselves of ARPLE, on-line and on-demand, via the company's client-server Ethernet technology. With it, Apple has replaced 75% of the company's former classroom training with just-in-time, multimedia learning platforms, and it aims to reduce this to zero as soon as the technology to do so becomes available.

Using Just-in-Time Training

Kanban, a Japanese just-in-time parts delivery process, named after the Kanban order cards originally used on Toyota's production lines, allows a team of workers who need a part to request and receive it immediately from another team. Extending this idea to training, just-in-time delivery of knowledge and skills, known as *kanbrain*, promises to accelerate learning because it enables employees to learn the skills they need when they need them while still on the job.

Carnegie-Mellon University now teaches its engineering students advanced math concepts as they need to apply them, not in separate math classes. Similarly, workers acquire and apply skills and concepts more readily when they feel they need new knowledge and when the knowledge they acquire proves immediately useful on the job. The software industry has pioneered just-in-time instruction by including built-in help commands that allow users to ask for assistance when they need it and then access different levels of detailed instruction at their own pace. Just-in-time learning, delivered when and where it's needed, takes control out of the hands of the instructor and puts it in the hands of the learner. Adding video-servers and training materials into groupware networks provides on-demand training programs that users can access at their convenience. In addition to classrooms where employees learn about implementation by working through case studies, such as those described earlier in the Blue Cross Blue Shield Genesis group, progressive organizations use computer networks to structure meetings where employees can work together to solve problems and take advantage of opportunities. Increasingly, smart companies rely on formal training courses only to convey highly volatile information that's changing too quickly to make it worth saving.

Learning from Peers

Employees who understand the skills they'll need tomorrow, and who have calibrated the capabilities they possess today, can best determine when, how, and what they should learn. Regardless of the degree of technology used in training, smart companies know that people can learn as much if not more from their peers as well as from managers and specialists. Peer-level coaching by other team members provides one of the most effective and least expensive alternatives to formal training programs. On-the-job coaching works best in environments where people have clear performance criteria, well-defined standards for self-assessment, where more advanced team members have strong coaching skills, and where there's an incentive for them to teach other people what they know. Training should emphasize a developmental approach that focuses on helping people get better, rather than a remedial one aimed at fixing their failures. Most people embrace the former but resist the latter.

Having addressed the five key guidelines for implementation and continuous improvement, organizations undergoing a Rapid Redesign can finally turn their attention from anticipation and preparation to translating ideas into action. They're now ready to plan the details of implementation and continuous renewal.

Putting New Ideas into Action

The following issues should be addressed when planning how to implement the redesign recommendations: setting the stage, designing the strategy, implementing the recommendations, evaluating the results, and institutionalizing the redesign process.

Setting the Stage

Winston Churchill once said, "It's a mistake to look too far ahead. Only one link in the chain of destiny can be handled at a time." This notion must have occurred to Doug Cahill in February 1994, when the 34-year-old general manager of Olin Pool Products embraced a vision of redesigning his organization from 14 departments into eight core process teams. After telling his staff they could ponder the change for 15 minutes, he said, "We're going to figure this thing out as we go along." Knowing that his employees feared he might be replaced by someone new who would change everything back to the old way, Cahill got his boss to promise that he would stay at Pool Products for at least three years as mentor, coach, and custodian of the new vision. By eliminating titles and departments, Cahill forced his managers to accept responsibility for their work rather than for their jobs. He'd decisively set the stage for change, and as a result, sales and profits increased dramatically in 1994.

Managers who underestimate the symbolic impact of their own actions forget that, from an employee's perspective, any pronouncement from above that the organization urgently needs to redesign itself implies that changes at the management level should be evident immediately. After all, actions speak louder than words, and people's behavior, more than their pronouncements, reflect what they truly believe. As the English schoolboy jingle says, "The higher up the monkey goes, the more of his behind he shows." Everything that managers say or do sends a message. But too many delegate communication to others, assuming it's something employee relations or public relations people will handle. That posture ignores the fact that employees closely watch what their leaders do, particularly during times of major change. They naturally assume that what they see indicates and illustrates what management requires of them. Preaching the importance of teamwork but rewarding people who strive to rise above the crowd or encouraging risk-taking but punishing good-faith mistakes quickly sends the wrong message.

To set the stage for change, top executives should change their own behaviors before expecting others to change. They should ask themselves, "If we were running the business the way we say is important, how should we act? How should we attack problems? What kind of meetings and conversations should we conduct? Whom should we involve? How should we recognize, compensate, and reward appropriate behavior?" A review of the organization's existing policies and practices to see how well they conform to the new vision and operating philosophy usually makes clear the directions in which managers need to move. They should pretend the organization has already implemented the redesign recommendations, then immediately start acting accordingly.

Lawrence Bossidy, the CEO of Allied Signal, says, "My philosophy is that if you get the right people leading a business, that business will improve." Allied has 128 key jobs, and Bossidy changed people in 69 of these jobs in his first two years with the company. He encouraged those who wouldn't help raise the sails to jump ship. As Louis Armstrong once said, "There are some people that, if they don't know, you can't tell 'em." When replacing people who leave, make sure that new people can demonstrate the behaviors called for in the redesign recommendations. Using this criterion as a basis for staffing emphasizes that this is what the culture will value in the future.

If the recommendations require a reduction in force, using voluntary turnover (such as attrition or retirement) to gradually reduce the number of people minimizes the trauma. Voluntary approaches, however, risk losing the people who are most needed to build the new organization since the most qualified employees are the ones with the most options to go elsewhere. When people lose their jobs, the more educated they are, the less they tend to project their ills on to the outside world, and the more they're inclined to blame themselves, and to experience guilt and shame about their shortcomings. This cycle of self-blame often reduces their capacity to function, and they require considerable support to rebuild their diminished self-esteem.

In the midst of change, weak people cling to their jobs while strong people position themselves for advancement. Wise managers take care to show their strong people that the new vision will afford them wonderful opportunities to advance their careers, and make sure they understand the organization's new strategy for success.

Designing the Strategy

Invoking The 20% Solution means specifying only the essential components of the implementation, focusing first on what needs doing and deferring details about how to do it until all those who will carry out the redesign recommendation are fully involved. The specifics of the *what* should be emphasized from the top down, allowing the *how* to be developed from the bottom up. Those involved in developing the implementation strategy should ask: "Have we provided an incentive for everything that needs doing? Do the people who will have to make the implementation work value the incentives? Could high performance ever result in negative consequences for the performer? If so, how can we avoid this?"

Since no business strategy should ever lose sight of the customer's requirements, the organization should make sure to showcase them in evaluating the effects of the new way of doing business. Developing a partnership with employees, suppliers, and customers isn't an on-again, off-again affair because "When you dance with a bear, you can't just quit when you get tired."

Overstructuring the implementation of redesign recommendations limits initiative and learning on the part of the participants and presupposes that the organization can specify every detail in advance. By its very nature, radical redesign makes it impossible to tell people precisely what to do since none of this has ever happened before, and problems and opportunities seldom conform themselves to people's preconceptions. When the advisability of certain actions or processes seems uncertain, redesigners should follow Yogi Berra's advice: "When you come to a fork in the road, take it." Be willing to experiment and discard what doesn't work. An effective implementation plan helps people review the consequences of their actions later and learn together based on actual operating experience. The secret of successful implementation lies in developing relationships people can fall back on when all else fails. Even if they don't know what's likely to happen next, when employees trust each other and embrace the same vision, uncertainty and vulnerability encourage energy and involvement. People have more faith in the future when they have faith in each other. Unity, more than anything else, makes people act and work in the right ways as the implementation of redesign recommendations unfolds.

Implementing the Recommendations

In 1985, AT&T established a corporation in Morristown, New Jersey, to provide financing and leasing services for customers of its telecommunication products. AT&T Credit Corp. included two divisions: the General Markets Division, which handled high-volume, small-ticket business, and the Business Markets Division, which took care of small-volume, middle-to-large-ticket items. Both divisions adhered to traditional work design principles, emphasizing top-down hierarchical control, functional separation, and a high degree of task specialization. The General Markets Division subcontracted credit approval, funding, and collection functions to an outside vendor.

When, by 1989, it was clear that these traditional organizations were failing to perform effectively, AT&T Credit redesigned itself into four core geographic regions, each with its own separate profit and loss accountability. Twenty high-performance teams operated among the regions, each one handling all the customers in an assigned geographical area. Three specialty units served state and local governments, federal and network systems, and emerging businesses and new business sectors (phone centers, catalog businesses). Six support groups provided each region with marketing, financial, human resources, legal, information systems, and operations support. The organization also introduced a collective reward system providing bonuses for individual team members based on the entire team's ability to raise revenues, satisfy customers, meet AT&T's financial objectives, and reduce bad loans.

AT&T Credit Corp. implemented this new structure in three stages. In early 1990, the organization held a three-day meeting involving all employees. After learning about the redesign proposals, employees discussed the changes in greater detail as they explored their impact on specific areas. Following this, the organization developed plans to move employees into a new office environment and to integrate connections between its different computer systems over a nine-month period. During the third stage, a formal renewal process enabled people to fine-tune the new organization and to institutionalize redesign activities into a continuous improvement strategy.

During the nine-month transition period, employees at all levels asked many questions, especially "How will these changes impact me?" To answer these questions, support team members had to provide constant training, coaching, explaining, and reassuring. Employees liked the idea of fewer layers of management and greater involvement in decisions about how to run the business. Virtually everyone appreciated the opportunity to help design the teams, choose their members, and participate in setting their goals. Employees also recognized and valued their newfound influence on identifying and solving business problems.

Since its startup in 1985, AT&T Capital Corporation, as it's now known, has expanded aggressively, and by 1994, it had grown to encompass 11 strategic business units managing combined assets of nearly $7 billion. The fastest-growing leasing company in the United States today, AT&T Capital has maintained a sustained growth rate of 40% a year and has always met or exceeded its financial plans. As Hal Burlingame, a senior vice president of Human Resources for the AT&T Corporation, noted "It clearly represents a most attractive organization model for building the AT&T of the future."

Team members can easily link their own success and their team's success with AT&T Capital's success. Employees who previously pursued individual, parochial goals have shifted their thinking toward supporting broader team goals. Sales representatives no longer just do deals, because they have a clear incentive to do good deals, which fully satisfy the requirements of their fellow team members who approve credit. Better deals result in lower delinquency rates and fewer write-offs. Success all along the way facilitates the institutionalization of the renewal process.

Institutionalizing the Renewal Process

AT&T Capital Corporation has institutionalized organizational renewal into a formal quality process it calls Customer Success Planning (CSP). CSP helps the organization to continually reinterpret the needs of customers and other key stakeholders, as well as constantly evaluating team members' ideas for improvement. Using this process, the organization continually gathers feedback from end users to learn more about their current and future requirements, to see if customers' perceptions have changed and how satisfied they feel with timeliness, responsiveness, and service quality. The process also assesses if employee motivation and commitment remains at a high enough level, explores how to improve communications between different parts of the system, identifies new issues the organization should address, and generates suggestions about how to further improve employee commitment and productivity.

The CSP process operates in two stages. During its spring planning session, the company uses environmental analyses to reevaluate each business unit's mission and core competence, and to identify any strategic gaps. During the fall planning session, it relies on technical and social analysis tools to identify and address gaps in day-to-day operations. CSP quality assessment tools are built into each step of the analyses and come into play throughout the planning process. As a result the organization continually makes progress toward creating a better future.

Evaluating Progress

In the mid-1980s, Texas Instruments sold 25 high-speed antiradiation missiles (HARMs) a month to the Pentagon for $1 million each. Then the government decided it wanted 250 a month at a much lower price, and if TI didn't deliver, it would take its business elsewhere. As TI realized it couldn't afford the cost of hundreds of supervisors roaming the shop floor anymore, it gave hourly employees access to personal computers right at their workstations and taught them how to collect and relay the information supervisors had once collected. TI also created a tracking method called HARM mountain, which showed leapfrog jumps from 30 to 75, 75 to 150, and 150 to 300 missiles a month. Banners and posters announced targets and gains, and TI threw a party every time the organization reached a new level of production. Soon everyone from the shop floor on up to the vice presidents were constantly monitoring progress up HARM mountain.

Redesign implementation unfolds like a cross-country road trip. As you travel along, you keep your eyes peeled for signposts that tell you that you're making progress. Reliable indicators can reveal your present location and indicate where you should go next. To steer the implementation process, employees must measure the distance between current and desired performance. Before beginning, realistic expectations should be developed among all the key stakeholders about how soon positive results will be evident as a consequence of introducing new ways of doing business. Quite often, an initial dip in performance occurs during the early stages of implementation as employees experiment with and learn their new roles. If no one anticipates and prepares for this transition phenomenon in advance, people may attribute unexpected outcomes to fatal flaws in the redesign recommendations, and pressure the organization to revert back to its traditional practices.

One wrong turn in a transcontinental journey never proves fatal if you realize early on that you're off track and make the necessary course corrections quickly. Dealing with issues as they arise helps keep the environment free from lingering distractions, while ignoring issues only fuels their growth over time. It helps to identify whether problems are due to flaws in the redesign recommendations, flaws in the implementation strategy, or flaws in the introduction and application of new technologies. As the journey to the future continues, addressing these issues quickly helps to keep the organization moving, despite some inevitable surprises and detours.

Keeping the Sizzle from Turning into a Fizzle

Sir Brian Wolfson, the chairman of Wembly PLC, the company that manages Wembly Stadium in London, the largest sports and entertainment complex in the world, believes that "A bad idea well executed in the last world war managed to kill 6 million people. But a good idea poorly executed won't pull the skin off a rice pudding." In that vein, the successful implementation of the Rapid Redesign recommendations depends on using The 20% Solution to concentrate on a small number of high-leverage initiatives and overlapping processes to keep the organization continuously moving forward.

Each organ in the human body works in conjunction with all of the others. The lungs and the heart function in an intimate relationship. Liver failure damages the kidneys and the brain. Lack of attention to the whole can cause as much harm as the failure of any individual organ. People who pick and choose among the redesign recommendations, implementing only those they like and discarding those they don't, can't expect more than lackluster results. No one would try to drive a car without all the tires, or assemble a bicycle without both pedals.

Nothing works all the time, and one quick redesign or reorganization doesn't assure success far down the road. Workers who maintain the Golden Gate Bridge in San Francisco start painting at one end, and by the time they've reached the other end, they need to start all over again. Continuous renewal applies to organizations as well because, as we've seen, "the future ain't what it used to be." The renewal examples described in this chapter illustrate how leading-edge companies track their environment, reappraise their experiences, and capture the learning that allows them to keep their focus and maintain buy-in from key constituencies. Renewal, like faith, is a daily affair. It takes far more than getting people excited every now and then. It takes continually awakening aspirations, fueling dreams, and creating and adjusting the mechanisms needed to bring those dreams to life. Chapter 9 explores the kind of people, skills, and responsibilities it will take to manage the constantly evolving organizations of the future.

Redistributing Responsibilities in the Redesigned Organization

L arry Padilla loves the oysters at the Mayfair Hotel in downtown Los Angeles. Every day, the Mayfair offers a legendary buffet lunch and today, Larry, a senior vice president at nearby First Interstate Bank, has decided to show it off to a special guest. Larry manages a 150-person loan processing organization and has won widespread admiration for his management style and leadership qualities.

"I'm impressed," admits Padilla's guest, as he observes the lavish spread—Eggs Benedict, Oysters Rockefeller, smoked sockeye salmon, succulent pastries, and everything in between. "I guess I should have expected no less. You do everything with style."

Padilla grins. "I wish all my people felt that way about me."

"You know they do. You're just fishing for a compliment."

Having helped themselves to the enticing banquet, the two men settle in to eat their lunch at a quiet corner table. "Seriously," says Padilla's guest, "I'd like to hear how you developed your management style. Harvard MBA? Claremont seminars?"

Padilla picks at an oyster with a small fork as he pauses to consider the question.

"You know," he begins, "I've taken a lot of management courses over the years, but I'd say that most of what I've learned about management and managing people, I learned in the music business."

When a look of surprise crosses his guest's face, Padilla explains that he worked as a professional musician in his late teens and early 20s, and that he still moonlights as the leader of a band on weekends.

"As head of a band," he explains, "you don't spend your time telling people what to do, the way you might with a symphony orchestra. Instead, you figure out what kind of music you want to make, then you go out and find people with the basic skills it takes to improvise together. If you get the right people, the right instruments, what happens when you play often surprises and delights you. As the leader, I select and coach people, and I set the boundaries of what I hope to accomplish, but then I let them do their own thing. The results always amaze me."

Padilla pauses to savor an oyster, chewing thoughtfully. His guest leans forward. "But, thinking about organizations that continually need to redesign themselves," he asks. "What if your dreams change?"

"That's the beauty of redistributing responsibilities to the people who make the music. If our drummer comes up with an exciting idea, the band can swing right into it. Hey, I learn more from my people than they learn from me."

Managing Differently in Redesigned Organizations

Art Money, the CEO of ESL Inc., a $400 million, 2,500-person subsidiary of TRW, based in Sunnyvale, California, recently flattened the organization from seven levels to four. Now 25 senior employees report directly to him. "With that many direct reports, you obviously can't micromanage," observes Money. "Rather, you have to empower the hell out of the people who work for you. Set very clear and explicit boundary conditions and define where decisions must be elevated to your level. Leave everything within those boundaries up to their judgment." True to this management philosophy, Money meets with each of his reports every six weeks, mainly "to make sure we're still calibrated." Shunning micromanagment, not sweating the small stuff, stressing only what really matters, and focusing on delegation and empowerment could all serve as definitions of The 20% Solution. From the CEO to the maintenance staff, everyone shares responsibility for managing the business all day, every day, in the redesigned organization.

At USF&G, the Baltimore insurer, CEO Norman Blake Jr. makes a point of sitting down with the dozen people who report to him once a week at an informal Monday night dinner. Otherwise, he sees them for a monthly staff meeting and during the week only as needed. "They're not working for someone as much as running their own businesses," he says. Blake has found that by giving people a very broad charter and letting them run their own operations, they end up delivering far better results than they would if they were striving for the most aggressive goal he might have set for them.

In traditional organizations, talk about managers and managing usually refers to the relatively few employees authorized to make important business decisions. That elite corps alone shoulders responsibility for the organization's success or failure. In redesigned organizations, the elite corps now includes all the employees who make the music. When all employees have specific management responsibilities, their roles change dramatically. Rather than sitting in assigned chairs and following a conductor's lead, they constantly innovate and orchestrate the activities they themselves deem to be the most productive. In redesigned organizations:

1. Every employee participates in managing the organization.
2. Employees' roles and responsibilities are defined in terms of the organization's strategic, coordinating, and operating functions.
3. All of the organization's key stakeholders become intimately involved in directing its evolution.
4. Employees develop a broad range of skills and have a big-picture perspective.
5. Leadership responsibility cascades throughout the organization.

Preparing Every Employee to Participate in Managing the Organization

According to an ancient Chinese chronicle, "There was trouble in the State of Lu, and the reigning monarch called on Confucius to ask for his help. When the master arrived, he went to a public place, took a seat in the correct way, facing south, and all trouble disappeared." Woody Allen once noted that 80% of life is just showing up. In a fast-moving, lightning-struck, global economy, managing has become more complex, more sophisticated, and more critical, and just showing up won't get the job done anymore. Past experience doesn't count for much anymore either. According to Kenichi Omahe, who formerly headed up McKinsey's Tokyo office, people involved in managing organizations today need "torawarenai sunao-na kokoro," or "a mind that doesn't stick."

When change alters the rules, employees must act together with the coordination and collective awareness of a flock of birds or a school of fish. Managing the coordinated contributions of many people requires a complete redistribution of responsibilities, so everyone can understand and influence what the organization needs to do to constantly reinvent its future. In redesigned organizations, the traditional boundary between managers and nonmanagers blurs, as every individual participates in making decisions and shares their learning with others. Rewards should be designed to support and encourage such participation, and in some cases, employees may receive greater compensation than the people they report to. Although most current management development programs still focus on personal mastery for a favored few, redesigned organizations place all employees on the developmental fast track. The following guidelines can help prepare employees for their new management role.

Mastering Individual Crafts

Just like offensive or defensive coordinators on a football team, effective management involves studying the momentum on the field, searching for patterns that reveal how the players should respond. A team of people can succeed only when individual team members feel capable and self-assured. The self-confidence of those who have mastered their craft induces confidence in others. People who have never excelled at something won't recognize exceptional achievement and will likely remain satisfied with ordinary performance.

Developing New Skills

Franklin Lunding, who became president of Jewel Tea in 1942 at the age of 36, ran the company on the philosophy that "Executive responsibility involves assisting the people down the line to be successful. The boss in any department is the first assistant to those who report to him." Effective management helps people see the work that needs to be done, and provides ways for them to learn the skills that'll help them do that work in the most effective way. It teaches people how to take responsibility for getting decisions made themselves, rather than waiting for someone else to decide. It empowers ordinary people to achieve extraordinary performance by strengthening their strengths and overcoming their weaknesses.

Respecting Emotions

Effective management emphasizes listening more than talking because it helps build understanding of people's true feelings, hopes, and aspirations. Recognizing and responding to people's often unexpressed emotions goes a long way toward gaining their respect and cooperation. People care less about how much someone knows than they do about how much that person honestly cares for them. The very words reengineering and redesign may seem to suggest that organizations are machines, whereas, in truth, organizations function more like biological organisms populated by people than mechanical units of production. Management must pay as much attention to people's emotions as they do to process and structure.

Confronting Reality

Thomas J. Watson Jr. said he always looked to hire "guys who see and tell you about things as they really are. If you can get enough of them around you, and have patience enough to hear them out, there's no limit to where you can go." Contrary to popular belief, redesigned organizations don't thrive in cultures where everyone agrees on everything. Without impatient, persistent, and aggressive people, no organization can make much genuine progress. According to Thucydides, the Greek historian, Pericles of Athens "was enabled, by the respect others had for him and his own wise policy, to hold the multitude in voluntary restraint. He led them, not they him; and since he did not win his power on compromising terms, he could say not only what pleased others but what displeased them, relying on their respect." In other words, Pericles knew the value of telling people uncomfortable truths. Effective management fosters clear, direct, specific, and honest communication among employees, encouraging interactions that mix human considerations with toughness. Aggressiveness by itself, however, won't carry the day; even the saber-toothed tiger eventually became extinct. Mary Parker Follett, a leading management consultant in the 1920s, observed that "Management is the art of getting things done through people." Nothing serves management in redesigned organizations better than this age-old concept of building trust and creating conditions that encourage involvement.

Teaming Up to Pull in the Same Direction

Management should be especially concerned about values today because, in a diverse workforce, employees don't automatically have a sense of obligation to one another. If people share the same values, the bond between them grows stronger than if they simply follow the same orders. Effective management focuses on defining and inculcating a set of common values in the organization. People who assume more responsibility need more explicit principles to guide their decisions. The tough choices aren't between right and wrong, but between right and right (such as when confronting a fellow worker over poor performance, duty to the organization can conflict with loyalty to a friend). Overriding principles applied throughout the organization encourage the consistency, agility, and flexibility people need to move everything in the right direction.

Mastering crafts, developing new skills, respecting emotions, confronting reality, and teaming up to pull in the same direction all combine to create a healthy environment where people can accomplish the goals of the redesigned organization. None of these tactics will produce the right results unless people fully understand their new roles and responsibilities.

Reassigning Responsibilities

Redesigned organizations reassign responsibilities in terms of strategic, coordinating, and operating functions. They classify employees not as executives, managers, supervisors, and workers, but as strategists, coordinators, and operators, classifications that focus on what people do rather than on their traditional status and position. Authority should derive from demonstrated competence, and competence should determine what kinds of power people have at each level and in each function.

Some employees participate in the organization's strategic decision-making process, ensuring that everyone shares a dream with a deadline to propel them forward. Others coordinate current programs and initiatives, and develop new ones for the future. Still others direct and maintain the day-to-day operating processes that deliver added value to customers and stockholders. It takes the combined efforts of all these employees working together to make the organization successful.

The Strategic Role

In redesigned organizations, thinking and acting strategically involves three fundamental tasks: first, developing, articulating, and modeling a vision of what the organization aims to accomplish; second, matching the right people with the right assignments; and third, creating an environment where every employee knows what to do and develops the competence to do it well.

A compelling vision sustains people on both an emotional and an intellectual level. Effective strategists share their deep understanding of the business to help others envision what the organization needs to become in the future, then they help them break through barriers to get there. Orchestrating a common vision in an environment of continuous change requires intense interpersonal activity and enormous energy. Reflecting on the role of the strategist, Michael Walsh, the late CEO of Tenneco, once said, "You have to reach out and energize the enormous latent talents of the organization. These jobs are backbreakers." To maintain their physical and mental health, employees charged with this responsibility need a personal support system they can trust. They need someone to whom they can speak freely, someone who understands the issues they face and who knows firsthand the stresses of management and leadership. This confidant or mentor can be a colleague or a close friend from inside or outside the organization who provides emotional support as well as technical assistance in addressing specific business issues.

When Paul Allaire became CEO of Xerox Corporation in 1990, he appointed a team of six young Xerox managers to examine the kind of structure and practices the company needed to fulfill its purpose. Over a 15-month period, this Future Architecture team involved 75 other managers from throughout the company in a search for new organizational models. Together, they agreed to redesign Xerox into nine independent global business divisions, each targeted at a specific market such as small businesses, office document systems, and engineering systems. All the divisions sold their products through a Customer Operations Group, a mingling of sales, shipping, installation, service, and billing, which afforded customers a single point of contact with Xerox. Allaire then assembled an Organizational Transition Board, consisting of a broad cross section of the most influential senior managers in the company, and charged them with working out the details of these new businesses.

As the new organization took shape, Allaire formulated explicit guidelines about the kind of people needed to operate it. In effect, he wiped the old slate clean, then redefined the ideal characteristics that people would need to manage successfully in the new Xerox. This resulted in 23 criteria for evaluating key employees. In the old organization, only those at the pinnacle of the company's hierarchy engaged in strategic thinking, but in the new, flatter architecture, strategic thinking became the responsibility of the many rather than the few. In the old structure, strategists or planners seldom took any responsibility for implementing their plans. Now merely thinking strategically would no longer suffice. Rather, many employees would now be required to act strategically as well.

As Jack Welch, the CEO of General Electric, observed "Get the right people in the right jobs and you've won the game. We spend days and days on assessments of people, interviewing people, talking to people, picking out stock option recipients. We allocate money to projects and people to businesses. We don't do any product development, any pricing, anything like that. Our jobs aren't picking colors for refrigerators or designing crisper trays. We set the objectives. People lower down do a lot of figuring out how to get things done. This is not a rudderless ship. The objectives are clearly in focus." That sounds a lot like The 20% Solution in action.

Since its founding in 1901, Nordstrom, the Seattle-based retailer, has earned an exceptional reputation for customer service, value, and quality. The company ruthlessly weeds out job applicants who can't fully commit themselves to these concepts. To put the organization's objectives clearly in focus, and to create an environment where every employee knows what needs to be done and can do it well, the entire employee handbook reads as follows:

Welcome to Nordstrom. We're glad to have you with our company. Our number-one goal is to provide outstanding customer service. Set both your personal and professional goals high. We have great confidence in your ability to achieve them. Nordstrom Rules: Rule 1. Use your good judgment in all situations. There will be no additional rules. Please feel free to ask your department manager, store manager, or division general manager any question at any time.

Nordstrom's has taken The 20% Solution to the ultimate extreme.

The Coordinating Role

In a 1958 *Harvard Business Review* article entitled "Management in the 1980s," professors Harold Leavitt and Thomas Whisler predicted that the computer would do to middle management what the Black Death did to fourteenth-century Europeans. And so it has. John Opie, the CEO of GE Lighting, notes, "There are just two people between me and the salespeople. Information technology has replaced the rest." When redesign efforts remove nonvalue-adding tasks, traditional organizations usually find themselves with a number of underemployed employees. In such cases, many middle-level managers fear they'll fall victim to the 50-50 rule, which states that if you earn over $50,000 a year and are over 50 years old, you stand a good chance of losing your job. The redesigned organization must address this sort of fear or risk courting increased resistance to change. Also, if there are layoffs, the survivors usually feel reluctant to stick their necks out and behave in an innovative fashion.

Research by Henry Mintzberg, a professor at McGill University, suggests that top managers spend 78% of their time in fragmented conversational contacts with people who work nearby. A high percentage of these contacts occur ad hoc with peers in other functional staff units, half of them last less than nine minutes, and most deal with current issues. These findings support the fact that many managers distance themselves from customers, external stakeholders, and the environment that shapes their future. Rather than letting middle managers go, redesigned organizations can gain greater leverage by training and redeploying them to coordinating roles, freeing up people at the strategic level to spend more time with external stakeholders. Reassigned middle managers can also tackle formerly neglected long-term capability planning and development tasks.

In redesigned organizations, managing at the coordinating level involves three fundamental tasks: first, coordinating tactics, programs, and activities across the organization and its partners; second, defining and prepositioning the capabilities the organization will need to prosper in the future; and third, coaching employees to continually acquire additional skills and knowledge.

Adjusting to these new roles usually challenges middle-level managers who have traditionally been accustomed to getting orders from above and demanding compliance from below. Charged with new demands, they often feel they're living through the classic actor's nightmare of waking up in a bed onstage with no knowledge of the play or the script. To make the transition successfully, they need training, support, and role modeling from those to whom they report.

In 1991, when a group of IBM executives started up a new company called Lexmark International, they showcased Big Blue's bulky procedures manual, encased in Lucite, in the lobby. Having designed itself around cross-functional business teams, Lexmark wanted all employees to stay aware of the rules and constraints that had limited how they worked together at IBM. In redesigned organizations, employees at the coordinating level grease the skids between functions, enabling the organization to respond swiftly and decisively to resolve its problems and pursue its opportunities. In order to replace sluggishness and defensiveness with agility and flexibility, people need to stretch their allegiances across old functional boundaries.

When Eastman Chemical redesigned itself in 1993, it replaced several managers in charge of key functions with self-directed work teams. Manufacturing, for example, is now headed by a team of plant managers. The 500 senior managers agreed that functions shouldn't pursue missions of their own, but should support Eastman's business in chemicals, plastics, fibers, and polymers. As a result, all of the company's managers work on at least one cross-functional team, and most work on two or more on a daily basis.

Companies build great strategies on unique skills and capabilities. Prepositioning capabilities for the future requires looking outside the organization to study new developments, benchmarking competitors, learning from partners, identifying new products and services that will delight customers, and introducing new processes and technologies. In a continuously evolving environment, middle-level managers can carry out these tasks only if they distance themselves from the day-to-day running of the business, vesting this responsibility and authority in employees at the operating level who work directly with products and services. To develop these new capabilities, employees need coaching in new skills and work practices, and to broaden the organization's skill base, employees at every level must learn how to coach one another.

United Parcel Service discovered that many of its 35,000 managers fell short as coaches and teachers. When surveyed, only 48% of UPS employees gave their managers favorable marks for helping them develop new skills. Employees don't naturally know how to coach each other without special training, and successful coaching takes more than technique, it also requires healthy personal relationships. David Maloney, vice president for development at Carnegie-Mellon University, formerly coached the school's basketball team. As a manager, he finds himself missing the close bonds he once developed with his players. Roger Evered and James Selman studied the qualities of great coaches, like John Wooden, George Allen, and Red Auerbach, and they found that these great coaches shared the following characteristics:

- They focused on the development of each player and held a personal stake in their success and well-being.
- They believed in constant improvement.
- They didn't view success as an individual accomplishment, and continuously communicated with everyone who could contribute to a player's performance.
- They stressed honest, straightforward feedback, and modeled the qualities they demanded from others.
- They remained uncompromising in their approach to discipline, preparation, and practice, paying attention to the smallest detail.
- They obeyed the rules of the game, but didn't let the rules limit their thinking.

- ❑ They felt personally responsible for the game's outcome, but not in a way that robbed the players of their own responsibilities.
- ❑ They loved the game, and considered coaching a privilege.

Great coordinators, like great coaches, can tell their players that they've made a mistake without destroying the player's motivation. John Wooden, the legendary former head coach of UCLA basketball, said, "A coach must prevent, correct, or help, and not punish. He must make those under his supervision feel that they're working with him rather than for him. He must be more interested in finding the best way rather than having his own way, and be genuinely concerned about his players." In the end, of course, the game is won or lost on the court or, in the case of a business, at the operating level.

The Operating Role

In redesigned organizations, managing at the operating level involves three fundamental tasks: first, making the organization's vision operational; second, delivering error-free products and services; and third, making decisions based on what's right for the organization as a whole.

The clarity of the organization's vision, not the control of higher-level managers and coordinators, will guide successful frontline employees in the future. Tommye Joe Davis, a 58-year-old mountain-bred grandmother, manages a Levi-Strauss sewing plant with almost 400 people in Murphy, North Carolina. The Murphy plant cross-trains teams of workers to perform 36 tasks instead of one or two, and the teams participate fully in running the plant, from organizing supplies to setting production goals. They also set personnel policy and, as a result, the Levi policy manual there has shrunk from 700 pages to 50. "You can't lead by just barking orders," notes Davis. "I used to say 'You do this, you do that.' Now I say 'How do you want to do this?' You have to have a vision in your head of what you're trying to do."

John Walkush, the vice president and general manager of the award-winning North Pacific Paper Company in Longview, Washington, argues, "When you first start up a team-based, high-performance organization, you worry that employees may take you someplace you don't want to go. Over time, you learn that most people want the same thing you do. Everyone wants to be successful." Real success hinges on learning new forms of control, trading in certainty for speed, and giving teams freedom to act as they deem appropriate. Nimbleness is the only way to maintain control in a fast-changing environment. As the old saying has it, "In structure, there is freedom." Using The 20% Solution to classify decisions in the following four categories helps clarify which control decisions individuals should make on their own, which should be shared, and which should be delegated:

- ❏ "Now hear this: I must make this decision." (individual)
- ❏ "I must make a decision, but I need your input." (partially shared)
- ❏ "We must make a decision together." (fully shared)
- ❏ "You have a decision to make." (delegated)

The clearer the organization's intentions and ground rules, the easier it is for employees to evaluate and influence what happens around them.

Overcontrol kills invention, learning, and commitment. Too much prescription inhibits the organizations agility, flexibility, and problem-solving ability. In traditional organizations, managers tell employees how to do their jobs and allow them to make decisions only when the managers feel certain that employees will make the same decisions they themselves would have made. In redesigned organizations, managing occurs after the fact, allowing employees to make mistakes now and then because, in the long run, they'll learn and make more right than wrong decisions. Few people understand a job better than the person doing it every day. John Puckett, the vice president of manufacturing at XEL Communications, says, "That was one of my most difficult transitions. I always had a book I could manage by, where I knew everything about everything. I don't have that anymore. Giving up that control, that's one of the most difficult things people from a traditional management environment have to do."

In order to take control of fulfilling the organization's vision, employees must feel safe challenging authority. In redesigned organizations, managers must listen in order to lead, and employees must challenge in order to follow. Quality expert W. Edward Deming's eighth point in his 14 obligations of management specified that managers drive out fear. According to Deming, "It is necessary, for better quality and productivity, that people feel secure. Secure means without fear, not afraid to express ideas; not afraid to ask questions; not afraid to ask for further instructions; not afraid to report equipment out of order, nor material that is unsuited to the purpose, poor light, or other working conditions that impair quality and production." He might have added to this list fear of giving information, fear of not knowing, fear of failure, fear of reprisal, fear of giving up control, fear of change, fear of the unknown. Mindlessly adhering to policies or slavishly following orders often undermines the quality of products and services. Under certain conditions, people need to feel they can break the rules without fear of reprisal. Doing what's right for the organization should always outrule blind obedience to rules that no longer make sense in a rapidly changing world.

While a redesigned organization can't run smoothly without strategists, coordinators and operators can't run the business all by themselves either. They must draw all key stakeholders into the cause.

Involving the Organization's Key Stakeholders in Directing Its Evolution

A group of 10 senior employees from a major semiconductor manufacturer recently met offsite for two days to review their organization's prospects and plans. As so often happens in these meetings, each of the attendees knew the others but had rarely, if ever, talked to them in depth. "When we talk," one of them observed, "it's always about solving problems, or we come together to respond to a crisis. We never get to talk about where we want to see the business headed." After the first hour's discussion, it became clear they all shared concerns about the future, though more questions than answers had arisen about what actions to take. Many of their questions required additional information about customers, suppliers, and other key external entities. Somewhat disconcerted and frustrated by their experience, they consoled themselves that at least they'd figured out some of what they didn't know. That's always a promising start.

Successful organizations constantly redesign and reinvent themselves by creating great prospects for the future and then striving to fill in any gaps in their knowledge about their environment. Since today's organizations and their environments are becoming increasing inseparable, no organization can thrive without tapping into the accumulated knowledge in the heads of its stakeholders, both inside and outside the organization. Major changes in strategy stand the best chance of succeeding when they harness the collective intelligence of the organization, together with the vast knowledge of its stakeholders—customers, partners, franchisees, distributors, suppliers, government agencies, communities, and other important opinion groups.

Structural redesign can't possibly cause lasting change unless all stakeholders also change their frame of reference. Getting employees and stakeholders to work together takes a lot of effort, particularly when members of the organization grew up and became successful largely as a result of their own individual initiatives. Goss, Pascale, and Athos note in their 1993 *Harvard Business Review* article, "Risking the Present for a Powerful Future," "We have found, particularly in senior executives, an unwillingness to think rigorously and patiently about themselves or their ideas. We often find [them], perched like a threatened aristocracy, entitled, aloof, and sensing doom." People isolated from their environment usually feel insecure and fear making mistakes. They deny, deflect, and reject new ideas from the outside, and find it difficult to confess what they don't know in public. Abba Eban, the former Israeli foreign minister, commenting on the G7 summit of 1993, observed that although the leaders who attended represented an extraordinary concentration of power and intelligence, their meetings didn't result in much progress. He added, "Perhaps it's because each of the leaders is thinking individually, not collectively."

Knowledge is an asset that grows exponentially when shared. In today's uncertain world where it's increasingly difficult to find useful information, employees and stakeholders must conceptualize connections across complex business domains together as a way to build knowledge. The rate at which organizations learn by generating new knowledge provides their most valuable and sustainable source of competitive advantage.

Organizations learn best when no single point of view predominates. To create a culture that values multiple perspectives, people need to confront and support one another at the same time, maximizing both individual contributions and mutual collaboration, disagreeing with each other without being disagreeable, and acting as authorities without being authoritarian. In the world of redesigned organizations, employees and stakeholders must confidently think out loud, risking mistakes, and sharing incomplete ideas with each other in an open, nondefensive way. Even then, however, just sharing what each stakeholder already knows won't suffice.

To learn, people must articulate a theory (a set of propositions that lead to certain expectations), then act to test their assumptions by implementing the theory, and reflect together on the meaning of the outcomes. Their shared learning creates wisdom, allowing them to make the best use of their joint knowledge, experience, and understanding. As the French philosopher Montaigne said, "We can be knowledgeable with other men's knowledge, but we cannot be wise with other men's wisdom." Knowledge is a collection of facts, but wisdom comes from having a broad enough perspective to put those facts to use. Knowledge without wisdom is the assassin of progress.

Developing Broader Skills and Embracing a More Systemic Perspective

The once-accepted notion of the universal manager, possessing sufficient generic management skills to lead any group in any organization, has joined other discredited theories on the scrap heap of history. A generalist without any in-depth knowledge will flounder in today's technically sophisticated world. Lester Thurow, a professor at MIT, notes that financial managers running American steel companies a few years back didn't understand important new technical processes such as continuous casting. As a result, they decided to wait and see how the process worked in other countries before committing to it themselves. By the time they gained that knowledge, their companies had fallen too far behind to catch up. "You don't have to be a scientist," observed Thurow, "but you must read the material and know how to proceed." To be effective, employees in redesigned organizations need to understand, in detail, many aspects of how their organization makes its products or supplies its services.

In the past, technical employees developed specialized skills by delving deeper and deeper into narrow fields of inquiry and staying in one position for a long time instead of moving up or out. Traditionally, many won promotion and became managers because of their specialized expertise and their ability to combine analytical reasoning with intuition sharpened by years of experience. In the future, however, a narrow specialist will more likely be a liability rather than an asset, as environmental and technical complexity requires combinations of new and different skills to solve problems. Changes in engineering education already mirror this trend toward broader expertise. Carnegie-Mellon University has merged electrical and computer engineering into a single degree program. Cornell University has developed a combined civil and geotechnical engineering program. The University of California at Berkeley offers a four-year program in mechatronics, merging mechanical and electrical engineering. While redesigned organizations must prize technical capability at all levels, technical know-how alone can't carry them into the future. A high-performance culture demands new skills and capabilities that will enable specialists not only to solve problems themselves, but to help others learn what the specialists know. Doing so requires interpersonal skills.

In addition to providing people with supplementary skills, redesigned organizations must adopt different criteria for promotion. Organizations that promote people solely on their records as individual performers will often pick the wrong people. The traditional industrial model generally promoted highly structured, analytical, and action-oriented people. The new one will favor people with agility and flexibility, multifocused thinkers who can integrate many different kinds of information, get above the details of their own departments, and detect patterns and opportunities where others see only chaos. Research by Michael Driver at USC shows that math wizards display personality and decision-making traits that work reasonably well in corporations with rigid hierarchies, but not so well in organizations operating with loosely managed teams. People with high verbal scores may be better at coping with ambiguity and uncertainty because, as Driver points out, "Verbal types take in a lot of data, but instead of jumping to one conclusion, they proceed on intuition, relying on teamwork and using persuasion to involve others."

John Rau, the dean of Indiana University's School of Business, counsels his students to develop their skills along four dimensions. The first he calls traditional content, learning about functions such as marketing or finance. The second involves expertise in a business process such as distribution or product development. Third, he advises developing in-depth knowledge of a particular industry such as paper goods or health care. And finally, he recommends that students strive to perfect their process skills, such as communication and team leadership.

In redesigned organizations, success springs not just from what functional specialists do, but from their connections with other stakeholders. And it doesn't arise automatically from a vision of high performance. It comes by widely distributing leadership responsibility throughout the organizations.

Distributing Responsibility for Leadership throughout the Organization

It's difficult to break free of old ideas while continuing to rely on old language. Traditionally, organization charts have labeled employees as executives, managers, supervisors, and workers, with the underlying assumption that only those at the top of the hierarchy should provide organizational leadership. In contrast, redesigned organizations promote leadership at all levels. Knowledge and experience, not titles and seniority, dictate who will lead at any particular moment.

Bill Gore, the founder of Gore and Associates, worked hard to inspire leadership in others. He believed that "Leaders are those whom others follow," "Leadership is a verb, not a noun," and "Leadership is defined by what you do, not who you are." Strong leadership moves people from the present to the future, from zones where they feel comfortable to uncharted territory. It urges rather than coerces, inspires rather than conspires, fuels rather than controls. The strong leader abandons the hammer of force for the lever of influence.

In redesigned organizations, leadership differs from management although both remain important. Successful organizations operate on the belief that all employees must learn to lead if they're to respond promptly and profitably to problems and opportunities. Southwest Airlines began companywide leadership training in 1985, pounding home the company's five basic principles of leadership to all employees. Robert Haas, the CEO of Levi-Strauss and the great-great-grandnephew of Levi-Strauss himself, says, "At Levi's, what we're trying to do is syndicate leadership throughout the organization. We share as much information as we possibly can throughout the company. Business literacy is a big issue in developing leadership. You can't ask people to exercise broader judgment if their world is bounded by a very narrow vision."

In redesigned organizations, people who have mastered the practical skills of management must also learn the less tangible skills of leadership. It all begins with building trust.

Building Trust with Conviction and Credibility

"Convince people, take the message to their hearts, that's the essence of leadership," claims Percy Barnevik, the Swedish-born CEO of Asea Brown-Boveri. Effective leaders, secure and confident in themselves and their abilities, bring their experience and decisiveness to bear on their organization. They truly believe in the values they proclaim, and they courageously back up their beliefs with consistent, persistent action. They enlist people's emotions around a shared vision of the future, and they instill in others the self-respect that stems from accomplishment. Trust arises from the fertile soil of reliability and blossoms into credibility and earned respect. Respect invites others to open up and assures them that their ideas won't fall on deaf ears. Effective leadership involves much more than charm. An actor isn't a leader and fans aren't followers. Presidential speechwriter Peggy Noonan tells us, "You can...use charm to achieve your purposes, but charm isn't a belief, it isn't a guide. It can't tell you where you want to go, it can only help you get there." In a complex world, Murphy's Law frequently kicks in, and anything and everything can and does go wrong. When this happens, effective leaders keep their cool.

Keeping Cool

Effective leaders never rely on heroics to conquer problems. Instead, they instill confidence and pride in others. Rather than simply firing people up into a frenzy, they bring a sense of calm. They also create a perception of urgency that inspires people's efforts, then they support rather than direct those efforts. Shunning the temptation to pull rank or to issue autocratic decrees, they share their authority and work to get results through influence and persuasion. They remain evenhanded in dealing with people and demonstrate great confidence in other people's capabilities. They're human, but they set challenging standards and don't tolerate substandard performance. They believe that those who refuse to accept anything but the best very often get just that. Their faith in their people rests on a deep understanding of their needs, hopes, and dreams.

Understanding Followers

Nothing consumes more of a leader's time than gaining a deep understanding of his or her followers. Followers needn't love their leaders, although that can certainly help. A leader's power doesn't automatically come with a position but arises from what the leader makes of the position. Power flows from those who allow themselves to be led, and because others bestow this power, it isn't a controlling factor as much as a propelling force. Followers judge whether someone deserves respect and trust, and they don't submit to a person just because he or she holds a fancy title. Rather, they join the leader in the pursuit of a shared goal. Effective leaders engage people in a journey, leading in such a way that everyone on the journey helps shape its course. David Hume, the eighteenth-century philosopher, argued that people obey others for their own advantage. Similarly, people follow most reliably when they're convinced that what they're doing is right. Good leaders don't play a zero-sum game. What they receive doesn't subtract from what their followers receive. Both get by giving. This is the real secret of great American leaders such as Washington, Lincoln, and Martin Luther King who created opportunities for everyone to succeed.

Seizing Opportunities to Lead

Without World War II, no one would ever have known how well Winston Churchill could rally the English spirit. Effective leaders don't wait for others to discover them but constantly look for opportunities to lead. A little girl once told her teacher she was going to draw a picture of God. "But, Mary," the teacher said, "no one knows what God looks like." To which Mary exclaimed, "They will when I get through." Anyone who would accomplish anything worthwhile always feels far more confident about the eventual outcome than the facts would seem to justify.

Leaders move out of their comfort zones and walk on ahead of their followers. In redesigned organizations, they do so in order to help people free themselves from their attachment to established practices and to wrench them away from models and ways of working that have become familiar, comfortable, and obsolete. Paradoxically, the greatest comfort springs from discontent. Managing such paradoxes will preoccupy leaders in the future.

Managing the Paradoxes of the Future

At the Skippy peanut butter plant in Little Rock, Arkansas, you'll find no team leaders, no reporting relationships, no repository of power ensconced in the traditional executive suite. The company has divided up among the operating team members almost all the responsibilities that fall to managers and supervisors in traditional organizations. For example, in traditional plants, supervisors handle safety issues, keep track of attendance, and coordinate work assignments for each department. In Little Rock, operating team members, who are all salaried employees, assume these jobs as part of their regular duties.

Walter Wriston would like that setup. "The person who figures out how to harness the collective creative genius in his or her organization is going to blow the competition away," says the former chairman of Citicorp, who serves on the board of directors of General Electric, J.C. Penney, and Pfizer. He adds, "This takes entirely different skills from what it took to be a manager 15 years ago." Combined together, new skills, new managers, new people, new technologies, and new organizations provide the ingredients to create a wonderfully productive, profitable, and personally satisfying future. Before that future arrives, however, organizations must resolve a few perplexing paradoxes:

- Being in control means getting a little out of control.
- Although people will work in small groups, they'll have to stay in touch with many more people.
- Even though new technologies will allow people to communicate effortlessly with countless others, they'll risk becoming more isolated than ever before.

The final chapter explores how new technologies will impact the design of organizations to resolve these paradoxes in the years ahead.

Managing Organizations in an Age of Paradox

Susan DeLillo sets three pizza boxes down on the conference table and lifts the lids. "Who ordered the anchovies?" she asks.

The seven people gathered around the table constitute the entire headquarters staff of DeLillo's $40 million mail order business. Two years before, 70 people worked at HQ, but after instituting a Rapid Redesign, the company has retrained the bulk of the former HQ staff and reassigned them to the field, where they now interact directly with customers. Communications technology has made it possible for the firm to eliminate two-thirds of its office space, and the conference table functions as both lunchroom and nerve center for the operation.

"Love those anchovies!" exclaims Alan Platt, a cherubic man with curly hair, as he takes a big bite out of a pizza wedge, then leans back with a hearty sigh.

DeLillo smiles at Alan. "Can you say the same about your work?"

"You bet," he says. "You know, the other day, I realized I don't spend as much time on the phone anymore. I used to worry about what our people were doing out in the field, but now I see them doing a much better job interacting with customers than I ever did. Instead of all that phone work, I spend my time doing what really counts—the things that will help this company keep growing."

207

Rick Preston swallows a mouthful of pizza and chimes in, "This place is a lot quieter. I spend more time talking and thinking about what we're going to do next. Sometimes, I feel nervous that I'm not doing as much running around and busywork as I did before, but I know our ideas are making money for this company. Alan's right. It takes some getting used to, but The 20% Solution really works!"

Candace Carroll, a field agent on temporary assignment at HQ, puts her elbows on the table and leans forward. "Well, let me tell you what it's like out in the field. I miss the coffee klatches, and sometimes working out of a laptop gets a little lonely, but I love the freedom and the responsibility. I don't know if I could ever go back to the old arrangement. I tell my friends I've traded sociability, security, and boredom for independence, growth, and accomplishment."

"What about you, Susan?" Alan Platt asks.

DeLillo has thought long and hard about this question. She smiles. "When I started this company 10 years ago, we were so small I could feed the headquarters staff with three pizzas. Now we're 50 times as large, and I can still feed you guys with three pizzas. That's real progress."

Signs of Changing Times

Susan DeLillo nicely articulated one of the many paradoxes that surround redesigned organizations: the bigger the company, the greater the need for a smaller driving force to guide its growth. In the future, success will hinge on skillfully managing such paradoxes, and this will preoccupy giant companies as much as it does small startup organizations.

At IBM, for instance, rank once entailed many privileges. Says branch manager Linda Bodden, "To be a branch manager in the old days was to get the big corner office, a personal secretary, and a branch manager's desk, which was bigger than a marketing manager's desk." That was a big deal. These days, Bodden works out of client's offices assisted by a car phone, a beeper, and a laptop computer. When she visits the Cranford, New Jersey, IBM office every two weeks, she shares a small cubicle in an open space. The adjustment, she says, required "a cultural change." As Rick Preston so aptly observed, The 20% Solution takes some getting used to, but Linda Bodden would agree that the adjustment pays off. Though rethinking work is never an easy task, the results can be more than worth the effort.

Rethinking Work

Five thousand of IBM's 100,000 U.S. employees have been forced to become mobile in the past few years, and IBM plans to double that number in the near future. Many now share secretaries and take turns using communal desks. Between 1991 and 1994, IBM vacated nearly half of its U.S. office space—21 million square feet. Lee Dayton, IBM's manager of real estate, explains this fundamental change in thinking. "You have to explain to people very matter-of-factly that having a private office or a given office size is no longer an entitlement."

Peter Firestone, a senior manager with Ernst & Young's information technology consulting division, knows exactly how that feels. With no permanent office, he relies instead on clients to provide him with a desk while he works on their projects. When he needs to spend time at his company's San Francisco office, he tells the company's concierge when he's coming and how long he'll be staying. The concierge checks the computer to determine available offices, assigns Firestone a space, puts his name on the door, and programs the phone for his extension. Since Ernst & Young's auditors and consultants spend up to 80% of their time working outside the office, it doesn't make sense for everyone to have his or her own permanent space. Ernst & Young expects to save about $40 million annually by reducing office space once it installs the program nationwide.

Locationless selling requires no retail stores, locationless inventory requires no warehouse, locationless training dispenses with classrooms, locationless conferences convene without physical meeting places, and locationless managers work without an office. Using integrated computer and communication technologies, organizations will increasingly define themselves not by concrete walls or physical space but by collaborative networks linking hundreds, thousands, even tens of thousands of people together. This presents yet another paradox: more people, fewer offices.

Offices in the future will provide landing sites, where employees can stop and dock temporarily at a communal electronic desk. Everyone will share what they know, filing their information in databases that others can access. As these working arrangements become the norm, most employees will occupy front-row seats where they can watch firsthand how business gets done (or doesn't get done), and success will depend more and more on effectively managing electronic relationships.

Living in the Cyberspace Workplace

Keeping up with customers today demands speed on a global scale, which explains why, every month, H-P's 97,000 employees exchange 20 million e-mail messages. Workers share databases at H-P's 27 customer-response centers, and whenever an employee works on a file, the system instantly updates that file so that every center possesses identical information about each job at all times. In 1994, about 55% of the 2,000 largest companies in America were using some version of electronic mail, up from 30% in 1991. By 1995, the number of electronic mailboxes in large companies will approach 20 million, and by the first decade of the twenty-first century, it's estimated that computers will link 2 billion people (nearly a third of the earth's population).

Any relationship involves proximity, and computers create electronic proximity, connecting people together and allowing information to pass directly between them. When tools such as e-mail, teleconferencing, and groupware link people together, they encourage a more informal organizational structure and style, which allows people to work together regardless of distance, time, or physical boundaries. Workflow software helps people understand the individual steps that make up a particular process, and thus allows them to redesign that process. Meeting software allows participants in face-to-face meetings or video conferences to talk simultaneously by typing on PC keyboards. This not only ensures everyone a chance to take part in discussions, but since a group of people can type and read faster than they can talk together, it also speeds progress toward consensus. Scheduling software coordinates employees' calendars and figures out when they can all get together, and some software applications include electronic agents that help employees filter and sort through information in order to pinpoint precisely what's needed in a given situation. All these technologies facilitate the flat, team-based, networked organizations that have begun supplanting traditional hierarchical structures. Meet yet another paradox: organizing more people with less structures.

Networks provide easy links between departments and across internal and external boundaries. Access to uncensored and unfiltered information helps an organization see its markets more clearly. Rather than accepting someone else's interpretation of what a particular set of numbers mean, people can now access, sort, and analyze the data according to their own ideas. However, organizations can't take advantage of networks unless they free their people to act on the information they obtain. In order to leverage hard data, organizations must first resolve some soft issues.

Managing Electronic Organizations

As e-mail replaces so-called snail mail, organizations find it necessary to be explicit about the values they want to govern their networks. Should they permit anonymous communications, or should they forbid them? What constitutes free speech on-line? When does e-mail become junk mail? How will people deal with mailboxes overflowing with digital communiqués? To resolve such issues, Tandem Computer has organized its e-mail system into three classes. First-class e-mail involves one-on-one messages between named recipients. Second-class mail includes company-related messages that go to everyone in a particular area or to everyone in the company. Extracurricular messages (such as movie or restaurant reviews), relegated to third-class mail, can't be delivered until after five o'clock in the evening. Without such clear guidelines, the new electronic networks can create cultural problems that forestall the benefits of their economic efficiencies.

With all these new organizational arrangements comes the challenge of dealing with unfamiliar issues. The 20% Solution suggests classifying the main issues into three categories: maintaining balance and harmony; managing large-scale social processes; and making progress in a way that genuinely benefits people. Each revolves around a paradox. Manage them, or they'll end up managing you.

Striking a Proper Balance

Mother Ann Lee, the founder of the Shakers, insisted that "Every force evolves a form." Change focuses redesign, and sound redesign creates a form that flexibly and agilely harnesses change. As the gathering forces of a new century swamp the old, new forms of organizations will arise. The best, like the designs of Shaker architects and furniture makers, will balance sparseness and functional excellence with an appreciation for the needs and dignity of the user. Similarly, organizations in the future must find ways to balance the need for change with the need for stability.

Balancing Change and Stability

When the pace of change speeds up, it multiplies the number of roles people must play and increases the number of choices they must make. Time no longer exists for extended pondering of current problems or situations. As Alvin Toffler points out in *Future Shock*, the hidden conflict between the pressures of acceleration and novelty forces people to make faster decisions while, at the same time, compelling them to make time-consuming choices. Increasing the number of choices increases the amount of information people need to make smart decisions, and this, in turn, slows down their reaction time. Such paradoxical demands can produce maladaptive behaviors that erode people's health. Change carries with it a psychological price tag, and the more radical the change, the higher the price. Accelerating change and its corresponding information overload leads to dysfunctional stress and psychological disturbance, conditions that thwart the flexible and agile response people need to function effectively.

On the other hand, sustainable, self-directed, healthy change becomes possible when those involved own the change and understand what to do and why. By adhering to the precepts of The 20% Solution, people can harness, steer, and pace change, and avoid wasting their time on trivia. Ownership demands involvement built on the stability of trusting relationships. Building trust means taking the time to undo obsolete conventional relationships as well as structuring new relationships around a common understanding of the future. As time deepens the basis of these relationships, change becomes possible in faster and faster time frames, and on a larger and larger scale. Organizations need to take the time to develop their people's capacity for change before they can hope to sustain continued forward momentum. It takes time for people to develop new models and strategies that enable them to recognize, invent, experiment with, learn, and even discard responses to the many paradoxes that they'll encounter in the future.

Shortcutting these processes will create little more than the illusion of progress. Activity alone doesn't mean accomplishment.

Some people resent change and seek equilibrium; others welcome novelty and love the excitement of disequilibrium. While no simple formula can resolve these two elements of paradox, absolute surrender to either of them invites disaster. Thus the question arises: Will the future control you, or will you control your future?

Retaining Control by Giving Up Control

In a dynamic environment, the most intelligent control gives local units the freedom and ability to adapt on their own, to evolve in their own direction, and to influence the direction of the organization's overall evolution. For people to find the best way to pursue the organization's vision, they must gain independence, and the smart organization values and safeguards that independence above all other qualities. Feedback on performance, supported by rewards for success, provides the key to self-control and self-governance.

Organizations driven from the bottom up must relinquish central control, allowing themselves instead to be fueled by the collective pattern of a multitude of simultaneous actions. In this sort of system, an organization can structure and stimulate and coordinate change, but it can never fully contain it. Redesigned organizations are guided rather than controlled by using positive feedback, applying force at key leverage points, and taking advantage of mistakes and learning to identify and pursue new ends. Learning from small failures today helps to avoid big failures tomorrow, and today's apparent error may turn into tomorrow's cutting-edge innovation.

Emerging sciences such as molecular nanotechnology promise biological machines that will eventually adapt and evolve on their own without human oversight. If and when this comes to pass, people may find themselves giving up control to intelligent machines. Until then, rigid, hierarchical organizations will find new organizational mechanisms like e-mail and the virtual office to be a cultural earthquake. Traditional managers will feel uncomfortable commanding people they can't see, let alone allowing them the freedom to make mistakes. The new breed of managers will, instead, apply what they've learned about working in small groups to managing the efforts of ever-larger groups.

Managing Large-Scale Social Processes

In a fast-moving global economy, successful organizations will need simple new social processes that allow them to overcome the complications and chaos that usually accompany large-scale complexity. Diversity offers one of the surest solutions to this particular paradox.

Learning to Engage with Many Different People

During the 1980s, the 500 largest companies in the United States eliminated over 3 million jobs, but at the same time, the American economy added 18 million new ones. Those jobs arose in small companies, which will continue to form the backbone of the future. By the end of the 1990s, an estimated 85% of the American workforce will work for employers with fewer than 100 employees. Paradoxically, however, while more people will work in smaller organizations in the future, they'll network with a far greater number of people. Interactive programs will bring together people with similar interests, regardless of where they work and live. The resulting interaction among many different individuals will help build a common database, thus creating a broader collective awareness of problems and opportunities, and generating an exponential number of novel possibilities for dealing with them. It will also facilitate the sharing of experience, while at the same time sending the message that each person counts.

These interactions will entail certain complications, such as distance (coordination across different time zones), intermittence (some people may not possess a complete picture of what's going on), or cultural differences (organizations have different norms and operating environments resulting in unique patterns of communication and behavior that may be difficult for those unacquainted with them to understand). In a world of global partnerships, the Rapid Redesign techniques described earlier must incorporate the new electronic communication technologies. For instance, the San Francisco office of the advertising agency Young and Rubicam used a Lotus Notes version of Action WorkFlow to redesign how it created advertising campaigns. Because this system allowed employees to see immediately the core set of interactions involved, the company achieved dramatic performance improvements within months, reducing overtime, rush charges, and re-work, as well as shortening cycle times and enhancing customer satisfaction. As tasks engaging many people create larger work-groups, new technologies and processes must come aboard to help these groups work effectively.

Helping Large Groups Work Effectively

In a year-long experiment conducted at the Rand Corporation, two 40-member task forces were formed to make recommendations about how to prepare employees for the transition to retirement. One task force used the latest communication technology, the other didn't. Although both task forces formed a variety of working subcommittees, the task force with electronic communication created more of them, organized them in a more complex, over-lapping way, and continued to add new subcommittees as their mission became clearer. At the end of the project, members of the electronic task force had achieved more interactions, knew more people, belonged to more subgroups, and felt more involved than their counterparts in the nonelectronic task force.

The conventional wisdom holds that workgroups function best when they can meet face to face and include between 6 and 12 members. The globalization of business and the complexity of the technical processes required to operate today often dictate a much larger and geographically diverse membership. The new commu-nication technologies create conditions for effective dialog, help people understand each other's views and purposes, and expand their organizational world in much the same way as the telephone expanded people's psychological neighborhood in the first half of this century. People can now share thoughts and experiences across ever broader boundaries.

Common LISP, a popular computer language for artificial intel-ligence, came to fruition in 30 months through the collaboration of over 60 people from universities, government, and industry, who exchanged over 3,000 messages, ranging from one line to 20 pages, and made collective design decisions on several hundred distinct points. It would have been much more difficult to com-plete this task by any other means and would have taken consid-erably more time to do so.

Large groups allow people to accomplish tasks they could never complete on their own. However, since people accustomed to personal recognition and face-to-face contact can feel unrecognized and isolated in larger gatherings, organizations must pay close attention to people's needs as human beings.

Relating to People as Human Beings

The new electronic technologies require people to behave in ways they've never behaved before, such as working closely with people they may never meet in person.

Developing Relationships without Physical Contact

When setting up worldwide product development teams, Hewlett-Packard identifies all the key players, gets them in the same room, and asks them to design a lateral work system for optimum speed and effectiveness. H-P follows a very detailed and elaborate protocol for this, which starts by asking the development team to answer questions such as: How will different players in the process (who may live in different countries) interact together? Who should be physically co-located? (Experience suggests that functional specialists who remain interdependent along the critical path should whenever possible be physically co-located for the duration of the program.) If co-location isn't possible, what arrangements can be made to achieve virtual co-location? In this case, what information technology will people use to communicate with one another? What are the best times to communicate? When will they come together in person? H-P has found that intermittent meetings in person provide contextual co-location, which helps people develop mutual sensitivities so they'll have the trust that will allow them to work together effectively.

Can people build meaningful personal relationships without regular physical contact? Although increasing bandwidth in computer-based communication systems allows the addition of graphics, sound, pictures, and video to establish social context cues, electronic communication won't likely produce the same experience as face-to-face communication. Electronic interaction is like learning a foreign language by reading a book while sitting at home, as opposed to visiting the country and living among its people.

Still, an increasing number of deep personal relationships have begun developing between people participating in on-line networks, many of which have even led to marriage. It appears that the more comfortable people become with the technology, the less of an impediment it becomes to relationship building. In some situations, the lack of social clues (such as gender, appearance, status, accent) allows people to interact more openly than they might in person, and the absence of certain social or personal distractions encourages a quick and comfortable intimacy. "If the other person is being honest with you, you don't have to pretend," says Frances Allen, who was living in New Jersey when she met her future husband, a Houston plumber, on-line in 1992. "You get to see the real person. You don't see a facade." Even so, complete dependence on virtual relationships can create feelings of personal isolation, yet another paradox the redesigned organization must manage.

Avoiding Personal Isolation

When people can obtain all the resources they need to do their jobs via their on-line information systems, they can complete an entire operation or process without involving others. With fewer reasons to interact with co-workers, employees can make their computer terminals their primary source of interaction. While this can make some people feel isolated and alone in an impersonal world, the technology makes it easier for others to extend the range of their interactions and allows them to join broader interest groups, both inside and outside the organization. While these new technologies may alienate some office or factory relationships, they may also strengthen bonds in the home or in the community. These new patterns of communication and interaction will, in time, undoubtably alter the structure not only of organizations but of society itself.

Will this be good or bad? What kind of a society will this create? Will people become more or less human as a result? If we assume, as the poet Yeats said, that thought occurs "in the mind alone," then isolated thinkers may create isolating organizations that separate people from meaningful relationships with others, and make it difficult for them to form healthy identities of their own. To avoid this trap, organizations must maintain a balanced perspective about people and technology. Most organizations suffer not because they can't solve their problems, but because they don't see their problems clearly enough.

Strange Things Happen on the Way to the Future

At the turn of the last century, the British government seriously debated doing away with the Royal Patent Office, believing that most significant inventions had already taken place. That was untrue, of course. In the 1920s, some futurists were predicting that by today everyone would fly their our own private airplanes and vacation on the moon. It didn't happen. In the 1950s, other futurists were predicting that today, people would work 30 hours a week and worry most about what to do with all their leisure time. Wrong again. In 1980, IBM determined the worldwide market for personal computers for the next 10 years would amount to no more than 275,000 units. In fact, that figure turned out to be 60 million units. Strange things invariably happen on the way to the future, and only 20% of the experts' far-flung visions of what's likely to transpire ever really occur. So, why waste time speculating on what organizations might look like 10, 15, or 50 years downstream? You can only invent the future, whatever it will be, by thinking about it constantly.

Collectively, the ideas presented in this book constitute a potpourri of ingredients for creating the organizations of the future, rather than a recipe. No single ingredient can make a meal, and different cooks will imaginatively create many very different meals. Success will accrue to those who pursue an energizing vision of what they want their organizations to do, to look like, to become, not to those who simply possess the best redesign tools and techniques. No two people see the future the same way. Consider the story of the two shoe salesmen who visited a faraway island. One phoned home immediately to say "I'm leaving tomorrow. No one here wears shoes." The other also phoned home, but said, "I'm not going to be back for three more weeks. No one here wears shoes."

In 1985, when he was president of *Esquire* magazine, Phillip Moffat wrote, "I have come to believe that everyone has to struggle with change, to take risks in the belief that what exists now as the work experience can become much better if we are persistent in our caring." We're fortunate to live in a time of great opportunity. While it's already painfully apparent that jobs in the information age won't afford people the cradle-to-grave security they once enjoyed, neither will they impose the same limitations on personal freedom, creativity, initiative, talent, and skill. The same traits that enable organizations to thrive in information-intensive environments also free up people to expand the limits of their capabilities, bringing all the freedom, self-control, risks, and rewards associated with acting as an entrepreneur.

Opportunities abound to create more human, more efficient, more socially responsive organizations, and deep down, most people welcome that change. In a 1994 study by Princeton Survey Research Associates that interviewed over 2,000 workers, 63% said they would like more participation in decision-making, and 76% said their companies would be more competitive if employees made more operational decisions. The workers also indicated by a three-to-one margin that they'd like to gain influence in the workplace by working cooperatively with management. A 1991 study of salaried workers laid off by General Electric during the previous two years found that 38% were self-employed, earning less than before and with fewer fringe benefits. However, almost 90% felt better about their current work than their old job at GE, and said they hoped to keep working independently for as long as possible.

There's nothing magical about entering a new century, but in our society, key dates provide important targets and benchmarks. The beginning of the twenty-first century clearly marks one of those dates. Will we be happier in the organizations of the twenty-first century? Since recorded history indicates that human beings have never felt totally happy, the words healthy and fulfilled might represent more realistic aspirations. Will our redesigned organizations perform more effectively? They will, if we free ourselves from the past and invent the future based on a heartfelt appreciation of people's potential for development. Unparalleled success will ride on the crest of our hopes, not our fears.

Experience shows that only those with the discipline to stick with their vision can make it come true. Even they can't achieve every dream or every goal in a lifetime. The 20% Solution can make more dreams come true faster by helping people concentrate on what matters most, on what boosts their energy, on what excites, delights, and fulfills them. There's no turning back. As the many examples in this book illustrate, the revolution has already begun. The exceptions are becoming the rule. The future is now.

Index